In the Hollow
of the Wave

University of Virginia Press

Charlottesville & London

Bonnie Kime Scott

IN THE
HOLLOW
OF THE
WAVE

*Virginia Woolf
and Modernist
Uses of Nature*

University of Virginia Press
© 2012 by the Rector and Visitors of the University of Virginia
Printed in the United States of America on acid-free paper

First published 2012

9 8 7 6 5 4 3 2 1

Library of Congress Cataloging-in-Publication Data
Scott, Bonnie Kime, 1944-
  In the hollow of the wave : Virginia Woolf and modernist uses of nature /
Bonnie Kime Scott.
      p.   cm.
  Includes bibliographical references and index.
  ISBN 978-0-8139-3260-6 (cloth : alk. paper) — ISBN 978-0-8139-3262-0 (e-book)
  1. Woolf, Virginia, 1882–1941—Criticism and interpretation. 2. Nature in
literature. 3. Modernism (Literature)—Great Britain. I. Title.
  PR6045.072Z8755 2012
  823'.912—dc23

                                                              2011042248

Dedicated to:

Evan Lee Jones,

Avery Thomas Kime Jones,

and Jasper Duval Scott

Respecting nature

for their future

But what after all is one night?

A short space, especially when

the darkness dims so soon,

and so soon a bird sings, a

cock crows, or a faint green

quickens, like a turning leaf,

in the hollow of the wave.

~Virginia Woolf,

To the Lighthouse

Contents

Acknowledgments

I would like to thank the following institutions for access to their collections and permission to reproduce images in their custody: University of Sussex Library, where Elizabeth Inglis was an invaluable guide; the Tate Gallery Archive's Photographic Collection; the British Museum of Natural History Archives Centre, for images of the museum in 1881 and of a nineteenth-century hummingbird case, and its division at the Walter Rothschild Zoological Museum in Tring, for images from Thoby Stephen's *Notes on Birds and Mammals Observed in England, Wales and Parts of Europe, 1902–1906;* the Modern Archives Centre, King's College, Cambridge; the New York Public Library, Berg Collection, and its curator, Isaac Gewirtz, for permission to publish a youthful image of Virginia Woolf from Julia Duckworth Hill's Album; the Mortimer Rare Book Room, Smith College, with special thanks to Karin Kukil, its director, for permission to publish images from Leslie Stephen's Photo Album; the Harvard Theatre Collection, Houghton Library, for permission to publish images from the Monk's House Albums; Special Collections, University of Delaware Library, for digital images of Hogarth Press books in their collection; Special Collections, San Diego State University, for digital prints from rare books in their collection; and Archives and Special Collections, Washington State University Library, Pullman, Washington, for digital images of sketches by Leslie Stephen. I thank Henrietta Garnett for permission to publish an image of Vanessa Bell's painting *View into the Garden* and woodcuts associated with *Kew Gardens;* Adrian Langdon for permission to publish his photograph of Godrevy Lighthouse; the Artists' Rights Society and the Yale Center for British Art for permission to publish an image of Duncan Grant's painting *Pamela;* and the Manchester Gallery of Art for permission to publish an image of John Everett Millais's painting *Autumn Leaves*. I thank the Society of Authors for permission to publish extracts from the writings of Virginia Woolf and images from the various albums cited above. Quotations from *The Essays of Virginia Woolf,* edited by Andrew McNewllie and published by the Hogarth Press, have been reprinted by the permission of the Random House Group Ltd.

My earliest memories testify to my parents' respect for and understanding of nature, whether I was planting my first seeds with Sheila Burton Kime, or identifying bird calls with Roy Milford Kime. The earliest phase of archival and site visits for this work was supported by my former academic home, the University of Delaware, with a General University Research Grant. My daughter Heather Scott, my son-in-law Damon Evan Jones, and my husband, Tom Scott, accompanied me across England and Wales collecting images and a better sense of place in summer 2000. Members of the International Virginia Woolf Society have been a constant support, deciphering and identifying Woolf's texts and sources, and listening critically to conference papers that tested out ideas. Particularly helpful was the 2010 Woolf Conference, "Virginia Woolf and the Natural World," organized by Kristin Czarnecki and Carrie Rohman. Two articles related to the book have appeared in selected papers: "Virginia Woolf, Ecofeminism, and Breaking Boundaries in Nature," in *Woolfian Boundaries: Selected Papers from the Sixteenth International Conference on Virginia Woolf,* edited by Anna Burrells, Steve Ellis, Deborah Parsons, and Kathryn Simpson (Clemson, SC: Clemson University Digital Press, 2007), and a keynote address, "Ecofeminism, Holism, and the Search for Natural Order in Woolf," in *Virginia Woolf and the Natural World: Selected Papers from the Nineteenth International Conference on Virginia Woolf* (Clemson, SC: Clemson University Digital Press, 2011), as well as "Green," in *Modernism and Theory: A Critical Debate,* edited by Stephen Ross (London: Routledge, 2009). The Modernist Studies Association provided an excellent venue for a collaborative seminar on nature as the other of modernism. Among individuals who have helped me clarify and present the work and ferret out answers are Jane Goldman, Elisa K. Sparks, Marianne DeKoven, Suzanne Bellamy, Pamela Caughie, Diane Gillespie, Beth Daugherty, Stuart Clarke, Barbara Gates, Suzette Henke, Patrick Parrinder, my student Michelle Garvey, and my daughter Heidi Cathryn Molly Scott, whose field is environmental literature.

My second academic home, San Diego State University, has provided one sabbatical and two Critical Thinking Grants, as well as willing and helpful colloquium audiences. Important technical support has come from Teddi Brock and Brittany Robinson. I am grateful to Paul Wong, dean of the College of Arts and Letters, for his fostering of faculty research in my own case and throughout the College.

Abbreviations

*In the Hollow
of the Wave*

Introduction

In people's eyes, in the swing, tramp, and trudge; in the bellow and the uproar; the carriages, motor cars, omnibuses, vans, sandwich men shuffling and swinging; brass bands; barrel organs; in the triumph and the jingle and the strange high singing of some aeroplane overhead was what she loved; life; London; this moment of June.

~Woolf, *Mrs. Dalloway*

"How fair, how strange," said Bernard, "glittering, many pointed and many-domed London lies before me under mist. Guarded by gasometers, by factory chimneys, she lies sleeping as we approach. . . . But we are aimed at her. Already her maternal somnolence is uneasy. Ridges fledged with houses rise from the mist. Factories, cathedrals, glass domes, institutions and theatres erect themselves. The early train from the north is hurled at her like a missile. . . . We are about to explode in the flanks of the city like a shell in the side of some ponderous, maternal, majestic animal."

~Woolf, *The Waves*

THERE IS NOTHING I can imagine that is totally independent of nature; despite the ravages of human-made pollutants, there may still be substances, forces, and living beings unknown or unaffected by culture. Nature enters a cultural arena, however, as soon as we think about it, and certainly when we write it, entering into discourse. Thus it is not very useful to make any separation of the two. Indeed, ecofeminist Donna Haraway has coined the blended term "naturecultures," breaking down the binary division between nature and culture that was long encouraged by Enlightenment philosophy, the rise of Western science, and the Industrial Revolution, fueled by capitalism.[1] Nature is an enormous system, of which humans are a demanding and ever more invasive, dangerous part. When in favorable balance, aspects of nature work together, providing conditions for sustainable life. Death as well as life supports this balance. Humans, particularly powerful ones seeking control, have manipulated natural conditions to favor their own perceived needs, goals, and superiority, usually to the detriment of nonhuman beings and less dominant peoples. We develop provisional concepts of nature that cultivate our understanding, either individually, starting at our earliest stages of cognition, or cooperatively, through our intellectual communities. Nature nurtures us by providing biological needs, by pleasing the senses, by offering the prospect of something to understand, and occasionally by lifting the human spirit above selfish individualism and immediate concerns into a cosmic sense of belonging, meeting, or becoming other than human. Nature provides a model for countless human rituals, narratives, and performances. We neglect it at our own peril and loss. This study joins the work of environmental and feminist thinkers who feel that we must discover a new, posthumanist pattern that escapes androcentrism and the nature/culture binary, and fosters richly varied, contextual, and relational thinking, holding in high regard all living beings.

Nature, as an inescapable aspect of being human, went dangerously unacknowledged in the twentieth century, as predominant cultures delighted and indulged in modernity—its various aspects including technical invention, urban development, rapid transport, global capitalism, militarism, and the empowerment of masculine assertion, based on Western values. Modernism, as an artistic expression of modernity, fits into this pattern, as demonstrated in many of its manifestos, and in its canonization via the New Critical tradition and successive forms of cultural studies. Despite their growing critique of the old modernism, proponents of the new modernist studies, and even feminists writing recently on Virginia Woolf, seem little more interested than their predecessors in modernist uses of nature.[2] From Susan Squier's *Virginia Woolf and London* and Jean Moorcroft Wilson's *Virginia Woolf: Life and London* to Pamela L. Caughie's *Virginia Woolf in the Age of Mechanical*

Reproduction, we have been reading for an urban, technical, and popularly cultural Woolf.[3]

Feminists have found serious obstacles in addressing, let alone embracing, nature. Why should women assign themselves to nature when, as Caroline Merchant has suggested, capitalist patriarchy and the scientific establishment have already done so, using this as an excuse for the domination of both woman and nature?[4] One of the major debates in feminist theory has been over essentialism, seen as reductive, bio- and matricentric, and determinist, as opposed to theories of social construction that contextualize and differentiate over time and geographical location. Both French feminist theory, with its interest in writing representations of the female body—sensitive to its rhythms, flows, and sexual difference—and early forms of ecofeminism that idealized the maternal figure of the earth goddess have been critiqued for their essentialisms.[5] By attending to various forms of difference as they intersect with the category of gender, feminists of the later second and recent third waves demonstrate skepticism of universals and are alert to ways that racism and homophobia have traditionally been "naturalized," or accepted as normal in nature. There is belated acknowledgment that women of color have been doubly subjected to cultural assignment to nature; same-sex love, on the other hand, has been "scientifically" classified as abnormal, or "unnatural."[6] "Uses" in the title of this study calls attention to nature as deliberate discourse, rather than essence or aesthetic decoration. The choice of "uses" rather than "discourse" reminds us that humans make everyday use of nature and may take advantage of it, as well as put nature into specialized language.

If nature and culture are taken in opposition, as they often are despite efforts of deconstructive and feminist studies to work beyond such binaries, then the turn toward cultural studies also tilts the balance away from nature.[7] Woolf has become a centerpiece of studies of gender (seen as a cultural construct) and modernism. *A Room of One's Own* is widely recognized as a founding text of second wave feminism and its cultural critique, with *Three Guineas* offering an even more radical challenge to patriarchy alongside fascism. Typical concerns of cultural feminists are Woolf's advocacy of a female counterpublic sphere where women obtain education and enter the professions, her pacifist reactions to war, her subversive queer/lesbian writing strategies, and her participation (and implication) in issues of racialism, imperialism, anti-Semitism, and class difference.[8]

Virginia Woolf makes her own contributions to urban, mechanistic concepts of modernism. She was tremendously eager to return to London in 1915 and 1924, following periods of recovery from mental illness, when her doctors situated her away from the city. She can be quoted saying that she prefers city to country walks. Indeed, some of her best ideas came while strolling through London. The Woolf of modernity walks city streets. She senses the pressure of crowds, the attractions of store windows and ads set in bold type, and the passage of time marked by the chiming clocks and the humming of machines. She attends the cinema, sets type for the Hogarth Press, uses a bicycle to get about in Sussex, rides in a motorcar, and spots airplanes overhead. Characters explore museums and go shopping in department stores, taking the lift for convenience. Favorite words, such as "incandescent," come from an electrified world. Woolf inhabits as she interprets her technological century.

Mrs. Dalloway's love of London is largely based on the rhythms and noises of modern commerce and technology, as is registered above in the first epigraph. The second epigraph, from *The Waves*, is complexly gendered. It takes on the perspective of Bernard as he is entering maturity and about to be married. His expression of confident masculinity resembles Ezra Pound's hypermasculine, vorticist plunge into the city.[9] "Fledged," a word that might normally describe young birds newly capable of flight, now describes houses on an outlying ridge of the city. London is feminized as a mother of epic proportions, about to be shot by an explosive shell. These troubling images only hint at the challenges ahead in this study. Still, it is well to remember that Woolf presents Bernard at various stages of maturity, and with changing ideas about his will and ability to control experience through language. Clarissa Dalloway turns from the vital rhythms of commerce cited above to the alternate rhythms of the park: "the mist; the hum; the slow-swimming happy ducks; the pouched birds waddling" (*MD* 5). Mist enters into both visions and remains one of Woolf's most connective images.

Natural elements infiltrate Woolf's London by way of the Thames, flowing along the architecture of the Embankment. The Botanical Gardens at Kew and the Regent's Park Zoo were frequent destinations throughout Woolf's life, and subjects of her fiction and essays. She knows that bones of ancient creatures lie beneath London's pavements.[10] Nature is organized and commodified in London's museums, in its great parks and gardens, replete with plundered, systematically named plants from empire, and in the flower shop Mrs. Dalloway reaches on her morning walk. In crossing Green Park, Mrs.

Dalloway has some of her most exalted thoughts about the possibility of life itself going on.

Similarly, technical and urban modes invade Woolf's country settings. Photo albums kept by Leslie Stephen, Vanessa Stephen Bell, and Stella Duckworth Hills favor the countryside and garden settings of family vacations, but we have these visual representations only because the family took up the camera enthusiastically. Trains, bicycles, and motorcars make liberating excursions into the country possible. Woolf's encounter with airplanes offered a disturbing "new pastoral of the aeroplane—pastoral because so strongly intermingled with breezes and country sights, lying so innocently 'among trees and cows,' but sinister, too, abrupting the familiar lie of the land, the ordinary clustering of objects" (Beer, "Island and Aeroplane" 165). The remaking of pastoral traditions is very much a part of modernism.

We frequently find a shuttling dialogic between city and country, culture and nature, in Woolf's life and writing. As she recalls in "A Sketch of the Past," the Stephen children alternated between London winters and St. Ives summers from early childhood until the death of their mother, Julia Stephen. Her first memory (likely set between these two places) "was of red and purple flowers on a black ground—my mother's dress; she was either in a train or in an omnibus, and I was on her lap. I therefore saw the flowers she was wearing very close; and can still see purple and red and blue, I think, against the black." A second first memory "is of lying half asleep, half awake, in bed in the nursery at St Ives. It is of hearing the waves breaking, one, two, one, two, and sending a splash of water over the beach; and then breaking, one, two, one, two, behind a yellow blind. It is of hearing the blind draw its little acorn across the floor as the wind blew the blind out. It is of lying and hearing this splash and seeing this light, and feeling, it is almost impossible that I should be here; of feeling the purest ecstasy I can conceive" (*MB* 64–65). Both memories are complex, involving rare proximity to Woolf's mother in the first, and her embryonic part in the beloved family seaside retreat in St. Ives, in the second. She goes on to imagine how she would paint a globular scene composed of semitransparent things, and she adds a slightly later memory of bees in the garden, where "all seemed to press voluptuously against some membrane" (*MB* 66; figure 1). Nature is fundamental to these first memories, but it is already mediated and reproduced—the flowers she identifies as anemones are printed on cloth. Though the waves, wind, and light are elemental, the acorn is of human creation, and the yellow blind, while it conveys the action of the wind, alters the light. Nature is implicated in culture from the start. Conversely, culture is invaded by nature.

Virginia and Leonard Woolf would replicate the Stephens' pattern of moving between city and country by maintaining both a Bloomsbury address and "Monk's House," which was in the village of Rodmill, adjacent to the River Ouse, in the Sussex downs. Woolf's novels move between country- and cityscapes, with even the exceptions proving the rule. *The Voyage Out, To the Lighthouse,* and *Between the Acts* are dominantly set in country places, but key participants have city addresses and memories. *Mrs. Dalloway* has London as its present location, but shuttles back in memory to the country house of Bourton. Her novels following the course of lives—*Jacob's Room, Orlando, The Waves,* and *The Years*—seem to require variation, with nature having a special claim at the beginning and the end of life, or playing particularly strongly upon certain characters. Movement between locations facilitates discovery in both character and reader.

Critics and biographers have placed different valences on more or less natural environments. Janice Paul attributes to Woolf the belief "that the English social machinery represses something natural and real. The contrast between natural and ordered places in her fiction recapitulates the separation between external social surface and internal personal feeling" (23). Despite Woolf's pastoral excursions, Paul finds Woolf "always returns to the city and the house" (39). Writing in the 1980s, and as yet untroubled by the feminist critique of essentialism, Elizabeth Abel described Mrs. Dalloway's Bourton as "an emotionally pre-Oedipal female-centered natural world," disjoined from her move to a "heterosexual male-dominated social world" (*Fictions of Psychoanalysis* 80). Something of this idealizing spirit is preserved in Hermione Lee's 1996 biography of Woolf. Lee opens with a country garden scene— the 1905 return of the four Stephen siblings to Talland House on holiday at St. Ives. Gazing through the escallonia hedge made famous in *To the Lighthouse,* they revisit what Lee, Leonard Woolf, and many others presume to be a childhood paradise.[11] In her 1989 study, *Virginia Woolf: The Impact of Childhood Sexual Abuse on Her Life and Work,* Louise DeSalvo challenges the idyllic representation of childhood in Cornwall, and with it the image of the benevolent earth mother that adheres to Stephen women and to Mrs. Ramsay in *To the Lighthouse.* Far from protecting her daughters, the mother as read by DeSalvo is complicit in male cultural control and its abuses. DeSalvo finds Woolf selecting natural images typical of victims of abuse in "A Sketch of the

FIGURE 1. Virginia Stephen as a child amid foliage. (Henry W. and Albert A. Berg
Collection of English and American Literature, New York Public Library, Astor,
Lenox, and Tilden Foundations)

Past"—an enveloping grape, suffocating duckweed, a wild beast, and a whirl-pool (125–28). She encourages us to look for mixed messages in nature.[12]

In approaching Woolf's uses of nature, it is important to resist false dichotomies. In his landmark study *The Country and the City*, Raymond Williams is careful to consider the historical interdependencies of city and country. He achieves a balance that often gets lost in urban-focused studies that quote selectively from him. Strict binaries and impermeable boundaries became suspect in deconstructive theory, and this thinking extends to recent feminist, ecofeminist, and allied postmodern and posthumanist theory. Starting with *Of Grammatology*, Derrida's deconstruction of texts focuses upon binary oppositions, often overthrowing their implied hierarchies. His *Dissemination* (with its seed metaphor and insistence on the merger of themes) and his essay "The Animal That Therefore I Am (More to Follow)" bring him closest to ecological concerns. Gilles Deleuze and Félix Guattari have also been instrumental to feminist and ecofeminist boundary crossing, particularly in *A Thousand Plateaus*, which expresses interest in humans becoming animal and makes use of natural figurations such as the rhizome to overcome hierarchical, filiative thinking and support a more holistic view of the world.

In addressing the revolutionary aspects of Woolf's uses of nature, it is helpful to have an array of feminist and ecofeminist approaches from which to choose. Chicana feminist Gloria Anzaldúa has encouraged investigations of cultural locations on and across borders, working to deconstruct boundaries of nation, race, and sexuality. Lesbian and queer theorists such as Greta Gaard have questioned the heterosexual bias that carries into designations of what is "natural" and "unnatural." Stacy Alaimo draws attention to ways that women have "negotiated, contested, and transformed the discourses of nature that surround them," and in some cases "inhabit nature as an undomesticated ground" (1–2), thus evading traditional cultural assignments. Feminists and ecofeminists have critiqued deconstruction and appropriated it for their own uses. For example, Rosi Braidotti carries Deleuze and Guattari's fluid theory of "becoming" into feminist studies of subjectivity, most notably in *Nomadic Subjects* and *Metamorphoses*. Donna Haraway quibbles with both Derrida and Deleuze and Guattari over the limitations of their approaches to nonhuman life, finding persistent divisions between animal and human, and binary preferences. Among various ecofeminist theories drawn upon in this study is the "feminist care tradition" in animal ethics, advanced by Carol J. Adams and Josephine Donovan. This is derived from Carol Gilligan's cultural feminism, which identifies a morality of relationship in women, expressed in her work *In a Different Voice*. The category of the posthuman, as developed by Briadotti, Haraway, Sara Whatmore, Diana Fuss, and Katherine Hayles, reacts to the androcentrism of traditional humanism.[13] In line with this work, Haraway has proposed the concepts of the cyborg and "naturecultures." With the former, she breaks down the division between body and machine; with the latter, she insists that a cooperative relationship must emerge between nature and culture, which have always been inextricably linked.

While Woolf's uses of nature may have tremendous appeal to early twenty-first-century environmental feminists, this study does not claim the current ecofeminist perspective as hers—nor could it be, given the changes to the environment and global economies that have arisen since her death in 1941. Ecofeminism as a term has been around only since the mid-1970s, its conception usually attributed to French feminist Françoise d'Eaubonne (Warren 21). Woolf's cultural affinities are apparent in her interest in a vast sweep of cultural history, shown most obviously in *A Room of One's Own*, *Orlando*, and *Between the Acts*. While we can derive a great deal from studies that seek her relation to the Romantics, to Enlightenment philosophy, Kant, phenomenology, or feminist activism, each of these is best understood as a partial approach to her very complex and variable literary project. Some are more integral to the weave of her work than others, and I hope to demonstrate the importance of Woolf's engagement with nature.

In Woolf studies, a scattering of articles has appeared—some in feminist and environmental journals and collections—showing that Woolf's handling of language and her perceptual engagement with nature make a good fit with recent ecofeminist thinking.[14] Elisa Kay Sparks has led us down various garden paths with Virginia and especially Leonard Woolf in beautifully illustrated conference presentations and publications.[15] The 2006 Virginia Woolf Conference had two panels concerned with Woolf and the environment, suggesting that this was a growing area of interest. Significantly, the 2010 Woolf Conference took as its title "Virginia Woolf and the Natural World," and a call for papers for an "Eco-Woolf" focus for the spring 2012 number of the *Virginia Woolf Miscellany* has gone out.

A study of Woolf's recourse to nature has to be an ongoing, multifaceted project, of which this study engages a limited number of aspects, organized in the thematically based chapters that follow, selecting from feminist, ecofeminist, and postcolonial theory as best suits each chapter. While urban, technical, and formalist studies of modernism have had critical blind spots, a shift toward nature in modernism runs its own risks of inattention to complex interrelationships. Although I cannot guarantee an ecofeminist Woolf, or a green world of pre-Oedipal delight in those of her novels most idealized by feminists over the years, I do find that nature plays a significant part in both the external and the internal dimensions of her life and work, and that it is inextricable from her language and ethics. Nature, as present in amazing passages of her writing, should be both puzzled over and enjoyed. I have no doubt that "common readers"—a group much valued by Woolf, as able to work independently from critics and scholars—have regularly engaged Woolf in this manner. I hope to engage them as readers of this study, as well.

Chapter 1, "Toward a Greening of Modernism," surveys a diverse set of modernist writers for the presence and play of nature in their works. Imagist, vorticist, and futurist manifestos and prominent formulators of modernism made considerable effort to control nature, associated with the feminine, and to make it "new." Still, modernists do recollect childhood encounters with nature, explore it from scientific angles, or use nature as access to a primitive or an inner self. The initial inventory of authors contained in this chapter— Wyndham Lewis, Ezra Pound, Gertrude Stein, H.D., Djuna Barnes, James Joyce, and D. H. Lawrence—sets a context for Woolf's own varied uses of nature. Numerous filaments of personal and publishing relations connect Woolf to the figures discussed here, or them to one another. So do debates about modernism's relation to earlier literary periods, most notably classicism and Romanticism.

Chapter 2, "Diversions of Darwin and Natural History," investigates Woolf's first exposures to nature in the post-Darwinian context that she shared with contemporaries such as Eliot and Lawrence. At the same time that she was learning to write, Woolf was being introduced to natural history by her father, Leslie Stephen, an Alpine climber, epic walker, devoted botanizer, and friend of the Darwins. She followed the naturalist occupations of her older brother, Thoby, whose collecting of creatures, ranging from Crustacea to Lepidoptera, are best known from *Jacob's Room*. The chapter's concerns include young Virginia Stephen's resistance to assigned natural pursuits such as gardening, which was prescribed for her health, her collaboration in the collection and identification of insects with her siblings, and her appropriations of and deviations from evolutionary narrative. Feminist science studies, including work that has recuperated and contextualized early women in science, guides the chapter.

The title of chapter 3, "Limits of the Garden as Cultured Space," suggests its argument that the garden is an ambivalent territory for Woolf. In her life, and for many of her characters, gardens ground early memories and assist coming into consciousness. Gardens promote detailed observation and enable conversations, somewhat freed from indoor restraints. However, as H.D. illustrates in her own garden poetry, women repeatedly experience imperfect freedom within private garden walls. As postcolonial theory has demonstrated, the very art of cultivation sets limits and hierarchies, and it draws upon imperial soil for its material. Respecting Woolf's immediate contexts, the chapter begins by visiting gardens and gardeners Woolf described in her letters and diaries and drew upon for her fiction. Woolf and her characters take full advantage of London's great public gardens as places to stroll or withdraw, often blending nature, culture, and self in their thoughts. Notable gardeners in her life include her aunt Caroline Stephen, whose garden was an early place of recovery for Woolf; her sister Vanessa, whose cottage and walled gardens can still be enjoyed at Charleston; and Vita Sackville-West, who is still appreciated for the gardens at Sissinghurst Castle (a National Trust property) and gardening advice published in numerous articles and books. At Monk's House in Sussex, Leonard Woolf proved an impassioned, if somewhat compulsive, gardener. Such real gardens contribute to witty anecdotes in Woolf's diaries and letters, and to fluid, symbolic settings for her novels.

Chapter 4, "The Art of Landscape, the Politics of Place," analyzes both aesthetic concepts and national identifications, while it contextualizes Woolf's experience of various landscapes from childhood on. Woolf was born to a set of artistic traditions via her mother's family. She was drawn into more contemporary artistic debates by the "sister art" of Vanessa Bell and her Charleston circle, which included art critic Clive Bell, critic/artist Roger Fry, and artist Duncan Grant. Woolf developed her own landscape art with reference to both realist and Post-Impressionist art. She was anxious not to sound like a fussy nature enthusiast recording the change of seasons or a travel guide cataloging the wonders of new landscapes. Her selection of preferred land- and seascapes became complicit with her political positioning, which gravitated toward the margins of the nation and reworked concepts of "Englishness."

Domestic, wild, and garden-variety animals, inclusive of insects, fish, and birds, as well as the "primitive," associated with animals and human "others," receive attention in chapter 5, "Crossing the Species Boundary." The chapter demonstrates ways that Woolf reacted to the gendered hierarchy and regulation of animals, handed down by the Victorians. Such discourse enters her fiction, serving as a commentary on gender roles and expectations. The chapter treats the menagerie of animal nicknames employed by Woolf and her intimates, and her rich experience of both companion animals and creatures viewed or hunted in the wild. Woolf wrote repeatedly about dogs, from an early essay on the family dog Shag to the well-known biography of Elizabeth Barrett Browning's dog Flush. Anticipating postmodern theories of becoming, and Haraway's ideas of companion species, she strove to cross the species barrier, apprehending life and death as a dog, or even a moth, might. Finally, Woolf struggled with false choices between feminism and environmentalism in reacting to arguments for the protection of birds, made at the expense of women.

The final chapter assesses ideas of order related to Woolf's writings. This includes a review of tendencies of Woolf criticism to find unity in her work, attention to her own scientific reading, and a comparison of her use of imagery to various ecological ideas of holistic order. Like early ecofeminists, Woolf reappropriated classical and pagan myths to explore the ideas of balanced and sustainable order. She focused on female figures, young and old, situated in direct relation to earth and water. A wide array of her characters develop complex natural images, which is one way whereby Woolf could explore what she famously termed "the dark places of psychology" ("Modern Fiction," *E* 4:162). Woolf's unlikely earth goddess figures and her troubled, marginal characters construct models of holistic environmental order.

Undeniable global warming, costly, diminishing supplies of oil, and the global spread of technological modernity contribute to our present cultural and natural crisis. One way to reach toward a sustainable future is to develop awareness of previous uses and understandings of nature. In this exploration of Virginia Woolf's uses of nature, I hope to demonstrate that Woolf's writing is both sustaining and renewable. Sustaining and renewing require questioning and resisting discourses and practices of the past, leading to a creative, concerted effort to apply to new circumstances what we find of use.

1

Toward a Greening
of Modernism

We want something that has been shaped
and clarified, cut to catch the light, hard
as gem or rock with the seal of human
experience in it, and yet sheltering as in a
clear gem the flame which burns now so
high and now sinks so low in our own hearts.
We want what is timeless and contemporary.

~Woolf, "Reading"

Yet the poetry often seems
to come in precisely at the
moment when the scientist
and the science, the method
and the newness go out.

~Woolf, "What Is Poetry?"

DESPITE THE CHALLENGES of modernity, nature has a persistent, even adaptive, presence in modernism. Furthermore, the reinsertion of nature into modernist studies contributes to ongoing debates concerning sources of aesthetic form, the development of personal identity, survival of trauma, and the rebalancing of power and resources in the light of post-colonial and antiracist consciousness. Modernists regularly make reference to nature, or its control, in their writing. Natural interests of specific writers vary, as affected by factors such as geographical location, gender, race, class privilege, spirituality, and awareness and acceptance of scientific theory. This chapter investigates ways that a small set of Woolf's companion modernists developed discourses involving or excluding nature. While it is hoped that this work will contribute to a greening of modernism, this chapter will also provide context and direction for the more intensive study of Woolf's uses of nature that follows. Modernist rejection of nature came in part from the preference of classicism over Romanticism, as well as attraction to new technology and science. But modernists also discovered the impossibility of rejecting the natural world, given powerful early memories of place and sensation, and the experimental satisfaction that comes with imaginative merger of human and nonhuman other—one of the basic tropes of ecofeminism.

The Classical Version:
Making It New through Technology

Modernist opposition to nature came largely from those who identified with a classicist approach, including the group labeled the "men of 1914,"[1] whose gender-biased version long enjoyed academic prowess. In manifestos and reviews, Wyndham Lewis, T. E. Hulme, and Ezra Pound conjure up formless, dark, decayed manifestations of nature to condemn what they consider inferior forms of writing; these they associate with decadence and the feminine.[2] Following the lead of Baudelaire, they turn toward urban settings. Science and mechanics, including the engines of war, furnish preferred masculine metaphors. Their gendering and diminishment of nature, and their goal to "make it new," are in keeping with the broad patterns of culture reported by Sherry Ortner in her provocatively titled 1974 essay, "Is Female to Male as Nature Is to Culture?" Ortner observes, "Every culture, or, generally 'culture' is engaged in the process of generating and sustaining systems of meaningful forms (symbols, artifacts, etc.) by means of which humanity transcends the givens of natural existence, bends them to its purposes, controls them in its interest" (72).[3]

T. E. Hulme, in his advocacy of classicism, provides a difficult scenario for incorporating nature into modernism. Classicism, as he defines it, is all about culture and its capacity to control expression. In his essay "Romanticism and Classicism," he sides with those who are suspicious of human nature: "Man is an extraordinarily fixed and limited animal whose nature is absolutely constant. It is only by tradition and organization that anything decent can be got out of him" (179). This contrasts to Romanticism, which is generally seen as the most nature-friendly of literary groupings. Hulme focuses his attack on Rousseau, citing the belief "that man was by nature good, that it was only bad laws and customs that had suppressed him." Hulme faults the Romantics for their recourse to the infinite and mysterious, and for finding god in man. In reaching for a metaphor suitable to his goal of "accurate, precise and definite description," he thinks first of an architect's variously curved wooden templates, but settles finally upon a springy piece of steel that can be bent precisely, using the pressure of the artist's own fingers. The goal with this implement is "to bend the steel out of its own curve and into the exact curve which you want. Something different to what it would assume naturally" (183–84). Hulme's favorite texture of "dry hardness" suggests that for him the best organism is a dead, or at least a desiccated, one.

Hulme does have some use for natural imagery and scientific understandings of nature. In "Romanticism and Classicism," he identifies humans as animals. He acknowledges Darwinian theory of the progressive development of species, but he prefers a scientific alternative of mutations. In place of the infinite, Hulme commits his art to "the light of ordinary day." This is a backdoor way of saying that observations of everyday appearances on earth are germane, even to classicism. When he wants to express the complex relations of the imaginative mind, Hulme's analogy is to a lithe natural being: "The motion of a snake's body goes through all parts at once and its volition acts at the same instant in coils which go contrary ways" (185). In *Further Speculations,* Hulme even asserts, "There must be just as much contact with nature in an abstract art as in a realistic one" (qtd. in Schwartz 60–61).

Hulme's ideas on classicism complemented the interest in immediate experiences and mental control characteristic of that founding group of modernist poets, the imagists. "Direct treatment of the 'thing' whether subjective or objective": this first principle, codified by F. S. Flint and endorsed by Ezra Pound, gives nature an entry as an objective thing. Indeed, imagists and imagist affiliates, from H.D. and Richard Aldington to Amy Lowell and D. H. Lawrence, regularly took entities (plants, animals, and landscapes) from nature for their poetry, controlling them as subjectively perceived objects in ways that were not always dry and hard.

In "A Retrospect," Pound intensifies the subjective aspect of the enterprise, centering more upon maker/perceiver than the potentially natural object. His "Image" presents "an intellectual and emotional complex in an instant of time" ("complex" to be read in the "technical sense employed by the newer psychologists") (60). In his analysis of Pound's celebrated haiku "In a Station of the Metro," Sanford Schwartz offers a double scenario: "Analytically, these visionary experiences are projections of the subject's emotions onto the object; phenomenologically, however, the visionary form is as real and objective as the natural object that inspires the emotion, and the two appear together at one instant in a vision of nature transfigured" (68). In the second scenario, nature both inspires and coexists with emotion, however important human control is to the actual production of art. With Pound, we find all sorts of historical and cultural controls in the processing of natural images, but the images remain.

On numerous occasions, Pound sought to edit nature out of modernism, shaping modernist form and history. He convinced T. S. Eliot to eliminate large segments of seascapes originally in "The Waste Land." For her influential little magazine, *Poetry*, Harriet Monroe favored American landscapes, against Pound's advice. Monroe's interest was consistent with her own environmental activism, dedicated to preservation of the American West, and backed by her writing of nature poetry.[4]

Wyndham Lewis, who conceptualized the notion of the "men of 1914," generally agrees with Hulme's classicism. He has his own way of structuring gender and art on vertical, hierarchical planes. This scheme assigns masculinity and art to dry surface articulation and the feminine, as nature, to damp and chaotic depths of being.[5] The title character of his novel *Tarr* groups "woman and the sexual sphere" with "jellyish diffuseness" that is the antithesis of Hulme's "dry hardness." These "chaotic depths" may imply common origins in primordial ooze, where the feminine is contained; art and culture must rise above this. Lewis's proliferation of technologically produced objects—girders, gears, and bits of metal bent to specification, as in his painting *Timon of Athens*—relates well to Hulme's flexible steel template for art.

Lewis's construction of gender conforms with his assignment of men such as Marcel Proust, Lytton Strachey, and Roger Fry to a degenerate, feminine category. His personal conflict while involved in Roger Fry's Bloomsbury-affiliated Omega Workshop may have influenced his thinking. Lewis was further offended that in the essay "Mr. Bennett and Mrs. Brown," Virginia Woolf detected "failures and fragments" in authors such as James Joyce. Accordingly, Lewis ensconces her as the presiding figure in an enfeebled feminine artistic realm: "So we have been invited . . . to install ourselves in a very dim Venusburg indeed: but Venus has become an introverted matriarch, brooding over a subterranean 'stream of consciousness'—a feminine phenomenon after all" (138). This territory is both natural and urban and includes the deep feminine ooze of stream of consciousness. The city has degenerate, rather than modern, form: Swinburne's decadent Venusburg, Eliot's squalid "unreal city" in "The Waste Land," and an effete Bloomsbury setting where Woolf presents "pretty salon pieces" (137). Here the visual system, generally prized as a perceptive channel, has become "myopic," and figures of myth and legend are declared decadent. Lewis does show some familiarity with Woolf's work when he registers her as a "symbolic landmark—a sort of party-lighthouse" (132). He satirizes "Prousts and sub-Prousts" who old-maidishly "shrink and cluster together, they titter in each other's ears, and delicately tee-hee, pointing out to each other the red-blooded antics of this or that upstanding figure, treading the perilous Without" (139)—the less sheltered world, even a wilderness where only the red-blooded males dare to work. Lewis charges that, in her account of modernism, Woolf misses what is robust and complete (read heterosexual and masculine) in Joyce and Lawrence (137) and in her own fiction offers "puerile copies" of the "realistic vigour" of Mr. Joyce (138).

In summarizing the action of "Mr. Bennett and Mrs. Brown," Lewis notes, without interpretation, that Mrs. Brown has been making conversation over the long-term effect of caterpillars attacking an old oak tree. That Woolf should come up with this natural drama in recording a fragment of dialogue spoken by the evasive Mrs. Brown suggests the effectiveness of invoking fragments of conversation overheard in everyday life, in modernist writing. Her complex natural image reinforces the situation that the elderly Mrs. Brown is facing, in an apparent attack by the demanding Mr. Brown.

In his querulous closing, Lewis offers an extraordinary mixture of natural and cultural metaphors to express his nausea over the power of the feminine mind, with Woolf as its adjudicator. "It has been with considerable shaking in my shoes, and a feeling of treading upon a carpet of eggs, that I have taken the cow by the horns in this chapter, and broached the subject of the part that the feminine mind has played . . . in the erection of our present criteria. For fifteen years I have subsisted in this suffocating atmosphere. I have felt very much a fish out of water" (140).[6] Is it the ooze of eggs, messing the carpet of the suspect salon, or the resentment that cows should show horns, rather than produce milk, that demands his control? Introduced initially as an "introverted matriarch," the Woolfian cow paradoxically evades maternity. I suggest that what oppresses Lewis is not the matriarch but the air of inversion, a queering of sexuality as well as gender, scripted as unnatural (the fish out of water), and classically equated with death and decay. Lewis was right in identifying Woolf's interest in depth and dampness, attributes associated with both death and primordial origins in her nature writing, and in her queering of both sexuality and expectations for the feminine.

Control and Loss of Natural Subjects in Eliot

T. S. Eliot, like Hulme, seeks to make more of the human animal through cultural control. After his conversion to the Anglican faith, such control increasingly involves religious icons and structures. Hulme introduced religion into his classicist program for combating human lapses. As Raymond Williams has noted, when Eliot's late works refer to nature, this is largely done to confirm the existence of God. Eliot shared Hulme's objections to Romanticism, his attitudes fed by Jules Laforgue, Irving Babbitt, and Charles Maurras. Eliot's celebrated "objective correlative," more so than Pound's "complex in an instant of time," controls the emotional response to some thing (often that subterranean feminine nature that so troubled Lewis), even as it uses the object's attributes to define the emotions. Eliot likes to formulate art in scientific terms. Thus, Hulme's pliable curves of steel have a counterpart in Eliot's filament of platinum, a catalyst that provides a useful analogy to the creative combinations achieved by the mature poet: "When the two gasses previously mentioned are mixed in the presence of a filament of platinum, they form sulphurous acid. The combination takes place only if the platinum is present. . . . The mind of the poet is the shred of platinum" ("Tradition and the Individual Talent" 88).

Eliot is not limited to his own controlled container, however influential this theory may have been. To the disgust of Pound and Lewis, Eliot gladly ventured into "Venusburg," playing the decadent in pale powder and eye shadow, and he set out to charm Bloomsbury. He published poetry and essays with Leonard and Virginia Woolf's Hogarth Press, and exchanged confidences about his art with her as they rode through London in a cab, or when he came as her guest to Monk's House. Many of the remarks about his work that proved most useful to biographer Peter Ackroyd were garnered from just such confidences, recorded in Woolf's diaries and letters.

Woolf and Eliot shared comparable post-Victorian childhoods in contact with nature. Both had parents of advanced age who entertained Darwinian ideas.[7] Eliot's childhood holidays in Gloucester, Massachusetts, on Cape Ann, offered him experiences similar to those little Virginia had at St. Ives in Cornwall. Lyndall Gordon, who makes a special point of the spirit of place provided to Eliot by Cape Ann, notes that he learned to identify seventy types of birds and various seaweeds. Eliot made an insect collection, combed through detritus on the shore, and examined crabs and sea anemones in costal rock pools. He learned to sail there, his parents feeling this would build up his delicate constitution. Young Eliot was fascinated by the yarns of fishermen, and he worked these into early school compositions and his mature work.

Winter meant a return to the city for Eliot, as it did for Woolf. His destination was St. Louis, where his father was president of the Hydraulic-Press Brick Company. The city offered his first riparian landscape, the Mississippi, as it ran among the factories, much like Joyce's River Liffey. Eliot planned to title his childhood reminiscences "The River and the Sea," and as Ackroyd notes, "These two natural forces run through all of his poetry, remembered even when they are absent in the landscape of desert or dry rock" (22). There was also a childhood garden in St. Louis, with a locked door in a wall, leading to a girl's school that he shyly visited. All of this is vaguely suggestive of the hedged garden Woolf explored in childhood at St. Ives, and of the psychological encounters of the children in the garden in *The Waves*. Of these children, Louis has been convincingly compared to Eliot, having a name suggestive of Eliot's St. Louis origin, a foreign (though Australian) accent, and a banker for a father (see Eder). Louis entertains images of the river as he departs London by train, bound to boarding school: "We are drawn though the booking-office on to the platform as a stream draws twigs and straws round the piers of a bridge" (*W* 20). Eliot's *Burnt Norton* has echoes of children's voices and partakes of the same privileged British garden sites that Woolf evokes throughout her writing, especially in *The Waves*.

The natural elements Eliot experienced, particularly in the summers at Cape Ann, survive as memories evoking lost possibilities in much of Eliot's poetry. "The Love Song of J. Alfred Prufrock" brings back the insect collection, but here the protagonist is the specimen trapped on the pin, rather than a curious collector. "Prufrock" recollects the crab, but as a bodily fragment, and a means of escape from a feminine society that does not understand him: "I should have been a pair of ragged claws / Scuttling across the floors of silent seas" (73–74). The poem ends with a timid walk on the beach, where mermaids sing to each other, but doubtfully to him. These fantasy females have the vivid experience of nature he lacks, riding on waves blown white and black by the wind, and "wreathed with seaweed red and brown" (127–28). In "Rhapsody on a Windy Night," memory's "clear relations / Its divisions and precisions" (6–7) have been dissolved by "lunar incantations" (4). This poem moves back and forth between images of nature and ones of city squalor, occasionally blending them "As a madman shakes a dead geranium" (12). Suggesting primitive origins of poetry, the street light "beats like a fatalistic drum" (9) and directs his attention toward feminine corruption as nature: "that woman / Who hesitates toward you in the light of the door" (17). He detects sand on the border of her torn dress, and the twist in the corner of her eye reminds him of

> A twisted branch upon the beach
> Eaten smooth, and polished
> As if the world gave up
> The secret of its skeleton,
> Stiff and white. (25–29)

Nature has some vigor in the recollected encounter with "a crab one afternoon in a pool, / An old crab with barnacles on his back, / Gripped the end of a stick which I held him" (43–45). The scene could as well be in the opening chapter of Woolf's *Jacob's Room*, where young Jacob climbs a rock "rough with crinkled limpet shells and sparely strewn with locks of dry sea wood" to retrieve "an opal-shelled crab" moving "on weakly legs on the sandy bottom" (*JR* 9). A list of lost natural images figures into Eliot's renunciations of "Ash Wednesday," many from his early seascape. He records "the lost lilac and the lost sea voices," as well as "the bent golden-rod," and "the cry of quail and the whirling plover" (196, 198, 200). "Dry Salvages" of *The Four Quartets* notes a loss to evolution, as the sea tosses "its hints of earlier and other creation: The starfish, the hermit crab, the whale's backbone" (18–19) on the beaches and offers "for our curiosity / The more delicate algae and the sea anemone" in seaside pools (20–21).

The pattern of lost nature takes numerous forms in "The Waste Land," a text well known to Woolf, who hand set it for publication by Hogarth Press. Pound cut many references to mariners and the sea by ejecting all but eight lines of part 4, "Death by Water." In what remains, we learn that Phlebas the Phoenician had known the gulls and the sea swell, but we are also instructed to dread nature, as we attend to the denuding of Phlebas's bones by sea currents, and are warned that the same could await any "who turn the wheel and look windward" (320). In earlier drafts, Eliot tells a disastrous tale of Glouces-ter fishermen whose ship is blown to oblivion in the Arctic (a trajectory sug-gestive of Ernest Shackleton's Antarctic wreck, cited in his notes). The voyage had started with benevolent conditions for creatures: "Kingfisher weather," the breeze so mild that "a porpoise snored upon the phosphorescent swell" (*The Waste Land: Facsimile* 55). When references to the sea return toward the end of the poem, it is the "hand expert with the sail and oar" and the heart . . . beating obedient / To controlling hands" (420–23) that approach the classical imperative, or the sort of control Mr. Ramsay would demand of a child at the helm of a sailboat in Woolf's *To the Lighthouse*. The voice of thunder works similarly, bearing the message of the *Upanishads:* "Give, sym-pathise, control" (*Complete Poems and Plays* 54).

Culture churns down many modernist rivers in both the global south and north: Conrad's *Heart of Darkness,* Woolf's *The Voyage Out,* Langston Hughes's "The Negro Speaks of Rivers," and Joyce's *Finnegans Wake.* The ri-parian landscape of "The Waste Land" runs through history as well as the urban environment, demonstrating how fragmentary and polluted modern experience of nature and self has become. We encounter "Trams and dusty trees" near Highbury (292–93) and "can connect / Nothing with nothing" on arrival at Margate Sands (301–2). Nature, if present on Eliot's river, "sweats / Oil and tar" (266–67) and is debased by paper wrappers, broken glass, and rats. Eliot would remind us in "The Dry Salvages" of *Four Quartets* that the river "is a strong brown god—sullen, untamed and intractable" by "dwellers in the cities" and "unpropitiated / By worshippers of the machine" (2, 10, 7).

Eliot's interest in "vegetation ceremonies" and the Fisher King, derived from James Frazer's *The Golden Bough,* provide a framework for the restora-tion of the arid landscape of "The Waste Land"—a place of red rock moun-tains and comparable architecture and humanity ("red sullen faces sneer and snarl / From doors of mudcracked houses" [344–45]), resonant with a decayed Europe. Aided by Chapman's *Handbook of Birds of Eastern North America* (cited twice in his notes), Eliot describes another loss: "the sound of water over rock / Where the hermit-thrush sings in the pine trees" (356–57)[8] It is the cock that immediately presages the long-awaited rain. Eliot's birds in "The Waste Land" include the kingfisher (reminiscent of the Fisher King) and the nightingale. The "jug jug" sound attributed to this bird (103, 204) is more closely related to Procne's "rudely-forced" (101, 205) abuse at the hands of Tereus in classical tragedy than to an actual bird call. Both of these birds were also significant to Woolf and were useful for connections with myths. Indeed, classicism offered a number of different options and its own rich connections to nature, a pattern we return to in the final chapter.

Sounding a more serious note about animal life are Eliot's Sweeney poems. For the Hogarth Press, the Woolfs set to print the unsavory café drama "Sweeney among the Nightingales." Most of the characters have animal traits, starting with Sweeney's simian apeneck and his spread knees (1). In "Sweeney Erect," he is compared to an orangutan. Carrie Rohman compares Eliot's human silhouettes to evolutionary charts common to Darwinian discourse (35). Sweeney may be primitive, or regressive, as a representative of the human. The other characters are no more exalted. A man in brown overlaps animal species when identified as a "vertebrate" (21), and Rachel tears into grapes with her "paws" (24). Nightingales sing of Agamemnon's tragic death (hinting that Sweeney too is at risk, and reminding us of Procne's tragedy and revenge). They excrete droppings on the ruler's shroud, suggesting that nature has little respect for cultural authority, or that natural processes eventually prevail. In her review "Is This Poetry?," Woolf selects as examples of poetry the two verses of this poem in which the nightingales sing. As quoted in the second epigraph to this chapter, she comments, "Poetry often seems to come in precisely at the moment when the scientist and the science, the method and the newness, go out" (E 3:56). This suggests that she had a different departure for modernism than the technical modernism espoused by Eliot, Pound, and Lewis.

Rachel Blau DuPlessis has drawn attention to racialized, Semiticized, gendered narratives in Eliot and to actions that undermine "female sexual choices and agency." As an example, she takes up Eliot's unfinished play, *Sweeney Agonistes*. In this work a Creolized Sweeney encourages a young woman to join him in primitive existence on a crocodile isle, where birth, copulation, and death rule the day (*Complete Poems and Plays* 79–80). The Conradian horror of it comes through allusion to missionary stew and a story of "a man [who] once did a girl in" (83), all played to the music-hall, minstrel chorus of a voodoo "Hoo / Hoo / Hoo" (85). DuPlessis finds that by using drumbeats, black diction, and elements of minstrelsy, Eliot, Vachel Lindsay, and Wallace Stephens both mock the African "savage" and appropriate his presumed sexual potency.[9]

Throughout his life Eliot recurrently sought and found relief in the country, often with female companionship. The newly wed Eliots rented cottages at Bosham and Marlow for several summers (1916–19), supposedly for the restoration of Vivien's health, though his was also in need of tonic. Eliot's return to sailing and her enjoyment of the garden introduced rare elements of fresh air to this difficult marriage.[10] The actress and producer Emily Hale, the first potential love of Eliot's life, shared country experiences with him. A poem that begins with the beautifully evocative phrase "Hidden under the heron's wing" was composed early in their relationship (Gordon). We can suspect Hale's presence in the many young women with flowers, who are ultimately denied love but made timeless in memory: the "Portrait of a Lady," which includes "a bowl of lilacs in her room" (42); "La Figlia che Piange," urged to "clasp your flowers to you with a pained surprise" (4); and the hyacinth girl of "The Waste Land." Hale spent many summers in England in the years between Eliot's marriages, and he joined her for country walks. Lyndall Gordon is amused by Eliot's letters on the subject, which "cast him as a cowardly, grown-up child, town bred and a nuisance on country walks because he fears the prongs of a bull lurking behind every tree" (399). Hale accompanied him to the setting of "Burnt Norton" while he was writing *Four Quartets*. In this work she shares the rose with the virgin, in Eliot's careful management of love in time. As Gordon has noted, the "unattended moment" that Eliot identified in his art at this stage bears comparison to Woolf's "moments of being," codified in her late memoir, "A Sketch of the Past." Such moments come frequently to those who are in relaxed immersion in a natural setting.

At mid-life Eliot assumed another role, remotely complicit with nature. As a respite from the World War II bombings of London, he resided part of the week at Shamley Green, Guildford, with Hope Mirrlees's family circle of women. Woolf's own involvement with Mirrlees included hand setting her poem "Paris" for Hogarth Press.[11] Again Gordon is droll: "Eliot enjoyed his position as prize domestic pet amongst women who cherished numerous cats and dogs" (367). Eliot's best-seller, *Old Possum's Book of Practical Cats,* confirms his sustained role play involving animals. I have remarked elsewhere that Pound's assignment of the "possum" identity to Eliot suits his capacity for playing dead (*Refiguring Modernism* 1:119). *Cats* is caricature, an important aim in Eliot's work, as he described it to Woolf. These verses often capture the movements and reposes of actual cats—as do his representations of cats in "Rhapsody on a Windy Night": "the cat which flattens itself in the gutter" (35), and the catlike fog of "Prufrock." These cats were "practical" in more than their personal exploits. Eliot could present his "Cats" as offerings that endeared him to others, without too much emotional involvement or risk on his part. Further, they allowed Eliot to construct categories as a way of controlling arrant behaviors. The cats' behaviors are very human, and suspiciously prone toward philosophy. They are of psychological value to the extent that they fulfill human fantasy. Both animal caricatures and more serious approaches to animal sensibilities compatible with ecofeminism emerge as important concerns of modernism considered further in chapter 5.

Joyce's Feminine Portrait of Nature

Though Wyndham Lewis championed Joyce's masculinity in repudiating Woolf, Joyce was more deeply interested in feminine depths and positive equations with nature than Lewis might have liked. Raised in Dublin and later the inhabitant of cosmopolitan capitals of Europe, Joyce is so obviously an urban writer that it may seem unpromising to go to him for a sense of nature. His large family was too far on the socioeconomic skids to afford extended childhood vacations in the countryside. He lived, however, in close association with animals that still frequented Dublin streets and was a short walk from the beach—an important landscape shared with modernists generally seen as closer to nature. The River Liffey was to him a female entity, Anna Livia Plurabelle, flowing from the remote countryside to dissolution in the sea in *Finnegans Wake*.

Representations of nature are frequently filtered through Joyce's characters and may vary with their level of maturity, education, or political beliefs, reinforcing the notion that nature is a discursive formation. In *A Portrait of the Artist as a Young Man*, Stephen Dedalus goes briefly to Clongowes Wood College, a privileged Jesuit institution whose "wood" discloses its rural location. Once there, Stephen is hardly a Wordsworthian child in nature. His Jesuit instructors support a controlled, classicist curriculum, reinforcing a strong patriarchal sense of sin. Stephen is plagued by social anxieties and spends much more time indoors than out. There is, however, something romantic to him about the peasant farmers of the region, who carry the aroma of the winter air and turf fires into the Clongowes chapel; Stephen gets pleasure from thinking of fields where turnips were dug, and with trees "beyond the pavilion where the gallnuts were" (62).

Joyce would return to the forest in the "Cyclops" episode of *Ulysses*, though in the service of a political satire rather than natural preservation.

The sixteenth- and seventeenth-century deforestation of Ireland is part of its colonial history, so it is not surprising that the Fenian zealot, the "Citizen," blusters that his barroom audience must "save the trees of Ireland for the future men of Ireland on the fair hills of Eire" (12.1262–63). This gendered discourse reserves the forest as a masculine preserve, set on feminine "fair hills." Narrative control shifts, however, and the Citizen's argument fades into the pageant of a fashionable wedding between the "grand high chief ranger of the Irish National Foresters, with Miss Fir Conifer of Pine Valley" (12.1267–69). Reflecting the rhetoric of the society column, this parodic discourse aims at a feminine genre, rather than environmental consciousness.

As the maturing Stephen returns to Dublin in *Portrait,* we experience fewer natural references until he becomes interested in female figures. Dumas and the Romantic poets provide his models for the feminine gendering of nature. Stephen begins to notice gardens and to imagine his own women within them. Having met Emma, Stephen feels that "another nature seemed to have been lent him" (83). Rebounding from episodes of lust, Stephen imagines himself "in a wide land under a tender lucid evening sky, a cloud drifting westward amid a pale green sea of heaven" in the presence of the Virgin—in effect his sky mother.

Stephen turns seaward as he anticipates an artistic, rather than a priestly, future for himself. The beach is an important setting for Joyce, not only in *Portrait* but also in both the "Proteus" and the "Nausicaa" episodes of *Ulysses.* The solitary Stephen is older than Jacob Ramsay as he wanders the shore, but children share the scene. "He was alone. He was unheeded, happy and near to the wild heart of life. He was alone and young and willful and wildhearted, alone among a waste of wild air and brackish waters and the seaharvest of shells and tangle and veiled grey sunlight and gayclad lightclad figures, of children and girls and voices childish and girlish in the air" (171). Despite its name, this "Bull" beach has strong feminine elements. The description is mannered, its repetitions calling attention to Stephen's own cultivation of nature in the scene, just as on an earlier walk to the beach Stephen drew words from his "treasure" to describe the color of clouds. The mannerisms of the young male writer are themselves open for analysis here, just as the methods of Woolf's Bernard, recording phrases in his notebook, would be in *The Waves.*

We turn next to Stephen's famous encounter with the wading girl, unabashedly moving before a gaze she returns. She provides material for his crafting of the bird girl: "Her bosom was as a bird's, soft and slight; slight and soft as the breast of some darkplumaged dove" (171). As he caresses each part of her body, some of its aspects avian, some girlish, she has an erotic appeal that occasions "excitement." The bird image used in relation to girls was also a favorite with Proust. But once Stephen's bird girl enters his soul, she becomes both muse and vocational guide to "the fair courts of life," a construction that takes us very far from Stephen's brief brush with nature. A far less critically regarded moment of communion with feminine earth follows:

> His eyelids trembled as if they felt the vast cyclic movement of the earth and her watchers, trembled as if they felt the strange light of some new world. His soul was swooning into some new world, fantastic, dim, uncertain as under sea, traversed by cloudy shapes and beings. A world, a glimmer, or a flower? Glimmering and trembling, trembling and unfolding, a breaking light, an opening flower, it spread in endless succession to itself, breaking in pure crimson and unfolding and fading to palest rose, leaf by leaf and wave of light by wave of light, flooding all the heavens with its soft flushes, every flush deeper than the other. (172)

A comparable flower vision, drawn from his coming into conscious life, is experienced repeatedly by Proust, whose flowers are one of his most insistent images.[12] Woolf offers a moment similar to Joyce's with the sensitive toddler, George, in *Between the Acts:* "The flower blazed between the angles of the roots. Membrane after membrane was torn. It blazed a soft yellow, a lambent light under a film of velvet; it filled the caverns behind the eyes with light. All the inner darkness became a hall, leaf smelling, earth smelling, of yellow light" (*BA* 8). These "moments of being," shared by Woolf, Proust, and Joyce, ground the young subject in a conceptual universe, starting with an erotic sense of union with a simple organic form. The experience resembles what Marianna Torgovnick identifies with "oceanic" feelings of ecstasy: "The West has tended to scant some vital human emotions and sensations of relatedness and interdependence—though it has never eliminated them. These sensations include effacement of the self and the intuition of profound connections between humans and land, humans and animals, humans and minerals, of a kind normally found in Europe and the United States only within mystical traditions" (*Primitive Passions* 4).

Toward the end of *Portrait,* Stephen is obsessed by the story of a young woman who opened her cottage door, and potentially her bed, to Stephen's friend Davin as he passed through the Ballyhoura hills. Like the bird girl, this image of a rural woman is converted to an animal, and appropriated by the artist: "the figure of the woman . . . stood forth . . . as a type of her race and his own, a batlike soul waking to the consciousness of itself in darkness and secrecy and loneliness" (182–83). Stephen leaves Ireland on a related but more masculinely defined project. Inspired by a bird of augury associated with the mythical Dedalus, Stephen vows to "forge in the smithy of my soul the uncreated conscience of my race" (253). With this art becomes a masculine, metallic fabrication, even a falsity, in an endeavor to "make it new." In "Modern Fiction," Woolf used Joyce as an example of her own generation of writers and their ability to get closer to life and consciousness. However, she was critical of a method that left one feeling "centered in a self which, in spite of its tremor of susceptibility, never embraces or creates what is outside itself or beyond" (E 4:162).[13] Her own attitude toward nature was to include this sort of embrace.

Repositioned Images of Woman in Nature: Gertrude Stein, H.D., and Jane Harrison

One has only to think of much-repeated phrases of Gertrude Stein to recall that she worked with natural images in new and tantalizing ways: "A rose is a rose is a rose is a rose" and "Pigeons on the grass alas."[14] Conscious of ways that moderns differed from previous generations, and that meaning of even so basic an image as the rose alters with time and situation, she repeats "rose" three times over, reworks the phrase, and eventually loops it into a continuous, inexhaustible ring.

Stein was no better liked by Wyndham Lewis than was Virginia Woolf— her major fault being a supposed obsession with time, shared by other modernists, including Joyce, as Lewis argued in *Time and Western Man*. He further attacked Stein on national and even physical grounds, her deliberate repetition degraded to a stutter: "Stein is just the German musical soul leering at itself in a mirror, and sticking out at itself a stuttering welt of swollen tongue" (104). Stein's modernist writing began well before doctrines on "men of 1914," imagism, and vorticism appeared. Having moved to Paris in 1902, she began *The Making of Americans,* the lesbian autobiographical work *Q.E.D.,* and *Three Lives.* Her highly experimental *Tender Buttons* appeared in 1914.

Woolf and Stein met in 1926, thanks to Edith Sitwell, herself eventually the subject of one of Stein's verbal portraits, "Sitwell Edith Sitwell." Woolf was never close to Stein; indeed, her remarks in letters and her diary are largely uncomplimentary. Still, the Woolfs published Stein's important theoretical essay "Composition as Explanation" as one of their series of Hogarth Essays in 1926.[15] Rachael Blau DuPlessis, in "WOOLFENSTEIN," suggests that *Tender Buttons* may have influenced the imagery of Woolf's *The Waves*.

While her childhood, unlike that of many modernists discussed in this chapter, was not obviously immersed in nature, Stein and her four older siblings enjoyed regular outings to Viennese parks during her early childhood. Once settled in Oakland, California, she and her brother Leo took to collecting insects and snakes. She could play in the family orchard and harvest fruit there. Stein's mother, Milly, raised chickens and sold peas grown on their grounds; there were a cow, dogs, pet birds, and a hedge of roses (Wagner-Martin 12, 19). Stein's "wife," Alice B. Toklas, though best known for her cooking prowess, was also a vegetable and flower gardener. She engaged in subsistence agriculture during the perilous sojourn of the two Jewish Americans in Vichy France during World War II. Two successive standard poodles called Basket and another named Pépé performed for guests, entering into the Stein legend. The dogs accompanied Stein on extended walks through the French countryside, mixing exercise with vital wartime contacts that enhanced security. Stein's careful observation of the manners and movements of her dogs, as well as those of cows and chickens, often find their way into her works.

Nature has considerable presence in the boldly domestic *Tender Buttons*, which is divided into sections entitled "Objects," "Food," and "Rooms." Into the "rooms" enter the moon, starlight, clouds, landscapes, air currents, and considerations of climate, often establishing a mood: "This cloud does change with the movements of the moon and the narrow the quite narrow suggestion of the building. It does and then when it is settled and no sounds differ then comes the moment when cheerfulness is so assured that there is an occasion" (507). Through juxtaposition, association, and circularity, Stein establishes, identifies, or reduces hierarchies and boundaries between human and nonhuman creatures, connecting their emotions. "CHICKEN" has four separate entries in the "Food" category; echoing dismissive systems of cultural value, it is pronounced degradingly "a peculiar bird," and "alas a dirty word . . . a dirty bird" (492–93). A greater sense of merger can be found in "A

DOG" from the "Objects" section: "A little monkey goes like a donkey that means to say that means to say that more sighs last goes. Leave with it. A little monkey goes like a donkey" (474).[16]

With Stein, flowers are especially suggestive of the physical qualities and cultural vulnerabilities of women. Though obviously enjoying its play with sound and repetition, "RED ROSES" can suggest a violated female body as well as a flower: "A cool red rose and a pink cut pink, a collapse and a sold hole, a little less hot" (472). Feminist commentary upon the patriarchal fetish of female purity, for woman or cultivated flower, might well be found in "A RED STAMP," with its juxtaposition of "lily white" and "dusty" flowers—the latter denied "grace" (whether religious or aesthetic): "If lilies are lily white if they exhaust noise and distance and even dust, if they dusty will dirt a surface that has no extreme grace, if they do this and it is not necessary it is not at all necessary if they do this they need a catalogue" (465). The syntax makes it difficult to determine if the pure or dusty lily needs the catalogue—though the pure white strain would seem to be the one to make the grade as a cultivar. The catalogue introduces the commercial element—the sale of flower or maiden—for marketing, complete with a red stamp of quality control. Stein may even encourage us to play with "exhaust noise," not just as an unusual action for the white lily, but as polluting products of modern technology encountered daily by women expected to remain immaculate. Still comes the assurance "a rose is a rose is a rose is a rose."

H.D., like Eliot and Woolf, had early access to the natural settings and images that would continue to populate her writing. In *Psyche Reborn*, Susan Stanford Friedman finds sources for images in "the harsh, northern seacoasts of Cornwall and Maine, the uncultivated fields and woods she roamed near her home in Upper Darby, and the flowers of the garden planted by her grandmother and enlarged by her mother" (2). Her youthful friendship with Ezra Pound places him in her natural environs, accounting for "Dryad" (wood nymph), his pet name for her in "Hilda's Book."[17] H.D. was able to embrace both classicism and Romanticism, her classicism tending toward the recovery of Sappho, and flourishing in feminist interpretations of mythical women such as Eurydice, Circe, and Helen—a phenomenon shared by Woolf, as we shall examine in chapter 6. Indeed, it offers an alternative classicism to that suggested for modernism by Hulme.

Sea Garden, H.D.'s first collection of poems (1916), contains exemplary verses of imagism (several published in Pound's *Des Imagistes*), but it also helps us sort out the merits of various naturally sensitive environments. Cassandra Laity finds that H.D.'s persona must leave the "cloyingly sweet" garden of "Sheltered Garden" for stormy settings by the sea (113). "Orchard" also suggests false values of cultivated spaces. H.D.'s speaker in this poem appeals with the god of the orchard to "spare us from loveliness" (6).[18] She has been susceptible to the first falling pear, going prostrate to catch it, feeling "flayed . . . / with your blossoms" (10–11). Her offering to the god is the imperfect, neglected fruits of nature. She may be escaping the idealized beauty of the female body, the fresh, perfect ripe pear. "Pear Tree" offers another attitude, in which the blooming tree has a more uplifting effect, with "silver dust . . . higher than my arms can reach" (1, 3).

The pear tree has numerous manifestations in modernist women's writing. Janie of Zora Neale Hurston's *Their Eyes Were Watching God* has an exalting apprehension of her own physical ripening as she sits under a blossoming pear. Katherine Mansfield uses a pear tree in full bloom to suggest female happiness and connection (though it proves to be a treacherous connection) in her story "Bliss."[19] In *To the Lighthouse,* the daughter Rose creates a still-life "arrangement of the grapes and pears, of the horny pink-lined shell, of the bananas" that reminds her mother of art depicting an undersea banquet, and the revels of Bacchus. When he helps himself to fruit, Mrs. Ramsay sees Augustus Carmichael as a marauding bee who "plunged in, broke off a bloom there, a tassel here, and returned, after feasting, to his hive" (*TTL* 97). Indeed, feminine sexuality is as vulnerable as the pear blossom to penetration.

The preferred and predominant setting of H.D.'s *Sea Garden* is a marginal one, where the sea meets the land. Alternatively, we can see it as liminal, a place where natural images are taken into the author's subjectivity and emotions. The novelist and critic May Sinclair said of H.D.'s work that "the fusion, the identity" of mood and object "is complete" (455). Eileen Gregory notes the "harsh power of elemental life" in the seaside gardens, including the emotional associations of salt and tears and the soul's engagement with the sea itself. This choice of flower seems complicit with the "dry hardness" of Hulme's formula (140). "Sea Rose" is "harsh" and "marred with stint of petals, and "stunted" (1–2, 9), its "acrid fragrance / hardened in a leaf" (15–16). Its position, however, "caught in the drift" and lifted / in the crisp sand / that drives in the wind" (8, 11–12) suggests the intensity of its experience, which is preferable to that of the single-stemmed wet rose. The amber husks of "Sea

Poppies," rooted "among wet pebbles / and drift flung by the sea / and grated shells / and split conch-shells" (9–12), have similar advantages over the fruits of the meadow, as does the "sea-violet / fragile as agate" ("Sea Violet" 3–4). These plants are survivors of physical trauma, and as such they are invaluable images for female would-be survivors.

In her own version of the imagist process described by Pound, H.D. is apt to make a complex of natural materials, at the same time emerging from a depressed, still condition and developing her own energies. An instance is her taking of the rose from the rock in "Garden," a vision akin to what Woolf is looking for in the first epigraph to this chapter. Her poem begins:

> You are clear
> O rose, cut in rock,
> Hard as the descent of hail.
>
> I could scrape the colour
> From the petals
> Like spilt dye from a rock (1–6)

This complex, demanding poem seems to require that the poet perform a geological process, breaking through stone and heat to produce the flower and fruit of her art. Such is the case, too, with waves and evergreen fir, whirled together in "Oread" to produce a spirit of exaltation in nature. Eurydice, pulled by Orpheus toward the earthly flowers she has sorely missed, then losing them to his arrogance, arrives at a better sense of self, having found the alternate, "the flowers of myself" (125). These contrast aesthetically to the black rocks of hell but emerge from them. She is now determined that hell must "open like a red rose / For the dead to pass" before she will be lost (134–35). H.D. moves from dialogue with nature and its gods into a more willful commanding of the self to work actively and deliberately with nature in a motivational form of art. Writing of "Hymen," H.D.'s friend Marianne Moore ponders the masculine "tendency to match one's intellectual and emotional vigor with the violence of nature." She finds in "the absence of subterfuge, cowardice, and the ambition to dominate by brute force" that we have in H.D.'s work "heroics which do not confuse transcendence with domination and which in their indestructibleness, are the core of tranquility and intellectual equilibrium" (352). Recovery through selection and combination of natural images is a process suggested in H.D.'s poems that we will encounter again via some of Woolf's traumatized female characters in the final chapter.

H.D. searches for communities where women were joined together—Sappho's Lesbos being the most important example, as Eileen Gregory has suggested. Her poems speak to nature, often addressing a nymph, or a god of the place, "Oread" being the nymph of the mountains, and "Orchard" having a resident god. Gregory finds that the flower poems suggest H.D.'s effort to connect with Sappho's world. There, rites for young girls found expression in various floral images—the moment of the opening flower, self-celebration of the erotic body, still accompanied by fresh emotions, and the woven garland recalling the union of souls among the company of girls. Finding roses in rocks, H.D. creates an enduring image of Sappho's world (135–36). The process is increasingly visionary and inclusive of inspirations from various cultures and religions.

In her later writing, H.D.'s explorations of the female body and sexuality approach ecstatic mysteries associated with goddess-centered religion at Elusis. Work not published in her lifetime represents the rhythms and attachments of what Julia Kristeva would term the maternal semiotic, from the expectant mother's perspective. H.D.'s "Notes on Thought and Vision," composed during her pregnancy, describe a balanced, nonhierarchical system of body, mind and over-mind, whose three components complement and even substitute for one another. Her metaphor for the over-mind, which she associates strongly with art (with Leonardo, the Athenians, and "the Galilean," Jesus), is "a closed sea-plant, jelly-fish or anemone," with "long feelers [that] reached down and through the body." The state of consciousness arrived at through the over-mind can be situated in the head, but equally well in the "love-region of the body," like a fetus. She reports, "It was before the birth of my child that the jelly-fish consciousness seemed to come definitely into the field or realm of the intellect or brain" (94).

The Eleusinian mysteries, providing a visionary route, are similarly codependent and related to natural metaphors. They begin with an animal, sexual stage, showing greater comfort with the erotic than do many doctrines of patriarchal religion.[20] Images from nature convey the understanding visionaries must achieve—for example, how dung relates to flowers. Nature also plays into the dramas of gods and goddesses: "Zeus Endendros—God in a tree; Dionysius Anthios, God in a flower; Zeus Melios, God in the black earth, death disruption, disintegration." H.D. addresses Aphrogenia (Aphrodite), whose "white pear-branch which broke so white against a black April storm sky" that the jealous Zeus raised his shaft to blast the tree. Jesus loved natural things such as "the sea-gull or some lake-heron that would dart up from the coarse lake grass." She concludes this section with a maxim: "we know there is a mystery greater than beauty and that is death" (100)—perhaps a sobering return to the mystery of male destruction or an admission of death as part of a divine cycle.

H.D.'s autobiographical novel, *Bid Me to Live*, begins in wartime London, where Julia's room is curtained and shuttered against the enemy. Its swirl-ing, repetitive narrative expresses her trauma over repeated displacement, a stillborn child, and potential loss of her husband to the war that so severely traumatized the early twentieth century. Later in the novel, she has aesthetic, gender-charged debates with Rico, a character patterned on D. H. Lawrence. Rico has all sorts of natural aspects, coming tanned from Cornwall: the mol-ten-lava content of his censored novels (76), and the white hyacinth of Dis, underworld husband of Persephone, to whom he likens Julia. Julia escapes the "city of dreadful night," exchanging the golden bough for a dead limb that falls across her path (109).

The novel's movement to Cornwall returns to the rugged seascape of "Sea Garden": "a country of rock and steep cliff and sea gulls," of stone circles left by the Druids and "ghost-flowers." She distinguishes her process from that of "Bloomsbury intellectuals" and Freud (*Collected Poems* 148). In Cornwall, she feels like engaging in ritual performance: "She wanted to lay flowers on an altar" (146). As part of a healing process, she senses that, "over and above the human hurt, hovered some other non-human, abstract perception" (148). She feels "enclosed in the elements; a fish out of water (she had been too long in London), back in water, she swayed across the sea-floor. The mist above, around her was the sea-mist, sea. Each separate twig formed to her imagination, another genus; twig, stalk were twig, stalk of other un-named but racially remembered flora" (149). She feels she is in a temple left from the Druids (149). H.D. suggests that vegetation provides a sacred and mysti-cal connection to harmonious, healing forces. Her reference to the scientific system of classification, "genus," even as she is operating via the imagination, suggests that she is devising a system of her own. She has previously asked Rico for the names of plants, but she now proceeds without them. It is tempt-ing to see in this an escape from logocentrism and classification worthy of an ecofeminist. "Racially remembered" suggests the Jungian unconscious, which is also evoked in "Notes on Thought and Vision." Particularly with the mention of the Druids, one suspects that "race" in this case means a region where a particular spirituality has been in place before.

The attraction H.D. felt toward maternal deities and classical rites was facilitated by her familiarity with the work of the classical anthropologist Jane Ellen Harrison. Harrison adds an interesting page to the modernist debates about classicism versus Romanticism because, as Torgovnick has argued, she offers a different kind of classicism, one well-known in her day but neglected in canonized accounts ("Bloomsbury Fraction" 138–41). In *Prolegomena to a Study of Greek Religion,* Harrison reaches back to the earliest stages of Greek tradition, and in archaeological artifacts, she finds evidence of goddess (Great Mother) worship, matriliny, and the predominance of the performing rites over the verbal narrative of myths. While the rational control of Apollo was the classical norm for the "men of 1914," Harrison, like Nietzsche, restores the companion values of Dionysis, which include ecstasy and proximity to nature. Originally seen as the son or consort of the Great Mother, rather than the son of Zeus, Dionysus serves as a liminal figure, reaching back from male-centered myths to the earlier female-centered rites, many of them using natural objects and settings.[21]

Harrison serves this liminal role in Woolf's *A Room of One's Own,* a text written soon after her death. J____ H____ flits through the gardens of Woolf's imaginary women's college (17). This comes as Woolf's narrative moves from the male-dominated preserves of Oxbridge to this more welcoming scene. Harrison was both a friend of Woolf's, via Cambridge and Bloomsbury links, and the lover of Hope Mirrlees, sharing in the creation of "Paris."

D. H. Lawrence as Naturist

D. H. Lawrence is probably the modernist most closely associated with a return to nature's vital principles, as he would state the connection. John Alcorn suggests that Hulme, Cezanne, and the Cubists spelled the end of a naturist tradition, asserting geometry over nature (115). Not surprisingly, he finds Joyce's *Ulysses* and Eliot's "The Waste Land" more concerned with art than nature; even Hemingway and Faulkner have only superficial interest in natural representation, in his judgment. Alcorn's definition of naturist is instructive: "The naturist world is a world of physical organism, where biology replaces theology as the source both of psychic health and of moral authority.

The naturist is a child of Darwin; he sees man as part of an animal continuum; he reasserts the importance of instinct as a key to human happiness; he tends to be suspicious of the life of the mind; he is wary of abstractions" (x). Alternatively, Roger Ebbatson assigns Lawrence to the traditions of the Romantics, the Transcendentalists, and Darwinian evolution. He finds that, for Lawrence's characters, individuation brings the tragedy of uprootedness from nature (33). Dolores LaChapelle studies in Lawrence a tradition she defines as the "future primitive": "awakening to richness and complexity of primitive mind which merges sanctity, food, life and death; integration with nature in a particular ecosystem"—an assessment that places Lawrence at an ecological forefront (xix).

As Raymond Williams has noted, Lawrence grew up in a colliery town, a "borderland" where industrial growth and squalor met farmlands and countryside. Both LaChapelle and Ebbatson take interest in the proximity of Sherwood Forest, Ebbatson associating that wood with Robin Hood and English pastoralism; LaChapelle, with ancient druidic magic. Indeed, Lawrence shared the Cornwall landscape where H.D. felt closest to the Druids. That Lawrence knew his botany is verified in *Bid Me to Live*, when Julia relies upon Rico to identify the unusual plants she is encountering there. References to flowers permeate Lawrence's correspondence with Amy Lowell, herself a devotee of the garden and the floral image, particularly in love poetry. John Worthen notes that Lawrence's collier father was an expert on wild flowers, fungi, and herbs, and LaChapelle imagines the elder Lawrence garnering mushrooms and poaching the occasional rabbit from the local gentry. At Lynn Croft, the Lawrences had a garden that delighted his mother, according to Worthen. But it was probably his woodland walks to the farm operated by Jessie Chambers's family that gave Lawrence his most exalted natural experiences. By 1900 he had acquired W. T. Gordon's *Our Country's Flowers: And How to Know Them*. Flowers, birds, reptiles, and trees receive their full measure in his poetry, his store enriched by travels in Italy and the American Southwest.

The Rainbow looks back through what Williams calls the "farming generations" and their natural way of life. He suggests that Lawrence's female characters turn their backs on nature, resisting its limits. In both poetry and novels, Lawrence assigns women to nature, the womb taking its voluptuous representation in all kinds of fruit. *Women in Love* is firmly grounded in nature, starting with the botanic metaphor of the withering bud, used by Gudrun to describe the discouragement of the young, early in the book. Flowers serve in a school lesson given by Ursula in which Birkin urges her to emphasize sexual difference, even of a floral sort. A simple flower serves as her peace offering when they quarrel, and flourishing flowers are used in describing her. Gudrun brings nature into her art; she carves birds and dances (dangerously) in the face of highland cattle. How Gerald Crich violently masters his horse becomes a serious commentary on his character; indeed, the horse became one of Lawrence's most important symbolic and mysterious creatures. The stars provide Birkin with an image of balance between individuals in their dual systems, but the moon, with its mother-goddess associations, confounds him, and he stones its image in the surface of a pond. Gudrun, on the other hand, senses an underworld of female power, her insight coming perhaps via Lawrence's own reading of Jane Harrison.

Lawrence's *Psychoanalysis of the Unconscious,* published several years after H.D. wrote "Notes on Thought and Vision," makes a comparable reassignment of vital functions of the mind to the womb area. The unconscious, according to this scheme, originates with the prime nucleus, located below the navel. Its first vital flow is with the mother; other centers are added later, and all are connected via magnetic fluxes. Lawrence joins H.D. in wishing to balance the brain with other body knowledges—a connection Woolf pursues in other ways, including her consideration of the effect of bodily illness on the mind (best seen in her essay "On Being Ill").

While Lawrence started out expressing affinity for evolutionary theory, he grew increasingly interested in vitalism and the primitive. Birkin views an African sculpture of a woman in childbirth in Halliday's rooms in *Women in Love*. It is the sort of sculpture that fascinated many Western artists and critics, including Roger Fry. Torgovnick argues that, starting with *The Plumed Serpent,* Lawrence re-genders the primitive as masculine. This is exemplified by the Indian lover of Kate, Cipriano, in that novel, and in "The Woman Rode Away," where an Anglo woman gradually yields to Native American sacrificial rituals. Lawrence finds power in collective rituals that are attuned with natural symbols; animals (particularly the bird and the serpent); oceanic, spermatic liquids; the morning star; and, most important, the masculine sun. In invoking ritual, however, he is sharing in an ancient desire for control of nature. Lawrence, like Mansfield, is a modernist whose passing, as a victim of tuberculosis, Woolf paused over with regret. Woolf felt that, distracted by Bloomsbury skepticism of Lawrence, she had not given due attention to his writing during his lifetime. His masculinism, and his tendency to erect gods from primitive sources, remained detractions.

Katherine Mansfield's Prelude to Woolf

Many modernists transport childhood memories of gardens into their works. Dorothy Richardson uses a garden recollected from childhood as a unifying device for *Pilgrimage*. This appears first in *Backwater*, where as an adult she recalls herself "toddling alone along the garden path between beds of flowers almost on a level with her head and blazing in the sunlight. Bees with large bodies were sailing heavily across the path from bed to bed, passing close by her head and making a loud humming in the air. . . . Sweet Williams smelling very strongly sweet in her nostrils, and one sheeny brown everlasting flower that she had touched with her nose, smelling like hot pepper" (317). Marylu Hill has compared this passage to Woolf's memories of bees in the apple orchard at St. Ives, recorded in "A Sketch of the Past" and *To the Lighthouse* (60).

Katherine Mansfield's *The Prelude*, like Hope Mirrlees's "Paris," was one of the earliest hand-set publications of the Hogarth Press. It makes much of gardens gradually embraced by the female members of the Burnell family when they move into a country house. Young Kezia and her mother, Linda, share their fascination with a large aloe plant growing in the center island of the driveway, leading to a moment of rare communion. Linda tells her daughter that the plant flowers only once in a hundred years, and she draws attention to its protective spines. The plant's strategy may appeal to a woman subject to much more frequent childbearing. Kate Fulbrook considers Kezia a Wordsworthian figure, as is appropriate to the "Prelude" of the title. The child explores the vast garden surrounding the house. She rolls down the orchard hill and finds presents for her grandmother; through Kezia, a catalog of plants is presented. The girl is introduced to the daily violence done to animals in country life, when the hired hand brings along a group of children to watch the killing of the duck to be served as dinner. The event is suggestive of the slaying of a chicken witnessed by Rachel in Woolf's *The Voyage Out*. Birds, whose songs mark the changing of the days in Mansfield's novella, also mark the interludes of Woolf's *The Waves*.

As numerous scholars have noted, Mansfield and Woolf had a "notoriously conficted" friendship (Moran 7). Woolf's diaries and letters record her uncomplimentary reactions to meeting Mansfield yet also register envy and respect for her abilities as a writer. Woolf was taken aback by Mansfield's criticism of her second novel, *Night and Day* (1919), for its failure to reflect the cultural "scars" occasioned by the outbreak of World War I.[22] Of their common interest in nature, Moran remarks, "Both made use of the natural world as a non-human frame of reference for their characters. Above all, their prose is remarkably similar—the choice and use of images, the shape of the sentences, the rhythmic cadences, even the way each evokes the natural world" (9).

Modernism Embraces the Animal: Djuna Barnes

The animal-human continuum has fascinated a number of modernists, as Margot Norris recognized in her 1985 study, *Beasts of the Modern Imagination,* which identifies "biocentrism" in Kafka, Lawrence, and Hemingway. To this list we could easily add Stein, Joyce, Eliot, and Mansfield, from the evidence above. More recently, Carrie Rohman has entered the field with *Stalking the Subject: Modernism and the Animal* (2009), which focuses upon Conrad, Wells, Barnes, and Lawrence, and Geoff Gilbert's *Before Modernism Was* includes a chapter entitled "Dogs: Small Domestic Forms." In her recent work, Marianne DeKoven has turned toward animal studies in both modernist and contemporary texts. The web, in one sense the artifice of the spider, was a controlling metaphor for *Refiguring Modernism* (1995), my own feminist post-postmodern study of Virginia Woolf, Rebecca West, and Djuna Barnes. The web finds form in tapestries of nature referred to in Barnes's letters and stories, and in her own illustrations of beast meeting human for *The Book of Repulsive Women* and *Ryder.* I found Barnes reminding us that "we have always had nature only as fabricated and deployed by culture" and insisting furthermore "that nature does not stay conveniently separate or 'other' from culture, and that evolution has not safely or permanently delivered human beings to civilization" (*Refiguring Modernism* 2:72). Despite considerable promotion by women of modernism, Barnes was noticed largely because both *Nightwood* and *The Antiphon* were published by T. S. Eliot at Faber.

Barnes had a far from idyllic childhood in the countryside at Cornwall on Hudson, where in a bigamous household her father bred numerous children with two wives. He left most of the farming operations to his family. The father in Barnes's autobiographical novel, *Ryder,* talks to animals, has riveting eye contact with them, and treats beasts pretty much on a par with his family. Young women are situated in a male agricultural imaginary, and they are apt to be taken sexually in the field. Little wonder that Amelia, one of the wives in *Ryder,* escapes to the woods. She seems to admire cycles of decay and regeneration that work apart from male intervention.

The wood is also a retreat for Nora Flood and Robin Vote in *Nightwood.* At the start of the novel, Robin creates her equivalent of an indoor jungle in which to array herself. In the confusing conclusion of this novel, Nora goes to a decayed chapel in the woods near Nora's American home. Robin had been terrified by the gaze of a circus lion, experienced when she first met Nora. She shares her final role in the church in the woods with Nora's dog. Robin enacts doglike behavior, at first startling the animal. Gradually the two bark, and move, and finally give up, to rest alongside one another, a ritual that brings the species barrier into question and suggests a mutual kind of exchange, such as Haraway seeks when species meet. In this ritual performance may lie the "caesura" that Giorgio Agamben theorizes for escaping human distinctions with animals—a space for new politics and philosophy, rather than the endless discriminations manufactured by what he calls the "anthropological machine." The joint quest of animal and religious communion found in *Nightwood* exists also in *Ryder,* her later play *The Antiphon,* and numerous stories. The setting of the church at the end of *Nightwood* accords with Togovnick's finding that many modernists move "from the idea of the primitive to spiritual emotions," citing Eliot's shift toward religion as well as comparable shifts in the work of Carl Jung, D. H. Lawrence, Isak Dinesen, Beryl Markham, and Georgia O'Keeffe—all subjects of Torgovnick's *Primitive Passions.* The wood, or the forest in Woolf's case, was a significant place for psychological discoveries, including, in the work of Jane Harrison, reaching back to primordial origins of forest people.

Barnes saw animals (or beasts, as she preferred to call them) as a subject for her cultural satire and verbal wit throughout her life. In her journalism on the circus, Barnes compared animals to marginalized sideshow performers, anticipating contemporary insights on commonly oppressive power structures. An article in which she holds the hand of a young female gorilla at the Bronx zoo anticipates Dian Fossey's *Gorillas in the Mist,* with its blend of empathy and critical edginess. Her beasts share human burdens. One such is an ox who sympathizes with a birthing mother in *Ryder.* They bear comparison to a vast range of American folk tales, including the mules in tales collected by Zora Neale Hurston.[23] The short, paradoxical, linguistically demanding poems of her final work, *Creatures in an Alphabet,* have something in common with Marianne Moore's neatly crafted verses, cataloging animals and their representations: "The Jerboa," "Tippoo's Tiger," and "A Jellyfish."

Connective Filaments

This small inventory reveals numerous debates and developing practices relating to modernist uses of nature in which Woolf was fully involved. Numerous filaments of personal and publishing relations, as well as written essays and reviews, connect Woolf to the figures discussed here, or them to one another.[24] Eager to pronounce their difference from their immediate predecessors, including the Georgians and the Victorians, modernists also lacked the Romantics' faith in the sublime. However, they could draw selectively from the past, appreciating Keats's relation to nature, for example, as did both Virginia Woolf and Amy Lowell, and mixing classicism with Romanticism, as did H.D. We find the Hogarth Press publishing poetry and prose with extraordinary images taken from nature, including the work of Mansfield, Mirrlees, Eliot, and Stein. Whether using nature in comparable ways or rejecting it, these modernists raise issues of control or gender stereotyping that Woolf could investigate further. The deep, dank, soft feminine areas of nature eschewed by Lewis offer an exploration of primordial origins and dark places of psychology connected to the mind, when turned over to H.D., Lawrence, or Woolf. What counts as classical to Hulme and Lewis is revised for Eliot, Lawrence, H.D., and Mirrlees through the alternate view of Jane Harrison, which included early forest rites, goddess figures, and matrilineal culture. Nature enters the consciousness of modernist authors and their characters as inquiring children, and proximity to the sea furnishes "moments of being" to all ages. Crafted too deliberately, such instances can become narrow and logocentric, an exercise of the artistic self, and worthy of satire, as in the figure of Stephen Dedalus. Mature women recovering from trauma make their own decisions about assembling complex natural images, perhaps connecting human to animal, as in Barnes, or polymorphous, queer, resilient flower images, as in Stein, H.D., Lowell, and Mansfield.

We might ask what happened to the work of writers who were more obviously centered in nature, but not classifiable as modernist. Vita Sackville West's award-winning poem *The Land,* her paean to the agricultural year, is an example, finding manifestation in Woolf's *Orlando.* Of the poets associated with World War I, Edward Thomas was probably the most influential for Woolf regarding aspects of nature. Peter Sacks notes that modernism was "not the swagger of 'make it new,' but the humility, attentiveness and open clarity of perception to 'find' it so" that characterized Thomas's writing (xii). Thomas, who has been hailed as a "prophet of ecocentrism" (Longley 109), attended to the cyclic continuities of the English countryside, particularly as experienced while walking along a road. He was aware of ways that perception of nature was tinged by the war that would take his own life in 1917. In "The Sun Used to Shine," Thomas follows a conversation between two walkers as they turn "to rumours of war remote." Even the nature they encounter bears reminders of the war, whether in an apple "undermined by wasps," in small flowers forming "a sentry of dark betonies," or in crocuses that seem to have "had their birth / In sunless Hades fields" (151). His "Old Man" and this verse echo in *Between the Acts,* Woolf's last novel, written at the outset of another war, and may have more immediately influenced her novels most touched by the First World War, *Mrs. Dalloway* and *To the Lighthouse.* Though hardly modernists, these poets were read by modernists and contributed to their attentiveness toward nature.

We now have the theoretical insight to consider the ways that nature itself is a cultural construction, variable with the ages, and highly political, as empowered intellectuals, or nations, seek to regulate or collect nature for their own ends. Modernism provides a fine example, and Virginia Woolf a case worth pursuing in depth.

Diversions of Darwin
and Natural History

There are in the Natural History Museum
certain little insects so small that they have
to be gummed to the cardboard with the
lightest of fingers, but each of them, as one
observes with constant surprise, has its fine
Latin name spreading far to the right and
left of the miniature body. We have often
speculated upon the capture of these insects
and the christening of them, and marveled at
the labours of the humble, indefatigable men
who thus extend our knowledge.

~Woolf, "A Scribbling Dame"

No currency has stood the
test of time like the Darwin
currency.

~Woolf, "In Any Family
Save the Darwins"

BY THE EARLY TWENTIETH CENTURY, the field of natural history had
yielded much of its authority to a more theoretical, discipline-based pursuit
of science situated in professional societies and the academy and, as feminist
historians of science have recognized, largely off-limits to women and people
of color.[1] Natural history still attracted the general public, including women.
These "common readers" of science might also apply "survival of the fittest,"[2]
or some other smattering of Darwinian evolutionary theory to daily discourse. For Woolf, the observers and collectors of nature were as interesting
as what they collected. Writing of the eighteenth-century naturalist Gilbert

White, she sets up with imaginary binoculars to study White as he watches migratory swallows: "We observe in the first place the creature's charming simplicity. He is quite indifferent to public opinion. He will transplant a colony of crickets to his lawn; imprison one in a paper cage on his table; bawl through a speaking trumpet at his bees" ("White's Selbourne," *E* 6:190). Woolf's novels, essays, and personal writings are replete with carefully delineated natural history enthusiasts and provide complex contexts and artistic angles for the study of nature. Woolf and others in the Bloomsbury circle had considerable respect for White. Edmund Blunden's *Nature in Literature*, published by Leonard and Virginia Woolf in 1929 as one in a series of "Hogarth Lectures," ends with a chapter that credits "The Selbornian" with the lasting popularity of natural history pursuits in England, and with literary influence on numerous British writers, from Darwin to Massingham (150–55). Woolf also attends to nineteenth-century women working on the peripheries of the science—figures who have also found their place in present-day feminist science studies.

Woolf's presentation of natural history amateurs begins in the first chapter of her first novel, her approach including parody and deflation of male authority. Rachel Vinrace compares Mr. Pepper to the "fossilized fish" she lifts from a basin (*VO* 19). Knowledgeable in many things, including zoology and Greek, Pepper has accompanied the group "either to get things out of the sea, or to write upon the probable course of Odysseus" (19). He accomplishes his own deflation in "a discourse, addressed to nobody, for nobody had called for it, upon the unplumbed depths of the ocean," proceeding "white, hairless, blind monsters . . . which would explode if you brought them to the surface, their sides bursting asunder and scattering entrails to the winds" (22–23). Pepper is prevailed upon by the ship's owner—Rachel's father, Willoughby Vinrace—to stop. Pepper's own physical description by Rachel and her aunt Helen falls short of a masculine heterosexual ideal, or even human evolutionary stature—quite the reverse of the tall and burly Willoughby. Pepper delivers his discourse by "leaping on to his seat, both feet tucked under him, with the action of a spinster who detects a mouse" (22).[3] Rachel and Helen metamorphose him into a "vivacious and malicious old ape" (17). Like Pepper, the ship's steward, Mr. Grice, launches into the "tirade of a fanatical man" concerning the merits of the sea, "with good flesh down here waiting and asking to be caught" to feed the hungry of Europe (53). Grice is certain that nature is there to serve human needs and pleasures.

Woolf was, however, deeply interested in the rapidly developing, theoretical disciplines of science—particularly the fields of biology and psychology, but also physics and astronomy. Though she may have made light of some amateurs, she was one herself, and what she saw and read influenced her. The family library visited in *Between the Acts* includes works by Eddington, Darwin, and Jeans (*BA* 20). On a 1907 vacation in Sussex, Woolf records a vivid impression of the moon seen through a telescope "like a globe of frosted silver with strange wrinkles & corrugations on the surface of the metal . . . , a visible token, shining in dead of night, that the sun was still blazing somewhere, in an August sky" (*PA* 368).[4] She attended programs of the London Film Society, whose offerings included the "Bionomics Series," featuring close-up and slow-motion photography of plants and animals.[5]

Women were more often the objects of, rather than the subjects conducting, science. As Marina Benjamin remarks in her introduction to *Science and Sensibility,* the doctrine of separate spheres was so established that it "arouse[d] no more remark than the statement of a natural law" (1). Still, women did learn scientific theory and play supportive roles, sometimes reconstructing the scientific narrative itself. Such women entered Woolf's imagination and populated her writing throughout her career. In *Mrs. Dalloway,* Clarissa's ancient aunt Helena "could not resist recalling what Charles Darwin had said about her little book on the orchids of Burma" (*MD* 175). Among Woolf's "Lives of the Obscure" rests her account of a specialist on destructive insects, Eleanor Ormerod. In *A Room of One's Own,* Woolf describes revolutionary content in Mary Carlyle's contemporary novel—two women characters sharing a laboratory as they engage in medical research. Woolf refers repeatedly to Mary Kingsley in *Three Guineas,* finding Kingsley's exploration of Africa in the service of ichthyology all the more remarkable considering that only £20 to £30 was spent on her education, and that for German language study (*3G* 6–7, 171). In her early novel *Night and Day,* Woolf offers Katherine, a heroine who prefers working in mathematics to preserving her grandfather's reputation as a poet, and in her penultimate novel, one of the characters, Peggy, becomes a physician. With this chapter I should like to consider the approaches to natural history encountered by the young Virginia Stephen, as well as her range of responses, which included disinterest, parody, concern with the obstacles women faced in science, and fascination with detailed observation of nature and the related narratives of science.[6]

A Natural History of the Stephen Family

Woolf's diaries, the Stephen children's family newspaper, family letters, and photo albums reveal a family enthusiasm for natural history that spanned the generations and the sexes. This interest has only modestly been attended to, as biographers have sought the environmental factors that produced Virginia's literary and Vanessa's artistic achievements. Leslie Stephen was an admirer of Gilbert White, the Oxford-educated country parson who meticulously studied the flora and fauna of his native village of Selborne and, like Stephen, appreciated the Sussex Downs. Books dating back into the nineteenth century, and very likely originating in the Stephens' library handed down to Virginia, included numerous titles featuring botany in general, butterflies, and birds, as well as less specialized works of natural history.[7] Notable are an autographed presentation copy of Darwin's *The Origin of Species* and a copy of his *Journal of Researches into the Natural History and Geology of the Countries Visited during the Voyage of the "Beagle"* (1879), with Darwin's inscription on an inserted paper: "From the Author with vy kind regards—."

Projects in natural history flourished during the long summer vacations in the countryside—at St. Ives while Julia Stephen lived, and subsequently at a variety of substantial houses in such places as the New Forest, Wiltshire, and Salisbury. Their leisure and the fine accommodations are reminders that the Stephens' access to nature was privileged. London offered the more formal resources of the Natural History Museum, walks in Kensington Gardens, and visits to the zoo in Regent's Park. Kew Gardens, with its collection of the plants of the world, was more remotely accessible. Brighton, where the family frequently visited relatives, had its own natural history museum and aquarium.

Although he did not consider himself a natural history enthusiast, Leslie Stephen brought home aspects of scientific exploration and evolutionary theory to his family. One of the reasons Stephen gives for his loss of faith is his reading of Darwin's *Origin of Species* (Bicknell 13)—an attitude that affected his life's work[8] and the belief system of his children. The elderly Charles Darwin and several of his descendants were acquaintances of the Stephen family.[9] Thomas Huxley, the noted popularizer of Darwin, was Stephen's close friend. Gillian Beer finds Huxley's style comparable to Woolf's in "its rapid shifts of scale and perturbation between metaphor and substance" ("The Victorians and Virginia Woolf" 105). Leslie was also acquainted with

Herbert Spencer and responded positively to a meeting with Mary Kingsley, who was accruing additional renown as a lecturer.

Stephen's expression of interest and respect toward Kingsley, recorded in a letter to his son Thoby, shows some acceptance of women in science, though details complicate the message. He reports meeting "the wonderful lady who travels all by herself in Africa, among gorillas and cannibals and in mangrove swamps." The mangroves are indeed important to Kingsley's account, but Stephen comes up with the gorillas on his own, and he makes the most of Kingsley's suspicions of cannibals, sensationalizing the account along typical lines of imperial encounter. He omits her intended purpose, the collection of rare fish, at which she had some success—three previously undiscovered fish bear her name (L 2:479). Kingsley's is one of the deaths he reports in his *Mausoleum Book*, pronouncing her a "genius," but appending a traditional moral tribute to a "good kind woman" (108). By the late Victorian period, botany (particularly orchids, ferns, and seaweeds) and insect collecting were established natural history pursuits for women,[10] so it is not too surprising that Leslie would encourage botanizing by Virginia.

As a child, Leslie Stephen was fragile, and seaside vacations in Brighton were recommended for his health. His love of flowers and his habit of talking to the animals in his Noah's Ark may have fallen short of Victorian norms for masculinity. A childlike love of animals persists in the sketches that ornament his books—a menagerie favoring dogs, cats, and monkeys, but also including pigs, parrots, wolves, lynx, chamois, kangaroos, lions, and an occasional bear, camel, fox, squirrel, crocodile, or owl (figure 2). Virginia Woolf recalls in her 1932 "Leslie Stephen" essay: "He would twist a sheet of paper beneath a pair of scissors and out would drop an elephant, a stag, or a monkey with trunks, horns, and tails delicately and exactly formed. Or, taking a pencil, he would draw beast after beast—an art that he practiced almost unconsciously as he read, so that the fly-leaves of his books swarm with owls and donkeys as if to illustrate the 'Oh, you ass!' or 'Conceited dunce,' that he was wont to scribble impatiently on the margin" (E 5:586).

As he grew older, Stephen was "obliged to be 'masculine'" and accordingly took up vigorous, long walks in the fenlands, along the Cornish coast, and in the Swiss Alps (Bicknell 11). Stephen's work as an editor of the *Alpine Journal* and *Cornhill* magazine allowed him to present various venues of science, including astronomy. He insisted that mountaineering be a companionable sport and had little sympathy for more scientific, militarily precise campaigns

FIGURE 2. Various animals sketched by Leslie Stephen in George Meredith's
The Egoist. (Books from the Library of Leonard and Virginia Woolf Manuscripts,
Archives and Special Collections, Washington State University Library)

launched on Asian mountains by the 1890s. In an essay entitled "A Substitute for the Alps," Stephen bemoaned the expedition leader enslaved to a "monstrous contrivance" for surveying, and "forced to be scientific, to collect stones and plants and insects, and to keep an elaborate diary recording his observations" (*Men, Books and Mountains* 208).

The aging Leslie Stephen led his children on expeditions where they hiked over the sand hills and sailed out of the harbor toward the now famous Godrevy Lighthouse in St. Ives (figure 3).[11] Later he chose summer sojourns near downs and fenlands, where his children continued outdoor exploits. His habit of long, observant walks was taken up for life by Virginia, who thought of her father when she bought her first good walking stick. Nigel Nicholson recalls that she would often walk six to ten miles by herself, thinking about her writing, exercising body and mind, and remarking on her return about a kingfisher she might have spotted.[12] Stephen's happiest letters to his absent wife and relatives report the young children's persistence with butterfly nets at St. Ives. As the children report in the *Hyde Park Gate News*, their mother was skeptical of a gift of setting boards presented by Jack Hills and disliked the idea of having caterpillars brought indoors (121). Leslie also records their visit to the "stuffed beasts" in the Natural History Museum (*Selected Letters* 2:287). Possessed with what Annan identifies as a "categorizing eye," he liked to identify flowers and plants on his walks (92). A letter to his son Thoby mentions cowslips and primroses as a matter of routine, shared interest (*Selected Letters* 2:301). The *Hyde Park Gate News* records his pleasure at finding a rare plant not previously encountered, and his creation of an album of pressed plants. Stephen taught the children "the different tribes of plants" (83). Virginia reports "botanizing with father" several times in her early diary, though he generally has to drag her away from her reading, and she complains of the heat. This sort of casual, mildly informed experience of nature would be shared later by Woolf's characters, such as Eleanor Pargiter, who botanizes on Wombledon Common in *The Years* (327).

Virginia Stephen's early diaries report expeditions to the Natural History Museum in South Kensington as early as 1897. The museum's grand Romanesque architecture, embellished with terra-cotta tiles representing flora and fauna, was designed by Albert Waterhouse and erected in 1873–80. Having opened in 1881, it was still a relatively new London attraction in Woolf's childhood. Its deep-set, rounded portal resembles the entry to a cathedral, representing the central position the sciences were taking in late Victorian

FIGURE 3. Godrevy Lighthouse and tidal pools, St. Ives. (Photograph by Adrian Langdon, Cornwall, UK)

life (figure 4). Woolf registers only tepid interest in her visits as a teenager, though it is difficult to say whether the nature of the exhibits or the rigors of the expedition, rather than an inquiry into nature, failed to please. En route, Virginia witnessed accidents to pedestrians in the streets, causing her obvious anxiety. As to the appeal of exhibits, we can reconstruct the sort of displays that greeted her. An 1887 *General Guide* to the museum cites Hobbes to define natural history as "the history of such facts or effects of nature as have no dependence on man's will." A decade later, the *Guide* explains that exhibits are intended to offer elementary, introductory material or demonstrate a systematic series, the former diffusing scientific knowledge and the latter participating in its advancement. Visiting in 1897, Woolf would have entered the vast Central Hall to find it dominated by the mounted skeleton of an enormous sperm whale. "Gallery" is an appropriate name for the displays in the wings, which arranged artistically mounted specimens, all labeled with their Latin, then their English, names. Its wall cases offered "many curious examples of nests, and of specimens illustrating ravages of destructive insects" and economic products derived from nature. Examples of the different groups were exhibited in systematic order in table cases, so as to give the visitor "a general idea of all and most interesting forms and their classification" (*1887 Guide* 44). An insect on display in the insect gallery was the red underwing—one of the moths most avidly quested by the Stephen children and later Jacob in *Jacob's Room*. Bugs were of sufficient interest to Virginia for her to make two trips in an attempt to see "a mythical underground collection of bugs" (*PA* 53). She and her brother Adrian fail on first try, but in June 1987, together with Vanessa and two Kay-Shuttleworth sisters, she is admitted.[13] This "insect room" housed the main collection of specimens, kept secure from fading and other forms of decay. It was really a collection of collections, some kept intact for historical interest, some broken down to demonstrate a systematic series. Reading between the lines of *Notes on the Various Collections of Insects in the Insect Room of the British Museum,* one can reconstruct a history of empire—Captain P. P. King, who collected insects as he surveyed the Straits of Magellan; the holdings of the East India Company Museum; and Rev. T. Blackburn's collection from the Hawaiian Islands. More concerned with the logistics of getting to the exhibit, and conversation with Miss Kay, Virginia found "nothing very wonderful" in the available insects (*PA* 94).

In an 1892 number of the *Hyde Park Gate News,* Virginia gives a stark, much more involving and dramatic account of a bird encountered on a sail to the Godrevy Lighthouse.[14] "Miss Virginia saw a small and dilapidated bird standing on one leg on the light-house. Mrs. Hunt called the man and asked him how it had got there. He said that it had been blown there and they then saw that its eyes had been picked out" (109). This is a far cry from what she would have experienced at the museum. A visit to the bird gallery would have presented cabinet after cabinet of stuffed specimens in pier cases. There was a special series concerning the nesting habits of British birds; photos from the 1890s show displays of gulls in water, parents on the nest, together with their nestlings, fulfilling a family narrative.

In today's museum, both insect and bird areas offer oversized explanatory models made accessible through interactive electronics; there are relatively few preserved specimens. Several period cases from the era of Woolf's youth have been retained for the sake of museum history. One enormous oval case explains bird anatomy, showing two small, splayed birds, displayed top and bottom, to reveal patterns in the growth of feathers. Partially dissected wings of various sizes reveal their structure and anatomy, as does a great array of dismembered beaks. Near this is a display case containing hundreds of types of hummingbirds, arranged on an intricate set of perches, shown as an

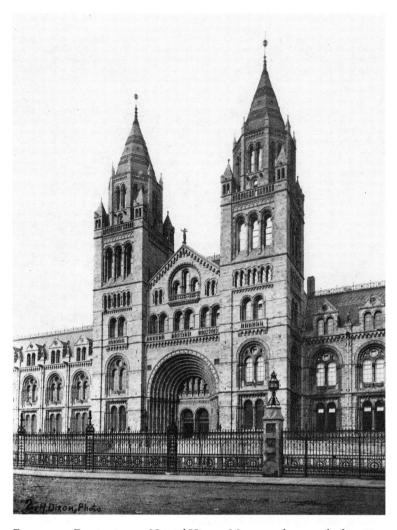

FIGURE 4. Front entrance, Natural History Museum, photographed in 1881.
(© Natural History Museum, London)

example of Victorian collections (figure 5). The need to have one of everything was still a strong part of the museum mentality throughout the nineteenth century, including the era when the Stephen children were visitors.
Their restraint is shown in another issue of the *Hyde Park Gate News,* which
reports on searching for bird's nests. Rather than take the eggs, they returned
"day by day to . . . see if the 'callow young' are hatched yet," and they enjoyed

FIGURE 5. Hummingbird case. (© Natural History Museum, London)

witnessing the feeding process. The article ends with the admonition, "Think oh children before you yield to the temptation which is before you. Imagine that you are the mother bird and you see some great giant before you. How frightened you would be . . . Think I implore you before you rob the poor bird of it's [sic] young" (59).

A favorite Stephen destination was the Regent's Park Zoo, an institution founded by Sir Stamford Raffles that opened its doors in 1828. Harriet Ritvo suggests that "Raffles' activities as a naturalist echoed his concerns as a co-lonial administrator: He made discoveries, imposed order, and carried off whatever seemed particularly valuable and interesting" (205). Raffles wanted his collection to "serve not just as a popular symbol of human domination, but also as a more precise and elaborate figuration of England's imperial enterprise" (206). Though the zoo had scientific ambitions and an imperial subtext, it also courted the public. Zookeepers sold buns and biscuits for feeding the elephants and the bears, as well as rides on the animals. The Stephen children fed the monkeys on numerous occasions, and on one notable visit Vanessa held a chimpanzee named Daisy in her arms (*PA* 12). Virginia reports on creatures in her journal, on one occasion finding baby crocodiles—"most delightful critters" (8); on another, she appreciates the klipspringer (12).

Woolf's depiction of her relationship with her father in "A Sketch of the Past" relies on zoo animals for its extended metaphor: "Suppose I at fifteen was a nervous, gibbering, little monkey always spitting or cracking a nut and shying the shells out, and mopping and mowing, and leaping into dark corners and then swinging in rapture across the cage, he was the pacing, dangerous, morose lion; a lion who was sulky and angry and injured; and then lying dusty and fly pestered in a corner of the cage" (*MB* 123). This betrays problems with both the zoo and the confines of Hyde Park Gate.

Woolf's brother Thoby is widely recognized as the model for the boy naturalists in her novels (figure 6). Jacob Flanders of *Jacob's Room* begins the novel capturing a crab and moves on to making careful observations of Lepidoptera: "The upper wings of the moth ... were undoubtedly marked with kidney-shaped spots of a fulvous hue. But there was no crescent upon the underwing" (23). Andrew Ramsay continues the tradition in *To the Lighthouse*. Leslie Stephen remarked in a 1902 letter to Mary Fisher, "It is very funny that he should have developed this thirst for natural history, considering how little encouragement he has had" (qtd. in Lee 115). Though his approach was more diversionary than scientific, Stephen did provide ample encouragement for botanizing and took obvious delight in the children's butterfly collecting. He pursued his son's interest with a visit to the bird museum at Brighton. Though Thoby's subject at Cambridge was classics, natural history was clearly his avocation, and perhaps as important a unifier with Virginia as his literary studies.[15] Writing to her brother in 1897, Virginia shares the "entomological news" of her aunt Caroline Stephen's back garden, a "miniature Kew" that yields a notable beetle pupa (*PA* 7). It can be inferred from a later letter that Thoby has fallen behind on an insect collection at school, and that Virginia and her team are prepared to collect the needed specimens (9). Bugs and chrysalises are among the booty brought to Thoby on one visit to his school (*HPGN* 133). Thoby's letters to Virginia, Vanessa, and his college friend Clive Bell make frequent mention of "bugging" and methodical bird-watching. This extended to conducting bird walks for working-class men in London, as Woolf mentions in her diary (*PA* 236).

The distinction between the naturalist and the hunter at the turn of the last century was not a neat one, as a young American girl discovers of her Audubon-like hero in Sarah Orne Jewett's 1886 short story "A White Heron." Sylvy encounters an attractive young man shouldering a gun who later describes how he has shot or snared, stuffed and preserved "dozens and dozens" of birds (1007). Despite his appeals, Sylvy keeps secret the location of the great white heron he is seeking. In *Woman and Nature*, ecofeminist Susan Griffin provides a particularly disturbing description of the hunting, shooting, stuffing, and mounting of an eagle, as an example of Audubon's methodology in painting his celebrated birds of America: "He used wires to pierce and hold together the body of the bird in the posture he desired and the result of his efforts created an effect whose grace and naturalness were later said to have rivaled life" (113–14). Something similar, no doubt, preceded the mounting of the Natural History Museum's display of bird parts. Gilbert White matter-of-factly describes shooting unusual birds that ventured into his area for accurate identification, and dissecting birds in order to inspect the food lodged in their crops.[16] We will return to Woolf and the subject of the hunt when we treat animals more thoroughly in chapter 5. Most relevant to this chapter is young Virginia Stephen's representation of a family form of insect hunting, conducted in the name of science.

On family holiday in Painswick in 1897, Virginia notes that Thoby had "set the Marbled Whites he caught yesterday" (*PA* 119). But there are further "mythical" goals, "Large Blues" sought at "a roman camp on the down" and a "mythical comma sought in the valley" (121). In mock-heroic fashion, Woolf's 1899 "Warboys" diary takes us on a memorable moth-hunt in Huntingdonshire, subjecting Thoby to the heaviest parody. In her account of "the most scientific way of catching moths" (144), the leader of the expedition is identified only as J.T.S., echoing the penchant for using initials in British academic publishing. Thoby is cast as a particularly methodical version of the great white male hunter. There is plenty of mockery in reserve for his bumbling accomplices, down to the dog, and for an imagined "temperance preacher who would find the text for many sermons" on the evil effects of treacle and rum on moth morality:

FIGURE 6. Thoby Stephen with shrimping net. (Leslie Stephen Photo Album, Mortimer Rare Book Room, Smith College)

Man, the hunter, starts forth in the following procession. Firstly of course the leader of the expedition, the renowned J. T. S. He wears a large felt hat, & muffled round him is a huge brown plaid, which makes his figure striding in the dark most picturesque & brigand like. In his hand he carries a glass jar—of which more anon. 2ndly appears a female form in evening dress, a shawl over her shoulders, & carrying a large stickless net. 3rdly the lantern bearer (none other than the present writer) who lights the paths fitfully with a Bicycle lamp of brilliant but uncertain powers of illumination. . . . 4thly Ad. L. S. a supernumerary amateur of no calling who takes little interest in the proceedings & is proficient in the art of obscuring the lamp at critical moments; 5thly Gurth the dog member, whose services are unrequired & unrewarded; being the first to investigate the sugar & having been convicted of attempts to catch moths for no entomological purpose whatever. (144–45)

These scientists manage to capture a huge, rare, red underwing, but Woolf extemporizes that "the whole procession felt some unprofessional regret when, with a last gleam of scarlet eye & scarlet wing, the grand old moth vanished" (145). Scientific organizations come in for satire in a later entry, where Woolf reports on a "Meeting of the Entomological Society," a family group to which her father and half brother George are assigned the respectable posts of president and librarian; she holds the multiple office of secretary chairman and treasurer. Thoby is "Larva Groom," conflating his dual interest in horses and Lepidoptera; as a final tease, she denies her younger brother, Adrian, any position on the committee at all.

The best evidence of Thoby Stephen's interest in natural history is the slim five-by-seven-inch leather notebook of natural observations, *Notes on Birds and Mammals Observed in England, Wales, and Parts of Europe, 1902–1906.*[17] He was working in the tradition of Gilbert White's journals, with the additional feature of his own drawings. Most of Thoby's reports concern bird watching, though he also notes the movements of foxes and rabbits. On right-hand pages, he routinely records the date and place of his observations, and lists the birds seen and any unusual markings or seasonal plumage. Left-hand pages are generally devoted to pen-and-ink sketches. Most remarkable among his written notes are records of favorite perches, bird calls, sounds, postures in the air or water, and dramatic incidents, as when one bird is attacked by another. As an example of his sensitivity to detail and movement, he remarks that "when a crow croaks it bows head and neck stretching head tight out." He then provides sketches offering two poses of the crow's head at different stages of this action. Elsewhere he observes, "Tufted ducks crest *not* conspicuous, bright light orange of eyes is—bill a fairly bright bluish—a bit of white shows when it swims." He might well have been writing a field guide. Thoby generally admires birds that fend off raptors; in one incident a kestrel rises with a group of lapwings, and one of them attacks it; in another a raven is held at bay by a group of daws (figure 7). He is a passive observer when working with this project. He finds nests all over London and counts the eggs, but he does not disturb or collect them, as is consistent with the children's ethics in the *Hyde Park Gate News*. His sketches are remarkable for the precision and assurance of their strokes, and for the adept representation of movement, character, and groupings (figure 8).

Thoby seems to have communicated with Vanessa about this notebook. She responds with interest to his record of nesting spots in London parks, and either teasingly or hopefully anticipates that he may make a book of these observations. Thoby's observations of conflict and the challenges of survival in nature anticipate the depiction of birds in his younger sister's writing. Readers familiar with Woolf's description of starlings settling in a tree in *Between the Acts* may find the following report by Thoby comparable: "Incredible number of starlings roost in a copse near Madingly. At about 6 parties of 20 or so or occasionally 100 begin to come from all directions & continue flying into the wood till about 8 when there is a starling on every twig & the music of their chattering can be heard ¼ of a mile off. Every now & then a cloud of them will rise with a noise like the sea and circle round for a few minutes and then settle again." Comparing Woolf's acute renderings of birds in texts such as *The Waves*, we find that interest in group versus individual behavior is typical of both brother and sister. Thoby gives attention to actual combat, while Woolf attends more to bickering among the birds, who exercise their most combative energies collecting a diet of worms and snails. Their interest in birds goes well beyond identification to include rich recording of behavior. Vanessa Bell's children pose for her album with butterfly nets, suggesting that natural history pursuits continued into the next generation. Julian wrote nature poetry and presented his aunt with a collection titled *Chaffinches* in 1929. Naturalist depictions of winter figure in two additional collections by Julian.

Entomological hunting and classification remained a resource for satire in Woolf's writing. Her 1916 review of a book on the eighteenth-century writer Eliza Heywood contributes the first epigraph of this chapter. As recorded there, Woolf recalls that the smallest of insects presented at the Natural History Museum "has its fine Latin name spreading far to the right and left." By analogy, Heywood is a "faded and antique specimen of the domestic housefly" who had to be researched, not "through airy forests," but in "dusty books

FIGURE 7. Thoby Stephen illustration, "Jackdaw Bullying a Missal Thrush," from *Notes on Birds and Mammals Observed in England, Wales and Parts of Europe, 1902–1906.* (© Natural History Museum, London)

from desolate museums" (*E* 2:22). One senses that Woolf leaves it to academics to find satisfaction from the smallest specimens.

Naturally Selecting Darwin

The precise observation, recording, and classifying of natural phenomena prepares the way for more elaborate narratives of science. The Victorian penchant for insect collecting, which caught up the Stephen children, provided evidence of variation, and this helped Darwin make the argument for continuing development of species. We know that Darwin was important to Woolf because, when she could salvage a few items from her bombed house in Mecklenburgh Square, she chose to take "Darwin." Gillian Beer, above all others, has worked out the Darwinian connections to Woolf. One reason for his adaptability to literature, as Beer explains, is that Darwin wrote

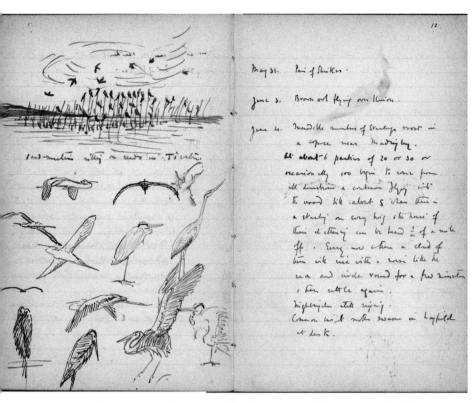

FIGURE 8. Thoby Stephen illustration, "Sand Martins and Herons in Flight," from *Notes on Birds and Mammals Observed in England, Wales and Parts of Europe, 1902–1906*. (© Natural History Museum, London)

in a language accessible to the nonspecialist, rich in analogy, metaphor, and myth, and he was steeped in English literature. Thus it should come as no surprise that he had many followers among the newly educated. Septimus Smith, a clerk who strived for an education in classes on the Waterloo Road, was found "devouring" Darwin (*MD* 83). Dorothy Richardson documents the same sort of interest for her character Miriam Henderson in *Pilgrimage*. In *The Tunnel*, as Miriam is accustoming herself to living in a room of her own in London, she settles into reading *The Voyage of the Beagle*, content that there would be "no interruption, no one watching or speculating or treating one in some particular way that had to be met. . . . She read a few lines. They had a fresh attractive *meaning*" (*Pilgrimage* 2:17).

Since the middle of the nineteenth century, Darwin's plots (to borrow a phrase from Beer) have offered a matrix for complex writing about nature, and the impetus for further scientific research. Beer senses Darwin's idea of overabundant fecundity of nature in Woolf's representations of the Victorians in *Orlando* (*Darwin's Plots* 123–24). She finds that Woolf's representation of the "primeval" forest in *The Voyage Out* owes something to descriptions in *The Voyage of the Beagle*. The primeval, which Beer also finds strongly expressed in *Between the Acts,* is a concept that links us to Darwin's consideration of origins. Of all the plots derived from Darwin, Beer argues that the analogy between ontogeny (individual development) and phylogeny (development of species) is "the most productive, dangerous, and compelling of creative thoughts for our culture" ("Woolf and Prehistory" 6). One good example of this is Bernard's soliloquy in *The Waves,* where he finds in himself "the old brute too, the savage, the hairy man who dabbles his fingers in ropes of entrails; and gobbles and belches; whose speech is guttural, visceral" (qtd. in *Open Fields* 144). In the sequence of childhood growth Woolf describes in "A Sketch of the Past," Beer finds an implication of evolutionary theory and determinism (*Darwin's Plots* 108). She credits Woolf with avoiding a triumphalist narrative of development, preferring the study of ways prehistory "permeates the present day" ("Woolf and Prehistory" 9). Extending from this notion, Joseph Kreutziger finds that in Woolf's two tales of snails, included in the early short stories "Kew Gardens" and "A Mark on the Wall," Woolf "registers the temporal process external to human will" (68), which accords with temporal aspect of Darwin.

Between the Acts has a great deal to offer in terms of natural history and Darwinian theory. Members of the audience gossip about "survival of the fittest." Evolution finds expression through Lucy's reading of an amalgam of H. G. Wells's *Outline of History,* his *Short History of the World,* and George Trevelyan's *History of England.* When we get to the Victorians in Miss La Trobe's pageant, Mr. Hardcastle is burdened with a fossil. "But it's nice for gentlemen to have a hobby, though they do gather the dust—those skulls and things" (114), quips Mrs. Hardcastle. She is equally concerned with laying out her picnic and ascertaining whether the new clergyman is free to marry one of her daughters. Children onstage engage in their own collection of butterflies. Turning to the still obligatory prayer, which includes an appreciation of nature, Mr. Hardcastle juggles beliefs in true Victorian fashion: "*Almighty*

God, giver of all good things, we thank Thee: for our food and drink; for the beau-
ties of Nature; for the understanding which Thou hast enlightened us (he fumbled
with his fossil). *And for thy great gift of Peace"* (116). Ironically, all indications
are that war is upon the audience in a novel set in 1939. An additional challenge comes in the distraction of the active "hindquarters of the donkey, represented by Albert the idiot" (116). Here is a toppling of the "natural order,"
socially contrived under God, with its ranking of species and intelligence.

The novel closes with a descent of man. The family sits near a darkening
window. Lucy is reading prehistory when "England . . . was a swamp." The patriarch, Bartholomew, blends in aspect and behavior with other species. "He
looked leafless, spectral, his chair monumental. As a dog shudders, his skin
shuddered." His sister Lucy arrives in her reading at "prehistoric man . . . half-
human, half-ape, roused himself from his semi-crouching position and raised
great stones" (148). It is predicted for Giles and Isa that "first they must fight,
as the dog fox fights with the vixen, in the heart of darkness" (148). The night
is evocative of "dwellers in caves." As "the curtain rose" and "they spoke," we
are left wondering what will evolve, or even if evolution is the useful term.[18]

Three decades of feminist scientific and environmental criticism have developed a rich and nuanced critique of the patriarchal aspects of Victorian
science encountered by the young Virginia Stephen. It is tempting to find
her anticipating this critique through parodies of patriarchy and through her
selection of subjects and writing techniques. Linnaeus, who provided a lasting framework for categorizing species, "brought traditional notions of gender hierarchy whole cloth into science" by using the male and female parts
of flowers to determine classes and orders, respectively, according to Londa
Schiebinger (125).[19] Flowers were established as sexual creatures by both Linnaeus and Erasmus Darwin (grandfather of Charles)—a framework D. H.
Lawrence takes into the classroom lesson concerning catkins in *Women in
Love.* We will investigate the queer sexuality of flowers further with Woolf in
chapters 3 and 6. The feminist geographer Sarah Whatmore, whose *Hybrid
Geographies* brings Linnaean scientific classification into question, notes that
species names, far from being systematically devised, were "chosen in any
number of ways (with reference to place, colour, body marking or shape, for
example)." This system of identification was promulgated throughout the "expanding scientific community associated with European colonialism" (Whatmore 20). This removed plants and animals from significant relationships on

earth; placing them back into the environment thus becomes an enduring challenge for scientists and artists alike, including Woolf.

Darwin has received both positive and negative feminist readings. Beer dwells positively on *The Origin of Species,* which she finds resistant to anthropocentrism, and thus to the hierarchies of human gender present in Darwin's other works and those of his promoters. Elizabeth Grosz and Carrie Rohman have noted favorably that Darwin's concept of species was provisional and indeterminate (Grosz 21; Rohman 3–4). In a mixed reading, Gates suggests that, even in *Origin of Species,* Darwin contributed to women's assignment to the nature half of the nature/culture binary by making nature the female heroine of his narrative (13). Darwin's insistence on the common origin of all humans in ancestral apes also challenged racist doctrines. Social Darwinism, however, rebounded against the democratizing aspects of Darwin's writing. Darwin's *Descent of Man* leaves more problems open to feminist concern. Though it declares that mental differences between animals and humans are "of degree and not of kind" (qtd. in Rohman 5), it embraces biological and social determinism to place women at a lesser stage of evolution than men, who are seen as physically and mentally more robust. This resonates with Victorian medical constructions of female weakness. On a more personal level, Darwin figures in the hard-hitting parody of patriarchy contained in Griffin's *Woman and Nature* (143–44). The demands Darwin posed upon his family, and particularly his wife, are comparable to the expectations Leslie Stephen had in later life of his elder daughters Stella and Vanessa. This Woolf describes in her letters, memoirs, and *To the Lighthouse.*

In Eliza Burt Gamble, Rosemary Jann has recovered an early feminist challenger to Darwin who strategically reread the evidence. Whereas Darwin had given primacy to male sexual differentiation, in *The Evolution of Women* (1894), Gamble argued for a more highly evolved, because more specialized and efficient, biological female. She also saw female altruism as a more evolved social value than the system of power and subordination of the patriarchal family—anticipating the more recent ecofeminist thinking of Carol Gilligan, which has helped set the script of "ethic of care" ecofeminism. Essentialism, which has been resisted in recent feminist criticism, is as strongly assumed by Gamble as by Darwin, as Jann concedes.

Feminist historians of science have noted ways in which women were excluded from the increasingly professionalized scientific disciplines. Huxley, for example, supported the ban on women's admission to the Geological

Society of London, which remained in place until 1904 (Gates 28). Herbert Spencer supported the belief that women's energies should go into procreation rather than mental activities (Gates 14). Similar anxiety over feminine mental exertion persisted in the rest cures Virginia Stephen would undergo from the age of thirteen.

Interpreting Victorian Women of Science

In Eleanor Anne Ormerod, Woolf recovers a fascinating Victorian woman of science, whose story demonstrates both personal survival and scientific critique (figure 9). "Miss Ormerod," an essay originally published in the American magazine *Dial* in 1924, appeared again as one of three "Lives of the Obscure" in the American edition of the *Common Reader*. To set up that collection, Woolf imagines herself in an obsolete library somewhere near the sea (a place resembling the summer vacation spots inhabited by her family). The 1904 volume *Eleanor Ormerod, LL.D., Economic Entomologist*, edited by Robert Wallace, is presumably one of the forgotten texts on shelves there. Woolf lavishes experimental form upon this essay, visiting Miss Ormerod's life at discrete intervals and from various points of view in six segments and a final coda.[20] The narratives, scenes, and dialogues are Woolf's construction from the book. The first three segments observe the child and young woman from a distance, assessing family and community contexts, as if constructing the case history of an outsider. With the fourth segment, the narrator moves closer to Miss Ormerod through free indirect discourse, understanding her passions and her frustrations with skeptics, and even addressing her, "Ah, but Eleanor" (*E* 4:136). Ormerod expresses herself in dialogues recorded in the last two segments. Readers must sometimes wait from one segment to the next to understand the scientific allusions and issues, but this is in keeping with an overall approach that adds layers of understanding to our experience of Woolf's characters.

Miss Ormerod's scientific achievements are both surprising, coming out of the home of a domineering country gentleman, and predictable, given the memorable first segment of Woolf's account. In this scene little Eleanor is left to watch a glass of water containing live grubs, and she does so with fascination and excitement, particularly when the grubs tear to pieces one of their own kind.[21] The little girl is not believed when she says what she has observed, the scene reinforcing cultural mores of gender; fortunately, this did

FIGURE 9. Eleanor Ormerod, portrait housed in the University of Edinburgh, published in *Eleanor Ormerod, LL.D., Economic Entomologist: Autobiography and Correspondence,* plate 29. (Special Collections, San Diego State University Library)

not discourage Ormerod's science. Woolf's brief dialogue between parents and child makes more of a point of paternal disapproval than Ormerod does in her own account, which suggests that "elders" disapproved (she had much older siblings to do that, as did Woolf). Woolf picks up on the limitations her brother Edward placed on her study of anatomy (136). Those familiar with Woolf's biography might think of George Duckworth's efforts to stress the importance of his younger half sisters' entry into society, rather than their aspirations in art and literature. As the chronicle continues, Woolf suggests through local gossips that Ormerod was unimpressed by rituals of courtship. "It was so difficult to make friends with a girl who could talk of nothing but black beetles and earwigs" (134).

In this essay Woolf is playing with the historical construction of nature that would later characterize the different ages of *Orlando,* including the plentiful vegetation and human fecundity of its Victorian phase. In 1835 the trees on the Ormerod estate in Gloucestershire are voluminous, and a troop of nine children accompanies their parents "past extremely old-fashioned sheep" into the grounds (132).

Woolf is more interested in the gender-inflected trajectory of Ormerod's scientific career than in her specific achievements as an agricultural entomologist. Although her knowledge of insects was publicly known by the time Ormerod was twenty-four, her career awaited her father's death at eighty-seven. This is not unlike Woolf's own career, which awaited Sir Leslie's demise. The section reporting the paternal death ends with an outspokenly feminist point: "Oh, graves in country churchyards—mature old gentlemen—D.C.L., LL.D., F.R.S., F.S.A.—lots of letters come after your names, but lots of women are buried with you!" (136). At forty-five, Eleanor was ready for a new life and scientific challenges: "There remained the Hessian Fly and the Bot"—the "harmful" insects Ormerod would study to control.[22] Woolf's narrative move to free indirect discourse brings us very close to Ormerod in this section. Take, for example, this declaration: "The only palatable object for the eye to rest on in acres of England is a lump of Paris Green. But English people won't use microscopes; you can't make them use Paris Green either—or if they do, they let it drip" (136). The testimony of a market gardener lets us know that she has finally found an appreciative following, as has the insecticide (arseniate of copper) "Paris Green."[23] In a memorable list, various destructive bugs mix with hallmarks of her career, as if on a par for attention with an honorary degree, the acquisition of foreign correspondents, and the resignation from her post as consulting entomologist to the Royal Agricultural Society, for reasons of failing health (140).

We move even closer to Miss Ormerod in the final segments, which record her in conversations. These show the fervor with which she pursued new passions, including persecution of house sparrows as worthless pests, and her efforts to deal with moth infestations of flour. We learn that Ormerod was attacked by humanitarians over the sparrows, and she felt frustration that scientists were not interested in such practical matters as ruined flour. Woolf is tolerant of both positions; she had tangled with pesky sparrows as a young gardener in London (an episode we turn to in the next chapter) and would differ with zealous bird protectionists over their rhetoric concerning the plumage bill (a subject for chapter 5). In crafting her essay, Woolf develops the brief mention of Ormerod's physician into a full-scale role as sympathetic listener for the final dialogue, a role Ormerod's editor might actually have fulfilled. Wallace had helped secure Ormerod an honorary doctorate at Edinburgh University, and he collected and edited her historical record. Valuing Ormerod so strongly, he might not have served the marginal position Woolf sought for Ormerod in her account.[24]

In these last scenes, Woolf also shows conventional elements. Ormerod perpetuates traditional rites of her genteel family. She misses Georgiana, the supportive older sister who became her companion for life. Ormerod drinks to the queen on her birthday, says prayers with the servants, and proclaims to Dr. Lipscomb, "Our lives are in the hands of the lord" (138). It was a good enough line, depicting the powerful foundation of religion in women's lives, to reuse for Mrs. Ramsay in *To the Lighthouse* (*TTL* 66). With these elements of the portrait, Woolf reminds us of the cultural distance we may experience, even in feminist recovery of women of science. Ormerod's work goes out into other elements of nature prized by Woolf. Her effort to protect trees, for example, is shared by the humble Mrs. Brown, who wonders, "Can you tell me if an oak-tree dies when the leaves have been eaten for two years in succession by caterpillars?" (*E* 3:424).

Woolf was aware of numerous Victorian women who were scientific collectors, including Mary Kingsley, who figures significantly in *Three Guineas*, as noted above. Ormerod's sister Georgiana, in addition to expertly illustrating her sister's articles on insects, was a member of the Entomological Society of London and had collected three thousand species of shells, as noted in the autobiography (3). Aunt Helena in *Mrs. Dalloway* represents Victorian female botanists who ventured into empire. Unlike the Victorian male, pursuing the heights where he can be "the monarch-of-all-I-survey," as Pratt detects him in period discourse (201), Aunt Helena descends for her discoveries of rare orchids. Mary Louise Pratt strikes this very contrast in describing Mary Kingsley, sliding down into the mangroves where she collected rare fish (216). These are the deep, damp regions eschewed in the masculinist modernism advanced by Wyndham Lewis, as discussed in chapter 1.

Aunt Helena is also a version of Marianne North (1830–90), a woman of sufficient wealth to finance her own world travel, with India and Ceylon among her destinations (figure 10). She went on to discover rare plants and painted them with near-scientific precision. Five of the thousands of plants North sent to the Royal Botanic Gardens at Kew entered the Linnaean system with North's name attached. In her chapter on North in *Place Matters,* Susan Morgan draws the connection between botanical and imperial projects, arguing that, despite a liberationist feminist discourse in her memoirs, North was complicit with scientific imperialism. Kew provides a grand public park, with pleasing vistas later evoked in Woolf's early diaries and fiction. But at its origin, it was a project for the mother country, drawing upon satellite gardens in the colonies for such saleable products as rhododendrons from the Himalayas, rubber from Brazil, and tropical medicines (Morgan 111–15). It may be the single best manifestation of Western scientific collecting and reorganizing of specimens of nature drawn from the entire globe. Botany, even as carried out in Southeast Asia, was an acceptable activity for women of the leisured classes, not being as obviously political as missionary work or geographical expeditions (Morgan 98–99). Botany had its social rewards as well. Sir William Hooker, the first director of Kew, and his successor, his son Joseph Hooker, had genial social relations with a number of women of science, including both Ormerod and North. North contrived her own enduring presence at Kew by donating the Marianne North Gallery, to be filled with her permanent display; the gallery opened in the year of Woolf's birth. An interesting connection to Woolf is that Woolf's great-aunt Margaret Cameron photographed North when she stopped in Ceylon, where the Camerons spent their final years. Woolf relied on North's memoir, *Recollections of a Happy Life,* for the final page of her essay "Julia Margaret Cameron." "'She made me stand with spiky coconut branches running into my head . . . and told me to look perfectly natural,' Miss North remarked" (*E* 4:383).[25] A more tenuous connection is that North has been quoted as saying, "I prefer vegetables," in a rejection of motherhood and heterosexual romance (Morgan 100). There is a curious echo in *Mrs. Dalloway* when Clarissa vaguely recalls Peter Walsh's remark, "I prefer men to cauliflowers" (3), at a time when he is pressuring her toward heterosexual romance.

Aunt Helena is "past eighty" and is treated with reverence at the culminating party of *Mrs. Dalloway*. Clarissa scouts out guests who knew Burma "in the seventies" and enlists Peter to talk with her, assuming "they used to be such friends" (174). The narrator zooms in close to Helena's thought: "At the mention of India, or even Ceylon, her eyes (only one was glass) slowly deepened, became blue, beheld, not human beings—she had no tender memories, no proud illusions about Viceroys, Generals, Mutinies—it was orchids she saw, and mountain passes and herself carried on the backs of coolies in the sixties over solitary peaks; or descending to uproot orchids (startling blossoms, never beheld before) which she painted in water-colour" (174). Woolf offers a decidedly mixed mental landscape. By dismissing viceroys, generals, and mutinies, Miss Parry would seem to be discarding the masculine politics of empire. Hers is a sentimental, personal account that romanticizes the landscape of the mountains, and even the coolies who hauled her over them—elements of imperial discourse identified by Pratt. Indeed, Pratt selects for the cover of *Imperial Eyes* an illustration of a European male, in full Western explorer dress, down to his stout boots, being hauled up an incline by a barefoot coolie.

Aunt Helena's landscape is otherwise unencumbered by people. She pretends to have found blossoms "never beheld before," when she probably owed finding them to native guides. By collecting rare orchids that someone would enter into the Western, Linnaean scheme of nature, Aunt Helena was participating in a form of imperial appropriation. As Pratt describes, "One by one the planet's life forms were to be drawn out of the tangled threads of their life surroundings and rewoven into European-based patterns of global unity" (31). Woolf's use of "uproot" in this description bears some suggestion of this deracination. Woolf's portrait of Aunt Helena suggests an aged and apolitical mind, focused intently on orchids, but also an obvious product of empire. Helena takes advantage of Peter's presence to tell him (probably not for the first time) that her now forgotten little book had gone into three editions.

For his part Peter feels handed off by Clarissa, his own colonial experience a convenient reason to select him as Aunt Helena's audience. He is reliving the worst evening of his young life, the night he realized that Clarissa would marry Richard Dalloway. Peter's memory shows he did have a relationship with Miss Parry; however, it paled in comparison to his drama with Clarissa: "There she sat in her white Cashmere shawl, with her head against the window—a formidable old lady, but kind to him, for he had found her some rare

FIGURE 10. *Marianne North at Her Home in Ceylon,* 1876, by Julia Cameron. From
Some Recollections of a Happy Life: Marianne North in Australia and New Zealand.
(Special Collections, San Diego State University Library)

flower, and she was a great botanist, marching off in thick boots with a black collecting-box slung between her shoulders" (*MD* 59–60). Sidelined, all he could do was talk inattentively about wildflowers with Miss Parry. "He had left her, Peter Walsh remembered, without a word in the drawing-room that night when Clarissa had asked him to come boating" (175). Earlier, Peter had recalled Miss Parry pressing flowers under a dictionary, which came to represent the accumulation of cultural mores that weighted down his youth. So convinced that she was a marker of the past, Peter had assumed she was dead.

Sally Seton's memories of Aunt Helena are less charitable than Peter's. As a girl visiting the family, Sally treats flowers aesthetically, cutting them at the neck to float in water, in a manner unacceptable to Miss Parry. It was an art of modern arrangement Woolf learned from her sister Vanessa. In *Jacob's Room*, Woolf had found an opportunity to satirize held-over Victorian family values through the vogue of Oriental paper flowers used in finger bowls: "About this time a firm of merchants having dealings with the East put on the market little paper flowers which opened on touching water. . . . Their fortunes were watched by eyes intent and lovely. It is surely a great discovery that leads to the union of hearts and foundation of homes. The paper flowers did no less" (*JR* 83).[26] Indeed, Woolf's generation, complicit with modernism, would find new arrangements for nature that move into different uses and understandings of it, from playful arrangements useful for domestic rebellion, to fossilized evidence of an ancient nature, to the plots implied by Darwin's theory of evolution.

The post-Darwinian plot extends into postmodern and even posthuman performances. Toward the end of the pageant in *Between the Acts*, "Children? Imps—elves—demons" holding mirrors and other reflective objects catch human forms, and amid the "jangle and din! The very cows joined in. Walloping, tail lashing, the reticence of nature was undone, and the barriers which should divide Man and Master from the Brute were dissolved" (125). The disorder increases with the surging back to the stage of actors representing the ages, their jumble of quotations relating to the hunter, the owl, the worm, and the butterfly (126). We find culture, linear history, and categories re-presented in "scraps, orts and fragments" (131). This may look forward to the "posthuman body," formulated by Judith Halberstam and Ira Livingston, and taken up by Donna Haraway, and a time when "the human body itself is no longer part of 'the family of man' but of a zoo of posthumanities" (Halberstam and Livingston 3).[27]

Limits of the Garden
as Cultured Space

The gardens gave off a murmur of bees; the apples were red and gold; there were also pink flowers; and grey and silver leaves. The buzz, the croon, the smell, all seemed to press voluptuously against some membrane; not to burst it; but to hum round one such a complete rapture of pleasure that I stopped, smelt; looked.

~Woolf, "A Sketch of the Past"

The gardeners sweep the lawn with giant brooms. We are the first to come here. We are the discoverers of an unknown land. Do not stir; if the gardeners saw us they would shoot us. We should be nailed like stoats to the stable door. Look! Do not move. Grasp the ferns tight on the top of the wall.

~Woolf, *The Waves*

THOUGH VIRGINIA WOOLF had only a modest record as a gardener, from her earliest years she recorded vivid impressions of gardens that held lasting significance. She was highly accurate in natural detail and imaginative with similes, metaphors, and modernist representation that included the influence of Post-Impressionism. Complex, interactive garden scenes permeate her novels and stories, many bearing hidden meanings. For Victorians, flowers might function as a code for things that could not properly be said or must be kept secret. Kate Greenaway's 1884 book *The Language of Flowers* decodes various flowers, trees, and vegetables, whereby (for example) ivy connotes fidelity and marriage, the oak leaf, bravery, and the white lily, purity and sweetness.[1] In Joyce's *Ulysses*, Leopold Bloom takes the pseudonym "Henry Flower" to conduct a secret correspondence with Martha Clifford, and he notes that women like the language of flowers because "no-one can hear" (5.261).

In Woolf's writing of the garden, we may find such important but censored subjects as sexual awakening, same-sex attraction, bodily and mental trauma, and resistance to patriarchal patrolling of boundaries, as well as delight in observation and pursuit of freedom. In early writing about gardens, Woolf was troubled about limitations she perceived in accounts by natural history enthusiasts—a group already encountered in chapter 2. As she began reconceiving them, gardens offered Woolf the fusion of natureculture theorized by Donna Haraway, for they housed not just flowers, but human products, designs, interactions, and conversations, and invited merger. Like the "common sitting room" so carefully observed by Jane Austen (*AROO* 66), gardens provided a place to study human behavior. As appropriate to feminist concern for women's lived experience, a tour through Woolf's actual and imagined gardens allows us to chart her feminist refiguring of garden space.[2]

Childhood's Garden

The earliest garden of Woolf's recollection was at St. Ives—largely the creation of her mother, Julia Stephen. The climate of Cornwall was mild enough for Mediterranean flora such as escallonia and yuccas to survive. Talland House had extensive greenhouses that ran between the front garden and the orchard, sheltering grapes and delicate flowers. A fine record of the layout comes from Leslie Stephen in his *Mausoleum Book*. He recalls its compartmentalized spaces and Julia's presence in what amounts to a domestic setting: "A garden of an acre or two all up and down hill, with quaint little terraces divided by hedges of escallonia, a grape-house, and kitchen-garden and a so-called 'orchard' beyond. . . . I can see my Julia strolling among her beloved flowers: sitting in the 'loo corner,' a sheltered seat behind the grape-house, or the so-called 'coffee garden,' where on hot days she would be shaded by the great escallonia hedge" (62; figure 11). Stephen made a strong, feminine connection between flowers and both of his wives, particularly in memorializing them. He chose cyclamen (a symbol of resignation or farewell)[3] to decorate his first wife Minny's gravestone.

Woolf's description of the layout of the garden in "A Sketch of the Past" is less organized than her father's, but it has the dynamism and sensual excitement of a young participant in the scene. Written toward the end of her life, this work is much more confident than her earliest diary accounts of gardens, to which we turn shortly. "Running down the hill, little lawns, surrounded by thick escallonia bushes, whose leaves one picked and pressed and smelt: it had so many corners and lawns that each was named: the coffee garden; the fountain; the cricket ground; the love corner, under the greenhouse; jackmanii grew there; . . . the strawberry bed; the kitchen garden; the pond; and the big tree" (*MB* 111). Woolf mentions elm and apple trees and a grassy mound, the Lookout Place, directing the gaze beyond the garden (114). The act of naming is part of the account. A remarkable impression of the garden, frequently cited by Woolf scholars and above in the first epigraph, comes earlier in the essay, as Woolf develops the concept of "moments of being." This "color and sound memory" comes from relatively early childhood and is "robust" and "sensual." She remarks, "It still makes me feel warm; as if everything were ripe; humming; sunny; smelling so many smells at once; and all making a whole that even now makes me stop—as I stopped then going down to the beach" (66). Enraptured by the scene that mixes fruits, blossoms, and leaves, Virginia joins in its ripeness and unity, pressed "voluptuously" upon by color, sound, and smell, in an aura of pleasure. There is no fear of having her membrane "burst," which might have betokened sexual anxiety. She makes no mention that bees can sting. To be so surrounded by pleasure, coming from multiple senses to voluptuous effect, is suggestive of the feminine imaginary famously evoked by the French feminist Luce Irigaray: "*But woman has sex organs just about everywhere. She experiences pleasure almost everywhere. . . . One can say that the geography of her pleasure is much more diversified, more multiple in its differences, more complex, more subtle, than is imagined—in an imaginary centered a bit too much on one and the same*" (103). The child makes deliberate use of her senses, to smell and look. A young explorer, she sets the garden in the larger context of the beach and the road. Her experience is far less protective, controlled, and confining than the garden Leslie Stephen uses to frame his wife.

FIGURE 11. Talland House, St. Ives. (Leslie Stephen Photo Album, Mortimer Rare Book Room, Smith College, North Hampton)

Creative Challenges of London Gardens

Nature first enters Woolf's diaries through gardens set in London. As noted above, Woolf was initially cautious with this material. In March 1897 she falls into a description of springtime in Kensington Gardens—"the almond trees out, the crocusses [sic] going over, squills at their best, the other trees just beginning to seed"—only to remark, "I shall turn into a country clergyman, and make notes of phenomena in Kensington Gardens, which shall be sent as a challenge to other country clergymen" (PA 55).[4] In this entry she both develops her satirical skills, aiming in this case at a fussy, competitive clergy, and looks for her own subject matter.

Woolf has other reasons to be cautious about gardening at home: "Father has taken up Doctor Seton's notion that I should be healthfully employed out of doors—as a lover of nature—and the back garden is to be reclaimed— that will be a truly gigantic work of genius—nevertheless we shall try" (PA 84). She offers both sarcasm and compliance. In Tom Sawyer's fashion, she allows the project to become more Vanessa's than Virginia's, humorously confessing, "I basely deserted her, when the worms and stones became too numerous, and the heat was too great" (85). Woolf offers details that show sensitivity to controlled elements of selection and design: "This desert place is under our hands, becoming a quite beautiful spot—There is one large round bed, which you see from the drawing room window, & another long one behind it against the wall. Both of these we planted liberally with half grown pansies, lobelia, & sweet peas. We are going to buy some grass seeds & cover the bare patch of earth which surrounds our beds" (89). The plan (more likely Vanessa's than Virginia's) is very much in line with the Victorian practice of bedding out colorful, decorative nursery-grown stock. The girls' choices for the central garden favor short plants, their layout visible from the drawing room windows. Locating another bed along a wall (where the sweet pea vines could be trained) is typical for an English garden, effective if the wall can block breezes or absorb and extend the heat of the sun. Sweet peas would remain a favorite with Woolf's character Mrs. Dalloway, who selects them at the florist's for her party.[5] The Stephen garden does not go unchallenged, however. Anticipating birds ruthlessly feeding in *The Waves*, Woolf describes sparrows with designs for her grass seed: "As soon as we had left the garden, the horrid little creatures swooped down twittering & made off with the oats" (96).

It is unsurprising that the gardening project at Hyde Park Gate was unpopular with Woolf. The enforced labor took her away from preferred activities indoors—particularly the reading program she mentions repetitively in her diary. Unlike the treasured garden at St. Ives, this one had no association with her mother, who had died two years earlier. Woolf learned that gardening was largely a matter of control, and that this struggle among genders, plants, and animals was part of what she wanted to record. Assigned gardening as a form of therapy, she could also use the garden to express ways that she felt coerced or regulated.

Though it compared poorly with St. Ives, nearby Kensington Gardens was of real consequence to Woolf, both in venturing forth as a child and in cultivating her art. Originally the exclusive hunting grounds of Tudor monarchs, London's Royal Parks were opened to courtiers by the seventeenth century, and by the eighteenth, commoners regularly visited them—provided they dressed well enough to satisfy Queen Caroline.[6] At her behest, the grounds were extended and given the natural look favored by the royal gardener Charles Bridgeman. Major features present in Woolf's youth include the

Broad Walk, once lined by elms, and subsequently by limes and maples. A statue of the young Queen Victoria was dedicated off the Broad Walk in 1887. Near Kensington Palace west of the Broad Walk is the Orangery, a structure with long windows and graceful brick arches, ornamented with classical busts and floral swags.[7] East of the Broad Walk, the Round Pond sits amid a wide terrace. This remains a hub for playful activity. The Long Water, farther east, emerges from the Italian Gardens, joining with the Serpentine, a major feature of Hyde Park that stretches beyond the West Carriage Drive. Less cultivated, this area provides a haven for butterflies and wildfowl. Botanizers have long frequented the Flower Walk, added in 1843. Lined with exotic trees brought from around the world, its variety of flowers changed with the season and the whim of the current gardeners.

Leslie Stephen went walking in Kensington Gardens with Julia Duckworth soon after she was widowed. It was convenient, since both lived nearby in Hyde Park Gate. Such strolls became a courtship and evolved into a family institution involving all of their offspring. "A Sketch of the Past" includes an extensive description of this terrain, as experienced by the Stephen children. Woolf vividly recalls two old women who sold items, such as air balls, at the entrance. The regular regimen of walks occasionally held terrors, as when an "idiot boy sprang up with his hand outstretched mewing, slit-eyed, red-rimmed" (*MB* 78), or when, encountering a puddle in the path, Virginia felt she could not step over it—a fear passed on to Rhoda in *The Waves*. The children exercised their creativity in this setting, having their own names and uses for various features. The wet, "derelict" ground behind the Flower Walk was a "swamp" where the older siblings discovered the corpse of a dog. They had a "crocodile" tree, named for a large exposed root, and enjoyed crunching shells distributed on the Flower Walk. On the round pond, Virginia sailed her model boat, a Cornish lugger, which was all the more remarkable for having survived a sinking, only to be recovered weeks later when the duckweed was dredged.[8] The uncultivated fields provided a setting for reading *Tit Bits* together. Devising long stories helped pass the time on twice-daily, obligatory winter walks.

In *The Years*, Martin Pargiter gives us a tour of Kensington Gardens. Walking toward the Round Pond to meet his cousin Maggie, Martin finds himself dissolving into unsubstantial images created largely by the play of light: "The sun dappling the leaves gave everything a curious look of insubstantiality as if it were broken into separate points of light. He too, himself, seemed dispersed" (229). Later, seated with Maggie by the pond, he gets a greater sense of control, finding (as Woolf's male characters are apt to do) the scene "admirably composed. There was the white figure of Queen Victoria against a green bank; beyond, was the red brick of the old palace; . . . the Round Pond made a pool of blue. A race of yachts was going forward" (231). Martin plays with perspective, as Woolf often does in landscapes. As he watches two of the model yachts avoid a collision and boys as they "dabble for minnows," life resumes "normal proportions" (232).

Woolf preferred the trees, the pond, and hidden places of Kensington Gardens to the more grandiose planning of Regent's Park, which had been laid out for the future George IV by John Nash in the 1820s. She regularly traversed Regent's Park to access the zoo, where animals look over the fences, as in *Mrs. Dalloway* (24). The Stephen children's *Hyde Park Gate News* celebrates the fact that the zoo can "drive away the business man's cares and give him something of the country's pure air for it is surrounded by fields and trees and though they are nothing to be compared to St Ives yet it has revived the tired eyes of many a city man" (141). Regent's Park plantings in Woolf's childhood would have been supplied by the Royal Botanic Society, featuring bedded-out flowers, massed for color and prized for exotic origin. Public parks can be a source of a nation's pride, expressing its character. The spectacle of Regent's Park fails to satisfy Rezia Smith in *Mrs. Dalloway*, as she compares its gardens unfavorably to those of her native Milan (23). The "stone basins, the prim flowers, the old men and women, invalids mostly in Bath chairs," and most especially the foreign Rezia and strange-looking Septimus, seem "queer" to Maisie Johnson, a young woman newly arrived from Edinburgh (25). For Woolf, gardens were already spaces for queering the conventional. In both "A Sketch of the Past" and *Mrs. Dalloway*, parks harbor a variety of visitors, cutting across classes, ages, some displaying disabilities, and including eccentrics and castoffs from society. Peter Walsh, jobless in middle age, whiles away the time in Regent's Park.

The Royal Botanic Gardens at Kew have assumed great importance for Woolf studies because of her innovative early story "Kew Gardens," published by Hogarth Press in 1919. Though she visited Kew occasionally in her youth, the gardens were more accessible during her early married years, being near Richmond, where Leonard and Virginia settled, south of the Thames (1914–24). Though its size has increased over the years, Kew has at its core two estates owned by the royal family. The botanical collection was started in

1759 by Augusta, Princess of Wales, mother of George III. In 1772 Sir Joseph Banks began collecting specimens for the gardens from around the world. As noted in the previous chapter, the primary mission of the gardens is scientific. Sir William Hooker, who became director in 1841, created its Department of Economic Botany, moving the institution toward capitalism and applied science. Charles Darwin formed a strong, lasting bond with Kew when he communicated his revolutionary theory of evolution to William Hooker's son, Joseph.[9]

Woolf represents a more popular sense of Kew as a place that attracts strolling couples. Modernist scholars characterize her story as an abstract study in color, light, movement, and words, which to some extent it is. Toward the end, we get a few distinguishing details of Kew. A young woman walking with her young man remembers "orchids and cranes among wild flowers" and the Chinese pagoda; we catch a glimpse of "the glass roofs of the palm house," which "shone as if a whole market full of shiny green umbrellas had opened in the sun" (*CSF* 95). A snail and various insects go about their business, free of scientific labels. Woolf gives us the snail's-eye view of "brown cliffs with deep green lakes in the hollows, flat blade-like trees that waved from root to tip, round boulders of grey stone, vast crumpled surfaces of a thin crackling texture" (91–92). She does not single out the rare, precious plants, and she generalizes the layout, offering an oval-shaped flower bed, its plants displaying heart- or tongue-shaped leaves and projecting the red, blue, or yellow colors of its flowers onto the ground. The natural elements of the setting play in with various human memories and overheard conversations. The motions of creatures and humans are in many ways comparable, leveling humans as only one part of the natural scene. If anything differentiates the creatures, the snail seems to have a clearer trajectory, and it travels alone. The light and heat, playing upon the flowers, the trees, and the passing people, eventually dissolve and merge them, equalizing and unifying elements in nature. The visual resemblance to a Cézanne or a Monet has been remarked on by numerous interpreters.[10] The people Woolf places in Kew think about more than botanical wonders. Several are eager to get tea. A young woman may prefer to think about the pagoda rather than the larger questions about her future that may be posed by her suitor at tea.[11] An old man (whom some see as an anticipation of Septimus Smith) is obsessed with communicating with spirits of the war dead via a battery-driven device. A woman walking with her husband recalls a first kiss as she painted water lilies in the park.

Since that kiss came from a gray-haired woman, the scene anticipates Woolf's story "Slater's Pins Have No Points," in which a flower also abets a queer, passionate experience between women of very different ages. Though the lights of multicolored flowers frame the start and end of Woolf's story, she also reminds us of mechanical elements in the environment—an airplane overhead and buses "turning their wheels and changing their gear" in the city beyond (*CSF* 95).[12]

Hampton Court provided Woolf a garden replete with historical features, ranging from the Elizabethan knot garden and maze frequented by Henry VIII, to grand avenues and fountains that came into favor in the eighteenth century. Many of Woolf's characters go there, with mixed results: Septimus and Rezia Smith have one happy excursion that ends badly, with Septimus declaring his wish to commit suicide. The entire cast of *The Waves* reassembles in middle age for dinner there. At this stage in life, Bernard feels less excitement about the excursion than he might have ten years earlier. Impressions of "summer afternoons, boats, old ladies holding their skirts up, one urn in winter, some daffodils in March—these all float to the top of the waters that now lie deep on every scene" (154). Louis is concerned with the sweep of historical time in which "the lighted strip of history is past," leaving "our Kings and Queens . . . lost in the abysses of time, in the darkness" (165). Walking separately from the others, he and Rhoda gather a composite message from night birds, trees, and electric rails. Their friends represent visitors to the garden over the centuries, including veterans returned from war (169–70). The happiest visitors may be Lily Briscoe and William Bankes. Despite failing to fulfill Mrs. Ramsay's marriage scenario, the couple visits Hampton Court every summer, admiring "the proportions and the flowers" (*TTL* 180). Its long avenue still holds for William the image of a young and beautiful Mrs. Ramsey "wearing a grey hat" (180).

After the younger generation of Stephens took up residence in Gordon Square, Bloomsbury, in 1904, the small parks lined with plane trees, laid out in the eighteenth century, claimed notice in Woolf's diaries. This interest redoubled when she and Leonard settled at 52 Tavistock Square in 1924. Strolling around the outside of this square, Woolf made up *To the Lighthouse*. The Woolfs walked their dog there, resisting an ordinance that required leashing. Though their home was destroyed during the bombing of World War II, Tavistock has come to be known as "peace square" in the years since Woolf's death (see Young). It contains a rock monument to the conscientious objectors of World War II, a cherry tree dedicated to the memory of victims of the bombing of Hiroshima, and a statue of Mahatma Gandhi. Also commemorated with a bust in its southeast corner is Dame Louisa Aldrich-Blake (1865–1925), surgeon to the Elizabeth Garrett Anderson Hospital and dean of the London School of Medicine for Women. Woolf's own bust, a copy of the Stephen Tomlin sculpture that also presides over her ashes at Monk's House, was erected in the southwest corner of the park in 2004 as part of that year's International Virginia Woolf Conference. On that occasion, some of the dog walkers, now confined to a nearby part of the park, yielded reluctantly to the strange crowd gathered for the ceremony. Whether by accident or by choice, terrorists could not have found a more ironic location than Tavistock Square to explode a bomb in a passing bus on the morning of July 7, 2005.

Tavistock has long been a square open to the public, but others, like Bedford and Mecklenburgh, are locked and accessible only to residents—an enduring expression of capitalist control. A woman with a social conscience in Woolf's story "A Man Who Loved His Kind" is haunted by the image of "a woman and two children, very poor, very tired, pressing against the railings of a square, peering in that hot afternoon. Can't they be let in? she had thought, . . . her indignation boiling" (*CSF* 197–98). The blend of nature with the commerce of the city is evoked in Woolf's "Street Haunting: A London Adventure":

> How beautiful a London street is then, with its islands of light, and its long groves of darkness, and on one side of it perhaps some tree-sprinkled, grass-grown space where night is folding herself to sleep naturally and, as one passes the iron railing, one hears those little cracklings and stirrings of leaf and twig which seem to suppose the silence of fields all round them, an owl hooting, and far away the rattle of a train in the valley. But this is London, we are reminded; high among the bare trees are hung oblong frames of reddish-yellow light—windows. . . . This empty ground, which holds the country in it and its peace, is only a London square, set about by offices and houses where at this hour fierce lights burn over maps, over documents, over desks where clerks sit turning with wetted forefinger the files of endless correspondences. (*E* 4:482)

Love and Conversation

Woolf had memorable experiences in private gardens, where visiting with friends and acquaintances encouraged her to write in terms of merger and transformation rather than control. Woolf's aunt and mentor, Caroline Emelia Stephen, had what Woolf called as a child a "miniature Kew" surrounding her cottage ("The Porch") in Cambridge. Woolf recalled "long hours of talk in her room with windows opening on to the garden" (*E* 1:268; figure 12)—a transitional setting from indoors to out that Woolf favored in her writing. This peaceful setting was a place of recovery from Virginia's 1904 breakdown. In memorializing her aunt, Woolf mentions that she spent "the last years of her life among her flowers and with young people round her" (269).

Woolf also was helped back to health at Violet Dickinson's home in Welwyn—a place she celebrated as a "magic garden" in the 1907 essay "Friendships Gallery." As suggested in this fantasy, the cottage and gardens Violet built for herself provided another space for jovial conversation, particularly among women. Aristocratic ladies assume the aspect of extraordinary flowers, with more than a hint of sapphism: "Ladies like flowers strayed from the beds, anemones and strange fritillaries freaked with jet, and certain straight tulips, tawny as sunset clasped by stiff green spikes, all kinds of flowers indeed, whose voices chimed like petals floating and kissing in the air; or creaked, as fresh tulip leaves creak when rubbed together, so that you long to crush the juice out of them" (282–83). Lady Robert (Nellie) Cecil stands behind the remarkable fritillaries (285). If of the *Fratillaria imperialis* variety, these flowers would stand three feet high, each stout stem surrounded by a dozen bell-shaped flowers, crowned by spiky leaves. Violet (whose name suggests a low and reclusive flower, but whose height was six feet) comes forth like this species as "a tall rod of a plant with queer little tassels always quivering and austere silver leaves which prick you if you don't know the way of them" (284). Woolf very likely encodes lesbian desire in the "queer," "quivering," and even the "prick." Sexuality here is fluid, and therefore worthy of the transgressive sense the word has assumed in queer theory. Though she represents Dickinson as a superb hostess, Woolf also captures her dear friend in a solitary and somber mood: "At times you would find her digging furiously in her garden or catching brambles by the neck as some deft animals catch snakes, and she would look at you with fierce melancholy and exclaim, 'Nobody wants me; but I'm very happy alone. Why should they want me? I

FIGURE 12. Caroline Emelia Stephen posed at her garden window. (Monk's House Album 1, MS Thr 557, Harvard Theatre Collection, Houghton Library, Harvard University)

don't know anythin'—can't do anythin' except weed" (290). Woolf would retain the idea of gardens as solitary, sad retreats in presenting the frustrations of early women writers in *A Room of One's Own*. By crediting Dickinson with the knowledge of how to treat the greenfly plaguing her roses, she attempts to ameliorate Dickinson's depression.[13]

Ottoline Morrell entertained a variety of literary and political figures on extended weekends at Garsington Manor, Oxfordshire, from 1915 to 1928. The garden featured a large grass terrace lined with yew hedges, with statuary interspersed. This led down to a spacious rectangular pool that reflected the images of nearby trees. Flowers bloomed amid boxwood borders. As in Woolf's *Orlando,* peacocks might stroll through the grounds. The manor house dated back to the Jacobean era, and for David Cecil it held a romantic aspect (8). Scenes from Aldous Huxley's *Chrome Yellow* and D. H. Lawrence's *Women in Love* have settings inspired by Garsington. Hermione Roddice, the hostess of Lawrence's fictional Breadalby, presents a notoriously negative image of Lady Ottoline, particularly when she knocks Rupert Birkin nearly unconscious with a paperweight. Receiving the full naturist treatment from Lawrence, Birkin retreats into the wood to roll naked amid sticky young hyacinths and flagellating firs (105–7).

Morrell's photographs in *Lady Ottoline's Album* show Woolf lounging in a chair, taking a smoke, reading, or enjoying the company of visitors such as Lytton Strachey. Guests are typically posed outdoors, against the background of the gardens. Woolf's treatment of the garden is ancillary to the people walking and conversing there. Thus in 1919 we learn of "young Lord de la Waar walking among the roses & cabbages" as "Gertler & Nelson strolled up another garden path." She covers the grounds with a series of queer conversations in June 1923: "I walked round the vegetable garden with [Lord David Cecil], passing Lytton flirting with Byam Shaw on a green seat; & round the field with [Edward] Sackville-West, who said he was better and was writing a better novel, & round the lake with Menasseh (?) an Egyptian Jew, who said he liked his family, & they were mad & talked like books" (*D* 2:244). Both her visits and her hostess get mixed reviews, however, due to the egotism expressed: "Thirty seven people to tea; a bunch of young men no bigger than asparagus; walking to & fro, round & round; compliments, attentions, & then this slippery mud—which interests me at the moment. A loathing overcomes me of human beings—their insincerity, their vanity" (243).

Woolf's lover and friend, Vita Sackville-West, was a consummate gardener, accustomed to cultivation on a grand scale from her childhood at the family's Elizabethan manor, Knole in Kent. In her later years Vita became a widely recognized expert on plants. Her weekly gardening articles appeared in the *Observer* (1947–61) and were collected in four volumes, starting with *In Your Garden* (1951). Her son Nigel Nicolson considered his mother a self-taught gardener, eschewing the notion that Gertrude Jekyll or any other gardening expert would have influenced her selection and distribution of plants (interview with author, 2000).

An early gardening venture for Vita had been at Cospoli, near Constantinople, where her husband, Harold Nicolson, was stationed in the diplomatic service. Like the imperial explorers who had stocked botanical gardens in the preceding centuries, Vita collected cuttings and bulbs on journeys abroad. She registers the vanities of gardening as she considers her Persian *Iris reticulata*: "There is a particular pleasure in bringing home plants which one has collected oneself in distant countries. Quite possibly that pleasure may plunge its roots in the fertile soil of vanity: 'Yes,' I should say, 'a nice group, isn't it? I collected the bulbs in the Bakhtiari country." But that would only be when strangers were present, forced to admire my garden" (*Twelve Days* 49–50). Vita also garnered Alpine flowers and sought bulbs for the flowers she had seen in Dutch paintings. Woolf and Monk's House benefited from a gift of Vita's surplus Dutch tulip bulbs.

The first of Vita's English gardens was near Knole at Long Barn, started in 1915. This was a setting for the romance of Vita and Virginia as it flourished in the late 1920s. After three days there in December 1925, Woolf wrote with imaginative similes of Vita: "She shines in Sevenoaks with a candle lit radiance, stalking on legs like beech trees, pink glowing, grape clustered, pearl hung" (*D* 3:52)—lines that could contribute later to *Orlando*. Vita also enjoyed visiting Virginia's garden, which served metaphorically as a disorderly place of vegetable passion. Writing to Vanessa Bell, Vita reported that "the garden was full of lust and bees, mingling in the asparagus beds" (qtd. in Glendinning 163). The threatened encroachment of a poultry facility encouraged the move of the Sackville-West-Nicholsons to Sissinghurst Castle, where their ultimate garden was begun in 1930. Sissinghurst was less frequented by Virginia, since it was developed after the period of her greatest intimacy with Vita, but her photograph remains there, enshrined on Vita's desk in the tower.

Vita's serious attempts at poetry, *The Land* and *The Garden,* honored the agricultural life of Kent in a Georgian pastoral tradition, quite removed from modernist technique. Woolf commented negatively about the manner and subject of *The Land,* which nevertheless commanded the Hawthornden Prize in 1926. Still, Vita's efforts at poetry move into *Orlando* as the poem "The Oak Tree," written and rewritten by the androgynous title character through the centuries. During their romantic involvement, Woolf had toured Knole, particularly admiring the trees in the surrounding area, named for this native flora, Sevenoaks. The estate represented in *Orlando* has a garden along the lines of Knole, where various courtyards are given over to unremarkable plantings. For Orlando, the formal garden is a territory to be avoided, as it disturbs him to think of his mother "walking out to feed the peacocks" (15). He retreats instead "uphill through ferns and hawthorn bushes, startling deer and wild birds, to a place crowned by a single oak tree" (18)—a location more conducive to solitary thinking. The setting is worthy of the androgyny the novel aims for, satisfying the later female Orlando as well as the original male one.

Art in the Garden

The artist and critic Roger Fry designed his own home, Durbins, in Guild-ford, which he occupied in 1910–19, and he enlisted Gertrude Jekyll to lay out the gardens. In her biography of Fry, Woolf pauses briefly over the garden: "A pleasing freedom seemed to prevail. There was time—time to look at the garden, with the flowers nodding over the pool; time for a walk to see a view he liked, though the country was only Surrey" (*RF* 141). Understandably, this garden became a subject for Bloomsbury painters, including several notable interpretations by Duncan Grant (figure 13).

Woolf's sister Vanessa was both painter and gardener, the latter art flour-ishing after her move in 1916 with Grant and her two sons to Charleston, a country farmhouse in Sussex. Vanessa saw fine elements in Charleston from the start, as she reports to Fry: "The pond is most beautiful with a willow at one side and a stone or flint wall edging it all round the garden part, and a little lawn sloping down to it with formal bushes in it [figure 14]. Then there's a small orchard and walled garden and another lawn and bit of field railed in

FIGURE 13. *Pamela,* 1911 (oil on canvas), by Duncan Grant (1885–1978). (Yale Center for British Art, Gift of Paul Mellon, USA/Paul Mellon Collection/The Bridgeman Art Library. © 2011 Artists Rights Society [ARS], New York/DACS, London)

FIGURE 14. Pond at Charleston. (Photograph by the author)

beyond. There's a wall of trees—one single line of elms all round two sides, which shelters us from west winds" (qtd. in Spalding 156). Vanessa takes as a matter of course the walled garden—an enclosure that allows for a different selection of plants depending upon the direction of each wall in relation to the sun. Fry has been credited with its plan, which offered a rectangular layout of gravel paths, running through large flower beds positioned on the north side of the house, where Duncan's studio, Vanessa's room, and the garden room were located. A lawn with a small rectangular pool ran from the house to the middle of the garden. Spaces were articulated to provide a variety of settings—as at St. Ives. Vanessa and Duncan developed an extensive cottage garden, accented with mosaic pavements and statuary provided by Duncan and others from the Omega Workshop group, blurring the boundaries of nature and art (figure 15).[14] Vanessa's garden contained considerable variety in height as well as type of flowers. Her "old-fashioned" flowers included red hot pokers, pinks, delphiniums, peonies, lavenders, daisies, phlox, stocks, achillea, columbines, goldenrod, Michelmas daisies, mums, and masses of roses (Brown 134).[15] Vanessa treated large globe artichokes like flowers, a floral/vegetable mix that makes its way into the garden in *To the Lighthouse*, when in "Time Passes" the garden runs wild and artichokes appear among

FIGURE 15. Cottage garden at Charleston. (Photograph by the author)

the roses (*TTL* 141). Outside her walled garden, Vanessa also grew fruit, vegetables, and herbs and kept bees, rabbits, chickens, and pigs to feed her family and visitors, fulfilling the present-day ecological goal of eating locally grown products.

Virginia was a frequent visitor to Charleston, sometimes bicycling from her home at Asham and later Monk's House. Vanessa's camera regularly captured Bloomsbury groups playfully posed together there. She preserved her mother's tradition of a garden of childish delights and nascent sexuality. Her three children pose nude, sometimes among fully clad adults (as in a photo of Angelica with Grant and Fry). Introducing another art to the gardens, the children acted in theatricals, appareled in flowing costumes (Bell and Garnette). Julia Stephen has a presence there in the form of a marble head sculpted by Baron Marochetti around 1863.

Vanessa's creations for the Omega Workshops included large, imaginative paper flowers. Her paintings, like those of Grant and Fry, regularly feature floral still lifes, flower borders, or a garden seen from a door or a window, as with Bell's 1926 painting *View into the Garden* (1926; figure 16).[16] Similarly, Virginia positions Mrs. Ramsay in a window, open to the garden, as the first setting of *To the Lighthouse*. Both sisters could have taken this from St. Ives, as Julia Stephen and her children are found posed at a similar window in Leslie Stephen's photo album (figure 17). Vanessa is attentive to the ways in which light shines iridescently through petals, and geometrical rhythms emerge from an assemblage of vases, picture frames, and furnishings in *Flowers in a Studio* (1915), a painting she presented to Virginia. At Charleston, Duncan and Vanessa had an abundant selection of the flowers with silvery leaves they preferred as subjects for their work. The garden also came inside in many of the designs with which they decorated the walls, woodwork, and furniture at Charleston, as well as the tile decorations on the fireplace at Monk's House (figure 18). Clive Bell had floral ornaments beneath his study windows at Charleston; Duncan Grant, a floral door; and Maynard Keynes, a table decorated as a lily pond.

Vanessa's use of flowers undoubtedly influenced her sister's and complemented Woolf's works, especially after the Woolfs' own Hogarth Press was publishing them. Vanessa supplied a woodcut in which flowers loom over and between a strolling couple as the frontispiece to the 1919 Hogarth Press edition of *Kew Gardens*. Inside, another woodcut features a caterpillar, black and white on each of its segments, arching around a butterfly in the leaves (figure

FIGURE 16. *View into the Garden,* 1926 (oil on board), by Vanessa Bell (1879–
1961). (© Bolton Museum and Art Gallery, Lancashire, UK/The Bridgeman Art
Library/© Estate of Vanessa Bell, courtesy of Henrietta Garnett)

FIGURE 17. Julia, Vanessa, Thoby, Adrian, and Virginia Stephen
with Shag outside the French window at Talland House, St. Ives.
(Leslie Stephen Photo Album, Mortimer Rare Book Room,
Smith College)

19). In a 1927 illustrated version of *Kew Gardens,* flowers and leaves surround
the words of the text (figure 20). Vanessa contributed numerous covers for
her sister's works, including *Jacob's Room, The Waves, A Writer's Diary, Granite
and Rainbow, A Haunted House and Other Stories,* and *The Moment and Other
Essays.* Writing to her sister about one woodcut, Woolf said, "I don't see that
it matters whether it's about the story or not" (*L* 2:258). On receiving a sketch
of it, Woolf was pleased to find it "just in the mood I wanted." But she goes on
to use "decorative" terms that could be seen to demean the effort. "As a piece
of black and white it is extremely decorative—you see my language is already
tainted" (*L* 2:259).[17]

Sally Seton's idea of floating the heads of flowers in a bowl of water in
Mrs. Dalloway likely came from an arrangement Vanessa had put out one day

FIGURE 18. Virginia Woolf reading, Monk's House; decorative floral tiles by Vanessa Bell. (Monk's House Album 5, MS Thr 562, Harvard Theatre Collection, Houghton Library, Harvard University)

FIGURE 19. Woodcut of a caterpillar, 1919, by Vanessa Bell. From *Kew Gardens*. (© Estate of Vanessa Bell, courtesy of Henrietta Garnett)

when Virginia was visiting Charleston. Poppies, generally associated with "sleep, dreams, and numbing relief" due to their narcotic effect (Barnette 150), are often featured in her paintings. The erect red hot pokers that figure so importantly in the garden scene of *To the Lighthouse* have their counterpart in Vanessa's 1926 painting of these robust orange and yellow flowers in a vase. Brought from the colonial territories of South Africa and Madagascar, the pokers may rise up to four feet. Their blooms comprise hundreds of small flowers radiating from a thick stem. When the Ramsays move from "the gap between two clumps of red-hot pokers" (71) to "the path where the silver-green spear like plants grew" (73), they are visiting some of Vanessa's favorite subjects (figure 21).

Woolfs in the Garden

In their own ultimate garden at Monk's House in Rodmell, Leonard and Virginia playfully named two elm trees after themselves (figure 22). Leonard was a methodical and earnest, if not inspired gardener, and an environmentalist, as suggested further in his attitude toward animals, which we will encounter

Kew Gardens

From the oval-shaped flower-bed there rose
perhaps a hundred stalks spreading into
heart-shaped or tongue-shaped leaves half
way up and unfurling at the tip red or blue or
yellow petals marked with spots of colour raised
upon the surface; and from the red, blue or yellow
gloom of the throat emerged a straight bar,
rough with gold dust and slightly clubbed
at the end.

FIGURE 20. Illustration by Vanessa Bell. From *Kew Gardens* (1927 edition).
(© Estate of Vanessa Bell, courtesy of Henrietta Garnett/Special Collections,
University of Delaware Library)

FIGURE 21. Woolf posed with red hot pokers. (Monk's House Album 3, MS Thr 560, Harvard Theatre Collection, Houghton Library, Harvard University)

FIGURE 22. Elms called Virginia and Leonard, Monk's House. (MS Thr 564, Harvard Theatre Collection, Houghton Library, Harvard University)

in chapter 5. He describes awakening from a night when he had slept outside in the garden at Asham House:

> In the night there was not a sound—I might have been miles from any other human being. Suddenly in the early morning there burst out a tremendous chorus as if every thrush and blackbird in England had started to sing round the house and every pigeon in Sussex had started "bubbling with content"—in Virginia's *Haunted House* "from the deepest wells of silence the wood pigeon drew its bubble of sound." When this ecstatic hosanna or alleluia woke me, I really felt, lying there on the ground, for a moment that I was submerged by the uncut grass towering above my head, the rose leaves above the grass, and the elms above the rose leaves. I wonder if it is age and its dullness of hearing, the spraying of crops, or insecticides which make it seem that there are now no such great convocations of birds in my garden, no such passionate bursts of song . . . as one knew 40 years ago. (*Beginning Again* 58)[18]

One senses from this that in the 1960s (when he wrote this) Leonard might have been a reader of Rachel Carson, whose *Silent Spring* (published 1962) drew world attention to the devastating effect of insecticides on the environment.[19] While living at Asham House early in their marriage, Leonard worked to revive its walled garden. Katherine Mansfield has preserved her sense of that garden as a special space of female bonding. In conversation, Mansfield offers a description of wild orchid cups in her own garden and receives columbines from Woolf. Virginia was working on her short story "Kew Gardens" at this point, having recently published Mansfield's story "Prelude," which also features garden settings, as noted in chapter 1.

Its garden was a major attraction when the Woolfs acquired Monk's House in 1919. Leonard recalls his positive early reaction: "The orchard was lovely and the garden was the kind I like, much subdivided into a kind of patchwork quilt of trees, shrubs, flowers, vegetables, fruit, roses and crocus tending to merge into cabbages and currant bushes" (*Beginning Again* 62).

Virginia shared this enthusiasm, telling Janet Case, "The point of it is the garden. I shan't tell you though, for you must come and sit there on the lawn with me, or stroll in the apple orchard, or pick—there are cherries, plums, pears, figs, together with all the vegetables. This is going to be the pride of our hearts" (*L* 2:379).[20] Both accounts celebrate the variety of the garden and its jumbled categories. Leonard, like Leslie Stephen, is concerned mainly with geography. Virginia anticipates meeting with intimates. She offers delectable fruits, as if for sensual enticement.

The house, which faced slightly north of due west, was set close to the village street, lending privacy to the garden behind, as did a churchyard to the east. The Woolfs acquired additional land, which they called the "terrace," to the north of the original parcel in 1928, hoping to ensure that they would retain a cherished view of the water meadows of the Ouse River. At about that time they became distressed about developers coming into the area. In December 1929 Woolf sits in her newly constructed bedroom admiring "two great views; sometimes sun over the brooks & storm over the church." She is furious with one "damnable Byng-Stamper & his power to sell the down to a syndicate to exploit." She admits to being "wrought up to protest" (*D* 3:274). The next February, she writes Ottoline Morrell to get the name of a man "connected with preserving the downs" whom she has met at Morrell's home. Woolf rants, "If I write my fingers off, I want to stop it. . . . It is one of the loveliest places in the world, and then they want to have a coast road and omnibuses—oh the damnable stupidity of the English middle class!" (*L* 4:139). Woolf's ideas of conservation betray class bias. But they do focus upon enduring environmental problems of suburban sprawl, tourism, and highway construction to meet the growing demands of the internal combustion engine.

Soon after the move to Monk's House, the Woolfs began acquiring books and pamphlets on plant selection and cultivation and on garden design.[21] Though probably acquired by Leonard, these would have surrounded Virginia on shared bookshelves. In 1925 Woolf boasts to Janet Case of a fine showing of Colchicums (Sparks, "Leonard's Vegetable Empire" 12)—showing success from one of their book purchases. The history of the garden at Monk's House has been carefully researched by Elisa K. Sparks, who appropriately considers it Leonard's project.[22] Virginia preferred to have the income from *The Common Reader* and *Mrs. Dalloway* go toward household improvements (13). She at times felt that the garden restricted her freedom to do other things. She records her complaints to Leonard in 1926: "I admitted that I had been irritated . . . by his assumption that we can afford to saddle ourselves with a whole time gardener, build or buy him a cottage, & take in the terrace to be garden. Then, I said, we shall be tying ourselves to come here; shall never travel; & it will be assumed that Monks House is the hub of the world" (*D* 3:112). The gardener, Percy Bartholomew, was an addition to the household servants, who had always been both needed and a source of guilt and tension for Woolf. As Alison Light remarks in *Mrs. Woolf and the Servants,* Virginia "joked about the quasi-feudalism" of Leonard's arrangements for the Bartholomew family. Leonard provided "his man" a four-room cottage lacking indoor plumbing, and few days off (Light 190). Revenues from *Orlando* (1928) helped to fund renovations of the garden and acquisition of additional land. Virginia consulted with Vita Sackville-West about purchasing Italian pots and statuary for the area surrounding a new lily pond in 1933. More typically, Virginia continued to foot the bills for remodeling the house, while Leonard financed new pathways, ponds, and terraces (Sparks, "Leonard's Vegetable Empire" 13–14).

Nigel Nicholson variously records the opinion of his mother, Vita, that "Leonard was attempting to construct Versailles on a quarter acre."[23] In some of her own descriptions, Virginia is equally prone to exaggeration for the sake of amusement. Leonard's methodical nature can be seen in his careful records of the productivity of each of the apple trees, as in later years he noted every time one of his rare cacti came into bloom.[24] Sparks notes that the fruit trees were indeed profitable in the early years and did well into the 1950s. She describes the couple's garden work along gender lines: "Leonard was always the chief planner, planter, and pruner. . . . Virginia's garden contributions were sporadic and consisted mostly of planting, weeding, and arranging flowers. . . . In times of crisis, she also helped with cutting back blighted potatoes and picking fruit" (12–13). Virginia tended potted plants inside, and might offer visitors such as Elizabeth Bowen cuttings for their own gardens. One of her last diary entries records Leonard's pruning the rhododendrons.

Even if she was not the planner or planter of the gardens at Monk's House, Woolf derived tremendous enjoyment from them. She conversed avidly with friends and literary acquaintances by one of the various lily ponds, set amid brick walks and garden urns and sculptures, often in the company of the current dog, a loosely grasped cigarette accenting her gestures. In many ways the garden provided a better space than the house, which visitors such as Nigel Nicholson and her nephew Cecil Woolf describe as encumbered with books and provisions for pets. A large proportion of the photographs of Woolf taken with friends at Monk's House are in the garden setting. The terrace gave Virginia a field for competition in lawn bowling, which she could take quite seriously, if still socially. She wrote in a garden "lodge," sharing the structure with apples, stored in the loft. Though the apples remained with her, in 1934 she relocated to a larger lodge, farther from the house, its windows looking across the water meadows. The garden was continuous with these meadows, where she regularly walked, collecting her ideas, always aware of the natural attributes of the setting. Thus, I think the garden provided an important sense of merger, with flowers and people, with Leonard's labors there, and with a broader, less controlled expanse of nature.

Women Characterized by Their Gardens

Woolf explores other gardens that she comes to through reading and writing, in order to understand the people who inhabit them. Numerous gardens house the frustrations of women at odds with society; they lack the sense of company that gave Woolf such pleasure in garden settings. In a 1910 review, Woolf describes the "mysterious spells" that the eccentric and increasingly isolated aristocrat Lady Esther Stanhope cast upon Mount Lebanon. There she "dug an elaborate garden" around her hilltop house and sat regaling her physician with memories of serving as Prime Minister William Pitt's housekeeper, and fantasies of saving the world from approaching catastrophes (*E* 1:327). Woolf leaves her "buried in a corner of her rose garden in the grave of a certain prophet, where she had no wish to be buried"—a place that reverted ten years later to a "thicket of brambles and roses" (329). Another of Woolf's early review/essays, written in 1911, follows Margaret Cavendish, Duchess of Newcastle, into retreat "to contemplate alone in the gardens at Welbeck" (349). Woolf regrets that her ideas (many of them original explanations of nature or science) were not subject to discussion there. Woolf returns to that garden more imaginatively in *A Room of One's Own*. The "loneliness and riot" of this literary predecessor seems to Woolf "as if some giant cucumber had spread itself over all the roses and carnations in the garden and choked them to death" (61). It is an objectionable image to those who have begun to reconsider the merits of Cavendish's scientific thought. But clearly, Woolf has moved beyond the meticulous natural representations of country parsons, to imaginative accounts that blur the boundaries between humans and the content of their gardens.

There is a more affirmative garden visit in *A Room of One's Own*, where Woolf memorializes "the famous scholar J____ H____," Jane Harrison, who had died the previous year. Harrison appears as a phantom in the garden of the imaginary women's college, which Woolf gives a botanic name, "Fernham."

She is spotted "on the terrace, as if popping out to breathe the air, to glance at the garden" (17). Like the garden devised for Cavendish, Fernham's violates the rules of realistic representation. Seasons switch from autumn to spring. The garden is "wild and open," accessible in ways denied the narrator at the men's college. This stirring of the imagination compensates somewhat for the idea lost when she was banished from the lawn reserved for fellows of the men's college.

The ways Woolf's characters apprehend flowers, or are described in terms of them, tell much about their personality and position in life. Woolf may invoke traditional symbolic meanings for flowers. This is true of *Mrs. Dalloway,* which offers Woolf's greatest number of floral references, many proving symbolic. Elizabeth Dalloway is annoyed that she is compared "to poplar trees, early dawn, hyacinths, fawns, running water and garden lilies" (131). The lily, flower of the Virgin, is appropriate to a young girl shown off at parties and thus set up for plucking on the marriage market. The hyacinth suggests the lesbian love of Miss Kilman, as it represents a young man loved by both Apollo and Zephyrus, who kills him in jealous rage. Unable to say "I love you" to Clarissa, Richard Dalloway presents her with a stiff bouquet of red and white roses, which he brandishes almost like a weapon. Here the association of the rose with the goddess of love, Venus, may be appropriate, though roses also have a connection to the Virgin Mary, reminding us of Clarissa's narrow bed, at this stage in her life. Roses also may subtly encode lesbian eroticism, or even war.[25] Mrs. Dempster, who sits in the park feeding crusts to the squirrels, works over her version of the common expression "Life is not a bed of roses," both because she wants to prepare the young Maisie Johnson for what lies ahead, and because she would like a modicum of pity for her sufferings. Roses enter her thoughts repeatedly before she arrives finally at "Pity for the loss of roses" (27). Sally hands Clarissa a single flower before kissing her in the garden and thinks of Clarissa with her hands full of flowers. When she reappears in middle age, Sally is associated with hydrangeas. The Greek word origin for this flower is equivalent to "water vessel," a choice based on the cuplike structure of its seed pods. Might Woolf have associated this with Sally's many pregnancies, resulting in five large sons, or with the taking on of water characteristic of middle-aged spread?

Mrs. Dalloway's response to the blossoms in the florist shop shows her knowledge of a variety of types. The scene is sensual, suggesting her merger with the flowers and the shopkeeper (whose observations blend into hers):

"Ah yes—so she breathed in the earthy garden sweet smell as she stood talking to Miss Pym" (12). She enjoys the flowers, first "with her eyes half closed," and after having opened them, she sees "how fresh like frilled linen clean from a laundry laid in wicker trays the roses looked; and dark and prim the red carnations, holding their heads up; and all the sweet peas spreading their bowls, tinged violet, snow white, pale." She is back in a garden with girls in muslin frocks and "grey-white moths spinning in and out" (13). Mrs. Dalloway has an organic, holistic philosophy regarding her place in nature and the world that we will return to in chapter 6. "Buds on the tree of life, flowers of darkness" sums up a moment of being as she reenters her home, greeted by her appreciative maid, hearing the cook whistling and a typewriter, feeling gratitude for Richard. But Woolf plucks away this blossom, as Clarissa discovers that he will not be coming home for lunch (28–29).

Women Seeking Freedom in Controlled Spaces

Woolf constantly makes us aware that even though gardens and flowers encountered in her writing may provide stimulus to the senses and a queer space for sensual exploration or lively conversation, they are also arenas of control and confinement. In *The Voyage Out*, Rachel Vinrace recalls "interminable walks around sheltered gardens" in suburban Richmond, where she was reared by her aunts (124); she welcomes the chance to join her father on a voyage to South America.

Some of the most memorable scenes of *Mrs. Dalloway* are set in the country garden at Bourton. In her first recollection of that childhood home, Clarissa is plunging "into the open air" through the French windows. In her psychoanalytic feminist study of *Mrs. Dalloway,* Elizabeth Abel tunnels back into Clarissa's pre-Oedipal development by constructing Bourton as a feminine, green world. Clarissa recovers this in rare fragments, having moved on as a married woman to what Abel construes as the masculine domain of London. Clarissa does construct something very powerful in her recollection of Sally's kiss as they walk in the garden. While at Bourton, Sally is in her element outside. While talking to "Papa" at the fireplace, "Suddenly she said, 'What a shame to sit indoors!' and they all went out on to the terrace and walked up and down. Peter Walsh and Joseph Breitkopf went on about Wagner. She and Sally fell a little behind. Then came the most exquisite moment of her whole life passing a stone urn with flowers in it. Sally stopped; picked a flower;

kissed her on the lips. The whole world might have turned upside down! The others disappeared; there she was alone with Sally" (34–35). But they do not have the garden to themselves. Peter interrupts their great moment with his remark, "Star-gazing?" "It was like running one's face against a granite wall in the darkness! It was shocking; it was horrible!" (35). "Sally it was who made her feel . . . how sheltered the life at Bourton was" and who helps Clarissa realize that "she knew nothing about sex—nothing about social problems" (32). The scene quickly gives over to old Joseph Breitkopf identifying stars, a masculine display of knowledge elicited at Sally's suggestion. The garden at Bourton thus offers only flashes of free thought and action.

We learn from Peter that he had his own sense of conspiracy with Sally, gained in retreat among the vegetables. The garden held his grief as well, set in the image of the "moon looked at from a terrace, ghastly beautiful with light from the sunken day" (41). He made a last effort to claim Clarissa by a fountain "in the middle of a little shrubbery, far from the house." He remembers the broken spout of the fountain "dribbling water incessantly" and "the vivid green moss." As in Clarissa's scene with Sally, they are interrupted. Perhaps more inclined to read and encourage heterosexual romance, Breitkopf goes away. Like the image of the granite wall Clarissa had of Peter, in this instance Peter feels "that he was grinding against something physically hard. She was like iron, like flint, rigid up the backbone" (63). Woolf's gardens can have painfully limiting walls.

While nothing matches Clarissa's response to Sally's kiss in the garden, it does have sequels decades later. Clarissa compassionately kisses Peter in her London sitting room, eliciting a surprisingly wild metaphor: "And Clarissa had leant forward, taken his hand, drawn him to her, kissed him,—actually had felt his face on hers—before she could down the brandishing of silver flashing plumes like pampas grass in a tropic gale in her breast" (45). This tall grass from the plains of South America also serves as emotional iconography when Rachel and Helen embrace in *The Voyage Out*. As a middle-aged woman whose life has moved toward a "narrow bed," Mrs. Dalloway still has occasional moments of "yielding to the charm of a woman . . . [,] confessing, as to her they often did, some scrape, some folly." As with Peter, this passion comes out of compassion. In this case it results in the extraordinary metaphor of "a match burning in a crocus" (31)—a complex construction, often read as lesbian code, to which we return in chapter 6.

Though it is modeled on the beloved garden at St. Ives, the garden of *To the Lighthouse* is far from idyllic. As the novel opens, Mrs. Ramsay and her son James sit in an open window that looks out immediately upon the terrace. This space is occupied by Mr. Ramsay, pacing back and forth, sometimes in discussion with the doting student, Charles Tansley. Stone urns drip with red geraniums nearby. While Mrs. Ramsay thinks Mr. Ramsay fails to notice flowers, he seems to regard them as a place from which his ideas emanate. James may be cutting out gardening equipment from a catalog, but he shows no desire to leave his mother's side and dig with real tools in the garden. But toward the end of the novel, as he sails with his moody, demanding father toward the lighthouse, James recovers a primal garden scene associated with his mother: "Everything tended to set itself in a garden where there was none of this gloom. . . . All was blowing, all was growing; and over all those plates and bowls and tall brandishing red and yellow flowers a very thin yellow veil would be drawn, like a vine leaf, at night. . . . He could see through it a figure stooping, hear, coming close, going away, some dress rustling, some chain tinkling" (188–89). This scene, with its yellow tint and vivid flowers, resembles the early moments of being recorded in "A Sketch of the Past." "Brandishing," whether of flowers or of grasses, serves Woolf in representing passion. "Rustling" and "tinkling," sounds associated with Woolf's own mother, later serve as attributes of the Angel of the House in "Professions for Women." James has another memory: "something flourished up in the air, something arid and sharp descending there, like a blade, a scimitar, smiting through the leaves and flowers even of that happy world and making it shrivel and fall" (189). This recalls his father's intrusion from the terrace to deliver his gloomy weather forecast, denying the possibility of sailing to the lighthouse. By equipping James with scissors and a huge claim to his mother's attention, however, I think that Woolf is suggesting that the masculine control of the garden was already well under way with James, even before his father intrudes, with metaphoric scythe in hand.

Standing on the lawn to paint a picture of Mrs. Ramsay with James, Lily Briscoe can see major features of the garden. She looks back at the house "starred in its greenery with purple passion flowers" (23). Violet jacmanna, a type of clematis, grows on a "staring white" wall (22). Her position is not secure or private: Mr. Bankes approaches to review her work within the parameters of Western art, Mr. Ramsay bears down upon them, reciting "The Charge of the Light Brigade," and Cam grazes the easel, not stopping for anyone (57). Lily's walks take us to the tennis lawn and the orchard—a place apart where Lily processes information, surrealistically. The branches of the celebrated pear tree contain her accumulated impressions of the Ramsays, with images dancing "like a company of gnats, each separate, but all marvelously controlled in an invisible elastic net" (28). Also contained is her impression of Mr. Ramsay, since among these things "still hung in effigy the scrubbed kitchen table, symbol of her profound respect for Mr. Ramsay's mind" (28).[26]

The Ramsays stroll every evening to the gap in the hedge with clumps of red hot pokers on either side, a lookout to the sea and the lighthouse. The couple is divided in its thoughts and metaphors—Mr. Ramsay thinking of the former freedom he'd experienced on the distant sand hills, before becoming the protector of his brood on a diminishing spit of land; she looking toward the town, where in social work she found purpose aside from her family.[27] As they turn to the "path where the silver-green spear-like plants grew" (73), Mrs. Ramsay has numerous concerns. Her husband doesn't notice that rabbits may be ruining her evening primroses (73). She cannot bring up the bill for repairing the greenhouse. But she can discuss faults of the gardener. She suspects that he never plants the bulbs she sends from London and indicts Kennedy with "incurable laziness. . . . If she stood over him all day long with a spade in her hand, he did sometimes do a stroke of work" (69–70). As a middle-class employer of servants, Mrs. Ramsay is in a position of power and can be oppressive; as a woman in her family, she is subject to her husband's power and oppression, unable to converse on economic and intellectual matters.[28]

Mrs. Ramsay's character is repeatedly essentialized in nature. Woolf's narrator, other characters, and Mrs. Ramsay herself all participate in this. To Lily, Mrs. Ramsay represents the dome of the hive to which she must return (54). At the critical moment when Mr. Ramsay intrudes upon Mrs. Ramsay and James, the boy sees his mother as "a rosy-flowered fruit tree laid with leaves and dancing boughs into which the beak of brass . . . plunged and smote" (41–42). Soothed by his wife, Mr. Ramsay is "like a child who drops off satisfied," but in another floral metaphor, "Mrs. Ramsay seemed to fold herself together, one petal closed in another, and the whole fabric fell in exhaustion upon itself" (42).

Mrs. Ramsay's own imagination abounds with natural images. Her husband resembles a sea lion at the zoo (36). Her children come in "fresh as roses," and she finds them "netted in their cots like birds among cherries and raspberries" (62). Comforting Cam, she takes a frightening pig skull and, by winding it about with her shawl, converts it into a bird's nest and then a mountain landscape, "with valleys and flowers and bells ringing and birds singing and little goats and antelopes" (117). At dinner, she listens to Mr. Ramsay reciting a poem that represents courtship in a garden. It supports her essentialist position, in terms of feminine fecundity, in the garden. *"Come out and climb the garden path Luriana Lurilee. / The China rose is all abloom and buzzing with the yellow bee."*[29] She imagines "the words . . . as if they were floating like flowers on water" out the window (112).

Extending this vision into her own random reading later that evening, Mrs. Ramsay "felt that she was climbing backwards, upwards, shoving her way up under petals that curved over her." Her sense of being is thus firmly grounded in the garden—a garden facing on the sea, stroked repetitively by the beams of the lighthouse (121). In these actions with words, Mrs. Ramsay adapts a language of nature to her own exploration of relationships and ideas—something that begins to escape from her natural and maternal essentialism.[30] Her sense of continuity with the natural world will occupy our attention again in the final chapter.

Mrs. Ramsay's garden figures recurrently in the modernist, experimental "Time Passes" segment at the center of *To the Lighthouse*—a segment that also mentions, with brutal abruptness, her unexpected death. The garden, like the house, gradually yields to larger forces of nature, which though flourishing, defy the human planting scheme. The nine intervals of *The Waves*, dispersed through a day in solar time, expand on that experiment, again registering the passage of time with brilliant natural images. Once the sun has risen sufficiently, the garden becomes a consistent element in the interludes, its images carried over into nine sets of soliloquies. *"The light struck upon the trees in the garden, making one leaf transparent and then another"* (3). By the third interval, the impersonal third-person narrative accommodates the viewpoint of birds, who have the prospect of a snail, apple leaves, and *"flowers making a light of flowing purple over the beds, through which dark tunnels of purple shade were driven."* Deeper down is an *"unlit world where the leaf rots"* (52–53). At this stage Woolf also introduces a potted plant, set on a windowsill of the house. This plant had a more central role in an early conception of the novel: "I shall have the two different currents—the moths flying along; the flower upright in the center; a perpetual crumbling & renewing of the plant. In its leaves she might see things happen" (*D* 3:229). The "she" is a mythic woman, preserved partially in a solar woman imagined lifting up the sun in the intervals; her vision among the leaves also seems dispersed into the perspectives of the six children Woolf brings to the garden of the final text.

The garden provides essential materials for the children's exploration and their imaginative play in the nine sets of soliloquies that work as chapters of *The Waves*. In her earliest perceptions, Susan focuses upon leaves. Rhoda notices the light on trees and grass. In the first extended soliloquy, the lonely Louis makes a strong connection to flowers set against "depths of green." He notices how their stalks rise from the hollows below; and becomes one with the stalk he holds: "My roots go down to the depths of the world" (6). Jinny's immersion in nature inspires her to dance like leaves and light.

In a more extended episode, Susan lays down her jealous anguish on the roots of the beech trees, in a ritual death. In an attempt to console her, Bernard proposes that they enter "the ringed wood with the wall round it" to stealthily inspect the private garden, Elvedon. There, to the fascination of the children, "the lady sits between the two long windows, writing." Bernard and Susan descend through the trees into an imaginary territory. Its "sleeping daws who have never seen a human form," its ringed wood, and even the name Elvedon suggest a Yeatsian fairy land, with its mixture of allure and threat. There are also very realistic apprehensions: "The ferns smell very strong, and there are red funguses growing beneath them." Elvedon is controlled at its center, having "the close-clipped hedge of the ladies' garden" where they "walk at noon, with scissors, clipping roses." Gardeners, cited above in the second epigraph, "sweep the lawn with giant brooms" and police the area. The children expect them to shoot if they detect intruders. Here rests a political allegory of possession and exclusion, not unlike those told in Victorian children's stories, such as *Peter Rabbit:* "We should be nailed like stoats to the stable door" (10). From a postcolonial angle, this tale of the big house, clipped gardens, and servile sweepers has been associated with an imperial mind-set.[31]

Of all the children, Neville is least inclined toward nature. Though intrigued by a brief view into a private garden, with steam rising from a tea-urn and "banks of blue flowers," what probably attracts him is "Fenswick with his mallet raised. . . . Suddenly descended upon me the obscure, the mystic sense of adoration, of completeness that triumphed over chaos" (51–52). He will retain the floral image to express moments of fulfillment, or use it to array an intimate scene. Neville has no wish to explore woods and fields, which carry too strong a message of heterosexual union: "Should I walk under beech trees, or saunter along the river bank, where the trees meet united like lovers in the water? But nature is too vegetable, too vapid. She has only sublimities and vastitudes and water and leaves. I begin to wish for firelight, privacy, and the limbs of one person" (36).

More closely associated with nature than any other character, Susan returns from school to her native farmlands. She is attracted most to open moors and fields. But she reproduces domesticity, including motherhood, and the maintenance of a garden, home, and servants: "For soon in the hot mid-day when the bees hum round the hollyhocks my lover will come. . . . What has formed in me I shall give him. I shall have children; I shall have maids in aprons; men with pitchforks; a kitchen where they bring the ailing lambs to warm in baskets, where the hams hang and the onions glisten. I shall be my mother, silent in a blue apron locking up the cupboards" (70–71). In the first chapter, she has seen that the kitchen garden is a scene for seduction between the scullery maid and the boot boy. In her maturity, she discloses also that "I am fenced in, planted here like one of my own trees" (139). She now leaves flowers on graves and snips her hollyhocks (a symbol of fecundity to Greenaway) while recalling the adventure of Elvedon. Visiting her during one of her pregnancies, Bernard feels oppressed by her prolific garden, "to me hateful, like a net folding one's limbs in its meshes, cramping," and he thinks "how we surrender, how we submit to the stupidity of nature" (199).

As a place for imaginative play, the garden sometimes betrays already imposed cultural values. Imaging exotic places and scenarios is an enterprise shared by many of the characters, female as well as male. In a favorite space beneath the currant bushes, where he likes to tell stories, Bernard constructs a "malarial jungle," the decomposing leaves translating into "an elephant white with maggots, killed by an arrow shot dead in the eye" (14). In the opening sequence, Rhoda makes petal boats to float upon a basin of water, and she uses a "head of Sweet Alice" to correspond to a lighthouse. Her boats take her to icy caverns and jungle islands with chattering parrots, playing out the adventures of the generations of male explorers in the Arctic and imperialists in Africa and Asia (11).

The garden also enters dreams. Rhoda recalls her own corner of the garden: "Travelling through darkness I see the stretched flower-beds, and Mrs. Constable runs from behind the corner of the pampas-grass to say my aunt has come to fetch me in a carriage" (18). This exotic grass, which we have already encountered as a passionate image in *The Voyage Out* and *Mrs. Dalloway,* is echoed in the image of her aunt's "nodding yellow plumes." But for Rhoda, there is no warm embrace; her aunt has eyes like "hard glazed marbles," diminishing any promise that the garden will furnish affection or release.

The greenhouse, which reached its greatest popularity in Victorian times, is perhaps the ultimate example of the controlled garden. Here, exotic and tender plants that could not survive in the open are cultivated for display and consumption. Mary Wollstonecraft uses the negative trope of woman as a hothouse flower in "Vindication of the Rights of Woman." Greenhouses in Woolf's works are disturbing regions. In *Night and Day,* Ralph Denham and Katherine Hilbery visit Kew, and he experiences confused emotions, brought about presumably by the bizarre flora on display. "He saw Katharine among the orchids, her beauty strangely emphasized by the fantastic plants, which seemed to peer and gape at her from striped hoods and fleshy throats, his ardor for botany waned, and a more complex feeling replaced it" (331). His turn from making a floral metaphor of Katherine to this "complex feeling" escapes nature/gender stereotyping. Clara hands grapes grown in her family's greenhouse down to Jacob, who will disappoint her as a suitor in *Jacob's Room* (62). Mrs. Ramsay is unable to disclose to her husband that it will take £50 to repair the greenhouse (*TTL* 69).[32] It even ages her: "grown old by her own fault. (The bill for the greenhouse and all the rest of it)" (101). In *Mrs. Dalloway,* Sally Seton goes from freely floating the heads of flowers in a bowl as a guest at Bourton to cultivating rare hydrangeas in an enormous greenhouse in the industrial north (183). Lewis, who has issues with his origins and status throughout *The Waves,* longs to have a glass houses with rare fruits when he retires to Surrey (123).

The greenhouse offers a significant setting in *Between the Acts.* Here, during the second interval, Giles Oliver seems to indulge in casual infidelity with Mrs. Manresa. In the first interval, the greenhouse sets the stage for mismatched attentions between the would-be poet Isa Oliver and William Dodge, a man of aesthetic and homosexual proclivities. In its artificial circumstances, they engage in a queer performance of gender. Dodge's original interest in seeing Isa "against an arum lily or a vine" in the greenhouse loses its effect as he redirected his gaze to her "hirsute, handsome, virile" husband

(73). For her part, Isa meditates upon a Swinburnian suicide narrative: "Fly away. I grieving say. Alone I linger, I pluck the bitter herb by the ruined wall, the churchyard wall, and press its sour, its sweet, its sour, long grey leaf, so, twixt thumb and finger" (77).[33] Isa picks up a knife lying in the greenhouse, to further dramatize her recitation. Dodge "saw her standing against the green glass, the fig tree, and the blue hydrangea, knife in hand." She breaks off the performance and they sit together: "The little grapes above them were green buds; the leaves thin and yellow as the web between birds' claws" (78). All is momentary and fragile as they begin speaking very plainly, never expecting to converse again. A sonorous voice of impending war adds, "The future shadowed their present, like the sun coming through the many-veined transparent vine leaf; a criss-cross of lines making no pattern" (79). Nature in this highly cultivated form fails to provide a new pattern, yet the setting does bring together conspirators against the troubling status quo.

Death and survival are intimately related in the garden. *Between the Acts* presents the dilemma of the snake choking on the toad it had intended to eat—both doomed to death. Death is one of the lessons, both resisted and embraced, in the garden of *The Waves*. Jinny kisses Louis, fearing him dead when she peers into the hedge and finds him there. Anguished, Susan flees to the beech wood, wanting to "die in a ditch in the brown water where dead leaves have rotted" (7). Neville associates a man found in a ditch with his throat cut with leaves of the apple tree, "fixed in the sky," glimpsed as he heard this ghastly story (15), and he is immobilized. Bernard is perplexed over whether he should remove a fly from a web or leave it for the spider to eat (8). In an interlude, one of the birds, *"beautifully darting, accurately alighting, spiked the soft, monstrous body of the defenceless worm, pecking again and yet again, and left it to fester"* among decomposing leaves (53).

Repeatedly in *The Waves*, Rhoda imagines her own death, constructing in effect an exit from the garden. She gathers and binds flowers into a garland, merging with them in an imaginary leap over a precipice to join the sea. "We may sink and settle on the waves. The sea will drum in my ears. The white petals will be darkened with sea water. They will float for a moment and then sink. Rolling me over the waves will shoulder me under" (151).

Among those who had sat and conversed with Virginia Woolf in the Monk's House garden was Rebecca West, also an essayist and novelist, and one of her appreciative reviewers. Having learned of Woolf's suicide, West imagined as a bad dream "Virginia walking out of that exquisite garden [Leonard] had made for her . . . and going down into the landscape they'd looked on together" (170).[34] Literary pilgrims still go to Monk's House, seeking her in that garden. As we shall see, however, Woolf's capacity for observation and her rich imagination were applied well beyond the garden, moving to wider spaces, other species, and fragile webs of connection, cycles, and systems of balance, including death in the balance of nature.

4

The Art of Landscape, the Politics of Place

Somehow or another, the windows being open, and the book held so that it rested upon a background of escallonia hedges and distant blue, instead of being a book it seemed as if what I read was laid upon the landscape not printed, bound, or sewn up, but somehow the product of trees and fields and the hot summer sky, like the air which swam, on fine mornings, round the outlines of things.

~Woolf, "Reading"

What I call "reality": a thing I see before me: something abstract; but residing in the downs or sky; beside which nothing matters; in which I shall rest and continue to exist.

~Woolf, *Diary*

THE ANNUAL MIGRATION of the Stephen family between London and Cornwall offered young Virginia contrasting urban and seaside settings, with differing balance and mixture of nature and culture. In her diaries, essays, and fiction, she made imaginative juxtapositions of scenes filled with people, and ones that pore over landscape as well as internal and external spaces. Giles Deleuze and Félix Guattari imagine that "to take a walk like Virginia Woolf" would mean "to be part of the crowd and at the same time completely outside it, removed from it: to be on the edge" (29). As noted in chapter 3, Woolf was anxious to avoid falling into the stale patterns and competitive attitudes she associated with an older generation of nature enthusiasts. Woolf began to express preferences for marginal geographical locations that stimulated her creativity and supported a sense of freedom. Pursuing heights and seeking out hollows or moors are landscape preferences she assigned to characters, and ones that can be read from gendered, postcolonial perspectives. Woolf was also in an excellent position to derive aesthetic ideas from landscape art, available in her family's connections to Victorian and Pre-Raphaelite painters. The Post-Impressionists admired by Bloomsbury painters were particularly important to Woolf for their sensitivity to light and color, cast on landscapes.

While the countryside seems the most obvious focus for studying landscapes, the city is also important. Representative of new directions in ecocriticism, Laurence Buell finds ways that modernists such as Joyce and Woolf reinhabit the city as an environment, citing Mrs. Dalloway's "porousness" in her flânerie as prime examples.[1] For Woolf and such influential critics as Raymond Williams, one must constantly move between city and country. Nature (or its loss) is implicated in both. Representation of landscape also changes over time. As Williams points out in *The Country and the City,* the British pastoral tradition reaches back to Greece, three centuries BCE, and changes with time and geographical situation. Williams locates a neo-pastoral in the "agrarian capitalism of the country-house," which sheltered many modernists, Woolf and her characters included. In Woolf's formative years, the blasted terrain of World War I encouraged new perspectives on pastoral traditions. Bloomsbury's conscientious objectors moved closer to the land as agricultural workers—among these, the painter Duncan Grant. Landscapes frequently depict people working the land, though only gradually have workers' perspectives become available. We have primarily "urban discourse about non-urban worlds, and a lettered, bourgeois discourse about non-lettered, peasant worlds," as Mary Louise Pratt has pointed out (34). One writing strategy in Woolf's early diaries and the *Hyde Park Gate News* was to assume a "cockney" (urban underclass) identity, particularly when observing the countryside. This choice relinquished authority as a rural observer, even as it distanced Woolf from her subject.[2]

The seaside town of St. Ives, Cornwall, was considered a family paradise by multiple generations of Stephen kin. By his own account, this was the scene of Leslie Stephen's "intense domestic happiness" through thirteen summers. He recalls Julia Stephen's catering for the expeditions he and the children undertook (*Mausoleum Book* 62). Woolf carried St. Ives into her fiction, much of it autobiographical. *Jacob's Room, To the Lighthouse, The Waves,* and "A Sketch of the Past" derive settings from St. Ives. Even Mrs. Dalloway conjures up "a morning—fresh as if issued to children on a beach" in that largely urban novel (*MD* 3). Landscapes helped Woolf, both in her own personal development and in defining her characters. Following Julia Stephen's death, perhaps because that place was so closely associated with her, the family ventured into alternate landscapes where the family stayed in houses borrowed from well-off friends. With these sojourns, Woolf added views of agricultural lands, fenlands, and classic English villages. As suggested in the first epigraph, her love of reading was "laid upon the land," the "product" of trees, fields, sky, and the circulating air. In struggling with landscapes, Woolf came into writing.

Though she was wary of the genre of landscape writing, Woolf's early diaries offer sketches of moors in various moods, clouds massed over the watery fenlands, and especially places where the sea meets the shore. The temptations and anxieties of landscape writing returned with later travel abroad in France, Germany, Spain, and Turkey. Woolf's lifetime habit of solitary walking furnished everyday landscapes, whether she strolled along the Thames in Richmond, or on the South Downs of Sussex. Nature was a player in her city walks, where trees completed with rivers for attention.

Woolf needed to work in something other than the pastoral, Romantic, realist, and naturalist traditions that preceded her, and to be more creative than the nature enthusiasts she occasionally mocked. Her review of Edward Thomas's *A Literary Pilgrim in England,* "Flumina Amem Silvasque" ("Let Me Adore the Rivers and Woods"), expresses relief that Thomas proceeds "on the most elastic and human principle" (*E* 2:161). As she notes by quoting it, Thomas cites Blake's anxieties about uses of nature in writing: "Natural objects *always did and do* weaken, deaden and obliterate imagination in me" (162).[3] This may have led to Woolf's striving for lively natural *subjects,* worthy of the imagination. Woolf further tested her organic relation to various settings and modernist use of images, similes, and other forms of figurative language. Her definition of "reality," contained in the second epigraph, is abstract but resident in the landscape, and it gives her an affirmative sense of existing and of going on. This blending with environment, rather than imposing the self upon it, accords with many strands of ecofeminism, including the work of Val Plumwood, Donna Haraway, and "ethic of care" ecofeminists.

Existing pastoral tradition posed challenges to Woolf's modernist and feminist sensibilities. A well-read literary critic on the Romantics, the Victorians, and the immediate predecessors she called the Edwardians, Woolf sought to connect literature to life as a modern experience, and hence in different relation to nature. Reflecting a prominent modernist concern, Woolf also cultivated an interest in the workings of the mind, including operations of perception and memory. Thus her writing can be analyzed in psychological terms, but also in relation to ecofeminist thinking, particularly where the perceiver merges intellectually and spiritually with what she perceives.[4] As noted above, postcolonial feminist theory draws attention to gendered landscapes and masculine scenarios of conquest that will also concern us here.

Woolf could survey English pastoral tradition back to the Elizabethans though Vita Sackville-West and her ancestral house, Knole. Vita practiced pastoral writing, in the form of Georgics, in her own verses concerning the landscape of Kent. Knole and Woolf's love for Sackville-West, of course, inspired *Orlando*—a novel that deconstructs, even as it celebrates, old England.

As she became increasingly aware of feminist and pacifist standpoints, Woolf grew skeptical of "Englishness"—national identification with a place often used to promote patriarchal and national projects, including war. In *Writing Englishness, 1900–1950,* Judy Giles and Tim Middleton hail the "richness" of early twentieth-century "debates about the nature of England and English identity" (4). They note the anachronism of many rural representations, which "had either disappeared in the first wave of industrialization in the nineteenth century or [were] being changed beyond recognition through the introduction of electricity, the impact of the wireless, increased mecanisation of agriculture, and the expansion of public transport and car ownership" (73). While invoking nostalgia for "old England," Englishness can also support a nation's economic, military, or imperial pursuits (12). Williams finds rural identification particularly pronounced for those who have given up a cherished site to serve in industry, war, or empire. In studying Englishness, Giles and Middleton quote the passage from *Three Guineas* in which Woolf questions "how much of England" actually belongs to women and proclaims, "As a woman I want no country" (*3G* 129).

In "DissemiNation: Time, Narrative and the Margins of the Modern Nation," Homi Bhabha identifies military and imperial pretexts of Englishness: "the 'deep' nation crafted in chalk and limestone; the quilted downs, the moors menaced by the wind; the quiet cathedral towns; that corner of a for-eign field that is forever England." Babha's quotation from Rupert Brooke's "The Soldier" reminds us of the "Englishness" that sent young men of Woolf's circle abroad to their deaths in World War I.[5] Bhabha extends imperial En-glishness even to the weather, which vindicates English power over the im-perial "other": "the heat and dust of India; the dark emptiness of Africa; the tropical chaos that was deemed despotic, and ungovernable and therefore worthy of the civilizing mission" (319). We might ask how Woolf rewrote landscapes supplied by Anglo-Indian family members, or Leonard Woolf's sojourn in Ceylon (now Sri Lanka). Woolf could bring Englishness and pas-toral tradition into her depiction of characters as they perceive and record landscapes, or slip it into the discourse of her narrators, often to satirical ends.[6]

Marianne Torgovnick has suggested that "the visual arts helped [Woolf] shape her ideas about nature and facilitated her development as a writer" (*Visual Arts* 125). Writing on Walter Sickert, a colleague of Duncan Grant and friend of Roger Fry, Woolf observed that "painting and writing have much to tell each other: they have much in common. The novelist after all wants to make us see. Gardens, rivers, skies, clouds changing, the colour of a woman's dress, landscapes that bask beneath lovers, twisted woods that people walk in when they quarrel—novels are full of pictures like these" (*E* 6:43). Such landscapes resonate to human behavior (love or quarreling). Woolf finds Sickert playing literary biographer, novelist, and poet in turn. Though she called him a "realist," she was sensitive to the formalism of his compositions and to his powerful use of color, derived from the Impressionists. The effect of his painting is visceral to an observer who, seeing like an insect, is "all eye" and drinks in color: "Colours went spirally through my body lighting a flare as if a rocket fell through the night and lit up greens and browns, grass and trees, and there in the grass a white bird" (188–89).

Woolf was in a good position to study various generational debates in the arts and to gather material for her own art. Little Holland House, home of her great-aunt Sarah Prinsep, was a gathering place for artists, including the well-known Pre-Raphaelites Dante Gabriel Rosetti, Edward Burne-Jones, John Everett Millais, and Frederic Leighten, and the photographer Julia Cameron, Woolf's great-aunt.[7] Cameron composed legendary and mythical scenes. *The Rosebud Garden Girls* is one of her better-known compositions. Woolf's play *Freshwater* recalls artistic entertainments staged at Cameron's home. Despite its comical distance, *Freshwater* demonstrates affection for Woolf's artistic ancestors. G. F. Watts, who specialized in a moralistic, high-arts style, was an early mentor for Vanessa, though by 1905 she and Virginia deserted his paintings, preferring the more current Impressionist artist James McNeill Whistler.[8]

Vanessa Bell's eventual style favored Post-Impressionism and the fauvists. Though engaging abstract forms, she avoided the futurist emphasis on urban and mechanical subjects and retained strong natural components. Several of her paintings move from an interior to an exterior scene, a juxtaposition also selected frequently by Virginia, as in the first epigraph of this chapter. Building upon Diane Gillespie's groundbreaking insights into the importance of Vanessa to Woolf's aesthetic, Jane Goldman argues that Vanessa's uses of color and light are more significant influences than the more widely discussed theories of "significant form" and "pure form." Attributed, respectively, to Clive Bell and Roger Fry, these too contributed to Woolf's ideas of the abstraction and composition of selected forms (*Feminist Aesthetics* 116).

Anxieties of Authorship: Early Landscapes

Woolf's memoir, "A Sketch of the Past," places significant early memories in Cornwall. The earliest surviving diaries (1897) allow us to follow Woolf's struggles with landscapes, and bear traces of the severe breakdown she experienced after her mother's death. She records self-critically having repeated tantrums, at which time she seems to have assumed the persona of "Miss Jan." Less obvious symptoms may occur in expressions of distaste for a geographical setting, or in natural metaphors for squalor, destruction, and decay. She disliked Eastbourne, where she had to chaperone the courtship of Jack Hills and her half sister Stella Duckworth (*PA* 27). Woolf describes a "black and rather inferior sea" at Bognor on another enforced vacation in service to the couple (31).

Family sojourns near old country villages offered greater diversion. Woolf admired the "flat fields & windmills & sky domes" of the fenlands, particularly when hung with clouds to spur her imagination (*PA* 162). Such views were visible from Moat House, Warboys, where the family stayed in 1899—a location that also fostered the Stephen children's moth collecting. Woolf revisited the fens in 1906, staying with Vanessa at Blo Norton in Norfolk in a setting suggestive of Elvedon in *The Waves*. This half-timbered Elizabethan manor house, dating back to 1535 (as indicated on an archway [figure 23]),

FIGURE 23. Blo Norton gateway. (Photograph by the author)

FIGURE 24. Blo Norton house and garden. (Photograph by the author)

was surrounded on three sides by gardens, with a shallow moat beyond (figure 24). Woolf's account of the place to Violet Dickinson suggests both irreverence and physical freedom: "Nessa paints windmills in the afternoon, and I tramp the country for miles with a map, leap ditches, scale walls and desecrate churches." The countryside was more quaint than beautiful, "as we say of things that are long and attenuated and more grotesque than shapely" (*L* 1:234). The remark probably bears a mischievous suggestion of Dickinson's own physical form.

Destinations inland evoked the long span of history, decipherable in landscape. The year 1897 found the family in a large vicarage (now a posh hotel) in the village of Painswick. Set at the edge of the Cotswold Mountains, Painswick offers stone cottages accented by window boxes and finely crafted stone carvings (figure 25). In 1903 the Stephens chose the stylish neoclassical Northampton House, with a well-tended garden to one side and stables to the rear. The house faces Wilton, the grand estate granted to the Earls of Pembroke by Henry VIII, and is not far from Salisbury Cathedral and Stonehenge—all providing material for Virginia's journal. Woolf sampled the moors when she stayed in Giggleswick on the Yorkshire Dales in 1906—a region where heather and sheep cover the limestone hills, and the more rugged

FIGURE 25. Painswick window box. (Photograph by the author)

slopes are marked with chalk scars. She was an ambitious walker, visiting the sprawling limestone Lawton Manor, which remains in splendid isolation, guarded by a pair of stone lions. Woolf developed a sense of sedimented history in walks across the dales: "You find strange fortifications on the moors, fosses & ramparts, so smoothly built & carpeted that either nature was the architect or some primeval man" (*PA* 302).

The "splendid wild country" of Manorbier, a resort on the Welsh coast where she stayed with family in 1904 and on her own in 1908, bore some comparison to Cornwall. She enjoyed walking on the cliffs and residing "in the shadow of a great feudal castle" complete with drawbridge and lofty towers (*L* 1:130). Reaching toward political commentary, she finds the surrounding land "markedly worn & poverty stricken, as though it could not support such a monster." Arrested in the 1840s, Manorbier would never become a "watering place." Despite the weakness of its coast, Manorbier's winds make her "think of the earth given up to this power tonight!" (*PA* 381). The sea offered dynamic contrast to the land: "perpetual movement, and a border of mystery, solving the limits of fields, and silencing their prose" (*L* 1:356). Woolf tells Vanessa that she can sit on the beach and "invent images from the shapes of the waves" (363)—a promising practice for the future author of *The Waves*.

The Sussex Downs, which provided Woolf's final favored landscape, were also instrumental to her coming into writing. Clay soil of the weald runs between the North and South Downs, allowing bushes and trees to root. Along the coast, grassy pastures give over to white chalk cliffs called the Seven Sisters. At Lewes, the River Ouze breaks through the downs, creating a port that has been in use since Saxon times.[9] Leslie Stephen cites with approval the landscape writings of Gilbert White and offers his own appreciation of the Downs: "The Downs have a singular charm in the exquisite play of long, gracefully undulating lines which bound their gentle edges. If not a 'majestic range of mountains,' as judged by an Alpine standard, there is no want of true sublimity in their springing curves, especially when harmonized by the lights and shadows under cloud-masses driving before a broad southwesterly gale" ("Country Books" 193).[10] White's observations, the subject of Woolf's own 1939 essay "White's Selbourne," were both imaginative in their analogy to vegetation and speculative about their formation: "I never contemplate these mountains without thinking I perceive somewhat analogous to growth in their gentle swellings and smooth fungus-like protuberances, their fluted sides, and regular hollows and slopes. . . . Or was there ever a time when these immense masses of calcareous matter were thrown into fermentation by some adventitious moisture; were raised and leavened into such shapes by some plastic power; and so made to swell and heave their broad backs into the sky so much above the less animated clay of the wild below?" (White, *Natural History of Selborne* 158–59).

One of Woolf's earliest and most pleasurable experiences of the downs came on a bicycle expedition out of Brighton. After a cautious start, she experiences unusual physical release as she rushes through the landscape: "When we had scaled the hill, which we did comfortably on our feet, behold a beautiful smooth descent of two miles & a ½ lay before us! Georgie, T. & A. flew down this with their feet up, but N. & I were more prudent—it was most exciting and splendid."[11] Labeling another bicycle tour "the famous Arundel expedition," she indulges in the mock-heroic mode, while setting preferences. Angmering was "a quiet sleepy little place, a swan sitting on its nest—most peaceful after Brighton glare" (*PA* 76). Englishness and serenity both reside here.

At seventeen, writing from the fenlands, Woolf goes more for effect in her diary, which treats sunsets and dramatic cloud formations, and is backed by research into *Kelly's Directory of Bedfordshire, Huntingdonshire, and*

Northamptonshire. This interface with travel guides, including their remarks on landscape, would persist through her final novel, *Between the Acts.* She continues to express caution about becoming a nature writer, but she also develops a sense of blending a city with a country consciousness. Woolf may already be imagining a yearly rhythm that allows both a city and a country existence, and a way to join books with nature:

> "I love the country best in books." I can never bring myself to believe in the felicity & simplicity of a country life. These speculations though belong to a cold brained critic in London. I am, at the present moment (the emotion is fleeting I know, so I must chronicle it) in love with a country life; I think that a year or two of such gardens & green fields would infallibly sweeten one & soothe one & simplify one into the kind of Gilbert White old gentleman or Miss Matty old lady that only grew till now for me inside the covers of books. I shd. be writing notes upon the weather, & I shd. turn to my diaries of past years to compare their records. (*PA* 137)

Woolf is beginning to recognize variation in her own attitudes, lending greater fluidity to her responses to landscape. Gilbert White and Miss Matty (an elderly spinster in Elizabeth Gaskell's *Cranford,* a novel about a northern village) were indeed content with small village life in the somewhat distant past. White's meticulous journals record the coming and going of seasons, the weather, botanizing, gardening, and especially observations of migratory birds.[12]

Woolf's "Terrible Tragedy in a Duckpond," recorded in a journal kept at Warboys, parodies the overdramatization of one strain of nature writing, with a touch of the gothic thrown in. Here a duck pond becomes an angry sea, and the doomed follow a fatal lunar path: "The angry waters of the duck pond rose in their wrath to swallow their prey—& the green caverns of the depths opened—& closed—The cold moonlight silvered the path to death" (*PA* 151).[13] Writing for her cousin, who shared in some actual mishap with a punt, Woolf creates a parody along the lines of Jane Austen's juvenilia, such as "Love and Freindship" [sic]. We have already experienced Woolf's inclination toward family comedy in her account of a family "bugging" expedition in chapter 2. In the fenlands that year, Woolf further imagines that "wondrous cloud bubbles" could be a form of amusement for "God babies" (*PA* 137), mythical figures that prefigure early drafts of *The Waves.*

In this same Warboys diary, Woolf shows an attraction to the picturesque elements of the harvest:

> We beheld the harvesters this afternoon as we rode back from Ramsey. On one side of the road was a corn-cutting machine sweeping down the standing corn; & on the other a field where corn lay all cut; & here & there women & boys were all tramping thro it heaping the corn into stooks. Even a little child not more than 4 years old was harvesting with its mother. It wore a bright scarlet frock, & trotted behind with a small armful of gleanings. One of the women harvesters was I should think almost 70 with white scanty locks, & a wrinkled sun burnt wind scourged face. There is some picturesque element in this country—harvesters, windmills, golden cornfields. Everything flat with blue haze in the distance, & a vast dome of sky all around. (139–40)

Woof prefaces this description with a sample of Vanessa's housekeeping trials, made worse when locals fail to provide dairy products and domestic labor while helping with the harvest. Virginia dwells instead on dangerous labor conditions—the perils of technology that only recently had made farming possible. "Should it stop work one day the water would well up over the fields & drown the Fen men" (156). Woolf displays distrust of nature altered and mechanized, and here comes as close as she ever would to watery tragedies depicted by Hardy. In her essay "The Novels of Thomas Hardy," Woolf would describe the farms in the down lands as a place where "Nature is prolific, splendid, and lustful; not yet malignant and still the Great Mother of Labouring men" (*E* 5:565).

In her finale to the Warboys journal, Woolf indulges in an aspect of nature writing so hackneyed that she had earlier sought to avoid it—the treatment of seasons. She describes, in subtle stages, changes in the field, the weather, and the hedges, quoting Tennyson's "Tithonus" on the woods' decay. Toward the end, the description turns to human involvement in the land; it is gendered and peopled with children, and takes on a mood of melancholy, offering a suitable text for comparison and contrast with Keats's "To Autumn":

> For me the definite touch that has spelt autumn is the subtle difference in the air. It brings with it odours of burning wood & weeds; & delicious moisture from the shaven earth; it is cleaner & more virile; it is autumn in its youth, before decayed woods & weeping vapours have

come to end its substance. We saw . . . weed burning on the hill. Look at the picture of Sir John Millais of children burning leaves & my theories will be revealed. I cannot attempt to explain in words the charm & melancholy, the colour & the interest, of the picture. (*PA* 161–62)

Notable here is her reference to landscape painting as a resource for her own description (figure 26).[14] Millais's girls burning leaves may have come to mind as Woolf composed a bonfire scene for *The Years*. Autumn in that work furnishes, not a "virile" phase, but a bold and spirited birthday celebration for mother and daughters. Little Magdalena "tossed a whole armful of dead leaves. She jerked them as high as she could, and the fire blazed up. A great fan of red flame flung out" (111). While *The Years* is one of Woolf's most urban novels, nature presides in its chapter openings, which are comparable to the nature-saturated middle section of *To the Lighthouse* and the interludes of *The Waves*.

Woolf's preference of place gradually moved to the margins of her island, where she favored hills with a prospect of the sea.[15] By 1903 she likened the downs to "to the long curved waves of the sea" noting that "man . . . has done nothing to change the shape of these breakers. . . . The villages have all sunk into the hollows between the waves; & the result is a peculiar smoothness & bareness of outline. This is the bare bone of the earth" (*PA* 192).[16] She gets down to a solid, skeletal framework, an essential shape and substance, muting human presence, while selecting an anatomical metaphor. By the time Woolf visits the cathedral town of Wells in 1908, she is assigning politics to landscape. The country around Wells "has to my mind one fatal fault—no sea. . . . When you see nothing but land, stationary on all sides, you are conscious of being trapped, on a flat board." She admits to inland beauties, "when the sun gleamed, great bones of green & brown earth showed in the middle of this scene, which was coloured like some drawing in brown ink. The kingdoms of the world lay before me, a rich domain, teeming in the folds with apples, & meadows, & little steeples."[17] Then comes a contrast: "In Cornwall, I never think of the kingdom, or the population—this view, stands for many I suppose, as a symbol of their mother England" (379). Already Woolf seems to be sensing that both mother and nation are figured differently for her, with images taken from nature working powerfully in that construction, and any liberation to follow. When, at the end of her life, Woolf returns to the inland English village for the setting of *Between the Acts*, she is again confronting

FIGURE 26. *Autumn Leaves,* 1856 (oil on canvas), by Sir John Everett Millais (1829–96). (Manchester Art Gallery, UK/The Bridgeman Art Library)

ideas of Englishness, by then in the light of emerging fascism.[18] Woolf's earliest diaries, attended to closely here, have the strongest landscape component of any of her writing, but in carefully parceled amounts, she would reuse her discoveries about the nature of landscape for the rest of her writing life.

The Art of Landscape

As suggested by her early tribute to Pre-Raphaelite John Everett Millais, art could provide a model for setting a mood or selecting the color of a landscape. Woolf may have been aware of Millais's own description of his intentions in his autumnal painting: "I intended the picture to awaken by its solemnity the deepest religious reflection. I chose the subject of burning leaves as most calculated to produce this feeling. . . . These kind of pictures are really more difficult to paint than any other, as they are not to be achieved by faithful attention to Nature, such effects are so transient and occur so rarely, that the rendering becomes a matter of feeling and recollection."[19] While Woolf can hardly be expected to share the religious symbolism of Millais, his sense of the limitations of nature, as the sole source of the desired image, seems in tune with her early strivings with landscape. Artists' choices let Woolf think about representing emotions, fleeting qualities of light, or depiction of basic forms, and how to extract and position them. Artists provided an example of the willful manipulation of a natural scene, from the act of framing a view to its material completion in brush strokes with oils.

Depending on whom you listen to, nature was supremely important or totally outmoded in modernist-period art. There can be no doubt of nature's importance in previous phases of English culture. The Romantics operated upon Edmund Burke's concept of the sublime, calling for the strongest possible expression of the emotions. Such emotions were frequently summoned by exalted experiences of natural landscapes. The Victorian Leslie Stephen still seeks the sublime from his Alps. A guide to one of the finest repositories of the Romantics, the Tate Museum, credits J. M. W. Turner for "his stress on the extremes of nature, storm or calm" (Wilson 73). Pre-Raphaelites combined detailed natural realism with symbolic, and frequently religious or moral meaning, as in Millais. A brochure for the exhibition "Art Nouveau, 1890–1914," at the Victoria and Albert Museum (2000), pronounced that "the natural world was the single most important source" for that movement; "Nature" anchored a section of the exhibition. Given the fact that the aesthetic movement flourished in urban centers, we see evidence of nature's penetration of modernity—even in entries to the Paris Metro, with their leaf and flower motifs. While they preserved some of the color harmonies characteristic of the Romantics, the Post-Impressionists Vincent Van Gogh, Paul Gauguin, and Paul Cézanne bought new elements to landscape, including experimental brushwork and a segmented handling of space.

Post-Impressionism entered England via the Bloomsbury figures Roger Fry, Clive Bell, and Desmond MacCarthy, whose exhibition "Manet and the Post-Impressionists" opened at the Grafton Galleries on November 8, 1910. This was one of the cultural watersheds marked by Woolf's essay "Mr. Bennett and Mrs. Brown," when "on or about December 1910, human character changed" (*E* 3:421). The Second Post-Impressionist Exhibition, organized in part by Leonard Woolf (1912), provided a venue for the British practitioners, including Duncan Grant, Vanessa Bell, Wyndham Lewis, and Frederick Etchells. Bell's formalist doctrine of significant form, published in *Art* (1914), with its concentration of line, color, motion, form, and combination of form as a means of summoning aesthetic emotion, would seem to bear little relation to nature. However, artists involved in Fry's Omega Workshop (1913–19) used natural motifs and landscapes, spontaneously rendered, in many of their designs for murals, screens, furniture, and textiles. Grant, for example, created both a table and a screen on a lily-pond motif. Equally prevalent were abstract and geometrical shapes, and designs involving the human body. Still, many of these were abstractions from natural materials. We find a flower or leaf grounding Vanessa Bell's 1914 design for an Omega rug (Shone, plate 92, 171). At Omega, and later in their own, signed art, Bell and Grant crafted still lifes involving fruits and flowers, and landscapes set in Sussex or the French countryside near Cassis.

Before turning to art as a career, Fry took his Cambridge degree in natural sciences. Richard Shone suggests that "the scientific rationalism that characterizes much of Fry's thought obviously found an alternative release in ... wilder aspects of nature, even when he was intent on taming them" (13). On the other hand, Fry wrote to his father in 1893 that he found his recent Suffolk landscapes "too detailed and literal and that for the final effect I must get away from Nature" (qtd. in Shone 57). *South Downs,* a bold landscape painted at Woolf's Asham House in 1914, is dominated by a rough and abstract, angular rendering of leaves at the top, and looks over to the valley of the Ouse, with Iford Hill as a long curve on the horizon. Shone calls it "one of his most vigorous assaults on the English countryside" (164). As he noted in the essay "Art and Life," by 1917 Fry found that impressionists such as Cézanne, Gauguin, and Van Gogh had freed artists from the need for skill in representation, requiring little more than unity in a work; this brought art closer to the "barbaric and primitive" (*Vision and Design* 7–8). This change in criteria could not easily be adopted by the "cultured public," many of whom responded with hostility to the supposed anarchy of the Post-Impressionist exhibition. Cutting through class and gender snobbery, Fry admitted in "Retrospect," a 1920 essay, that "one's maid . . . might by a haphazard gift . . . surpass one" in apprehending the new art (*Vision and Design* 192–93). Fry did not concur with Clive Bell's declaration that "representation of nature was entirely irrelevant to" achieving "significant form." "What I think has resulted from Mr. Clive Bell's book, and the discussions which it has aroused . . . is that the artist is free to choose any degree of representational accuracy which suits the expression of his feeling. That no single fact, or set of facts, about nature can be held to be obligatory for artistic form" (195).[20]

The most deliberate challenge to Bloomsbury artists and their uses of natural forms came from Wyndham Lewis following his defection from the Omega Workshop—an episode in his artistic politics introduced in chapter 1. His brief but influential journal, *Blast* (1914–15), relegated nature to an inferior, feminine position in the hierarchy of creativity and control—a tradition reaching back to Aristotle. Lewis's typical landscape was an urban, technologically-inspired grid-work (see Corbett 106). This view of masculinity and landscape failed to survive World War I. During the years 1920–50, Ian Jeffrey records "a history of constant negotiation between pastoral and modernizing tendencies, with the pastoral usually in the ascendant" (7). This formula suited Bloomsbury.

The influence of Post-Impressionists such as Cézanne on the representation of landscapes comes through clearly in *The Voyage Out*. Take, for example, the view from the ship *Euphrosyne* as it pulls into port.

> The little boat was now approaching a white crescent of sand. Behind this was a deep green valley, with distinct hills on either side. On the slope of the right-hand hill white houses with brown roofs were settled, like nesting sea-birds, and at intervals cypresses striped the hill with black bars. Mountains whose sides were flushed with red, but whose crowns were bald, rose as a pinnacle, half-concealing another pinnacle

behind it. The hour being still early, the whole view was exquisitely light and airy; the blues and greens of sky and tree were intense but not sultry. (88)

Various characters, and especially men, attempt to capture landscape in the course of this novel. Mr. Dalloway gives lessons on how to judge a view—opining that variety is essential. Mr. Fleming chooses the "views" his wife is to paint. Terence Hewet sees the mountains in terms of a watercolor. Helen Ambrose represents a native, exotic scene in needlework.

In writing her earliest memories in "A Sketch of the Past," Woolf reached immediately for the example of the painter: "If I were a painter I should paint these first impressions in pale yellow, silver, and green," though she quickly adds a dimension of sound that goes beyond painting. She begins with "a picture of curved petals; of shells; of things that were semi-transparent; I should make curved shapes, showing the light through, but not giving a clear outline. Everything would be large and dim; and what was seen would at the same time be heard; sounds would come through this petal or leaf—sounds indistinguishable from sights." The blurred abstract is landscape as perceived by an infant still attuned to sounds as in the womb, able to decipher shapes dimly. The views grow more "robust" as, looking over the gardens en route to the beach, the child is enraptured by the sensual murmur bees in the apple trees, by "red and gold" apples and "pink flowers; and grey and silver leaves" (MB 66).

From this same stock of landscape images comes much of *To the Lighthouse*. None of Woolf's works offers greater awareness of landscape, its perception and artistic rendition, than this novel. We learn that since the generation of Mrs. Ramsay's grandmother, painters have come to capture the seascape. Mrs. Ramsay and Lily Briscoe both comment on Mr. Pauncefort's style. Mrs. Ramsay thinks of "green and grey with lemon-coloured sailing boats, and pink women on the beach" (17).[21] Lily defies what Pauncefort has made "fashionable . . . everything pale, elegant, semitransparent" and instead is "faithful" to the bright violet of the jacmanna plant and the "staring white" of the wall (22). Neither woman is a realist, however; both place a premium on shape and color. Mrs. Ramsay imagines a wedge of darkness as she looks toward the lighthouse and identifies with its long third stoke. Lily lightly traces a grid on the surface of the canvas as she starts painting, seeking the shape and balance of her "vision," as well as its colors.

Lily's painting seems at first to be a representation of mother and child, echoing perhaps an undefined Michelangelo print in the background. The Madonna as a "subject of universal veneration" seems to be what Mr. Bankes expects in viewing the painting. He must adjust to the fact that Mrs. Ramsay and James assume a "triangular purple shape," finding this done "without irreverence" (55–56). Lily incorporates elements of landscape gardening, including tree, hedge, wall, and plants. But nature, like the revered, essentialist subject of mother and child, is controlled by abstraction. Lily suggests to Bankes that "the question [is] one of the relations of masses, of lights and shadows" (56)—an explanation that engages his scientific mind.

Famously, Lily does this painting twice. Whereas for the first picture Mrs. Ramsay is requested not to change even the position of her head, for the second, she is present only mystically for a brief, inspirational period. For both paintings, Lily composes more than what appears on her canvas. She is aware of nearby landscapes and perceives them as well in painterly terms. While doing the first painting, Lily thinks of the break in the hedge, guarded by red hot pokers, visited every evening by the Ramsays. Though originating with Lily, the description that follows moves closer to the emotions of Mrs. Ramsay, feelings that Mr. Ramsay may share. The prospect of the sea from the land liberates thought:

> It was as if the water floated off and set sailing thoughts which had grown stagnant on dry land, and gave to their bodies even some sort of physical relief. First the pulse of colour flooded the bay with blue, and the heart expanded with it and the body swam, only the next instant to be checked and chilled by the prickly blackness on the ruffled waves. Then, up behind the great black rock, almost every evening spurted irregularly, so one had to watch for it and it was a delight when it came, a fountain of white water; and then, while one waited for that, one watched, on the pale semicircular beach, wave after wave shedding attain and attain smoothly, a film of mother of pearl. (23–24)

Interestingly, the phallic rock offering a "fountain white water" yields to restful "mother of pearl" on the beach.

While painting for the second time, Lily is aware of the constantly changing seascape through which Mr. Ramsay, James, and Cam travel to the lighthouse. She looks to it to satisfy "some instinctive need of distance and blue." Her view synthesizes land and sea, "making hillocks of the blue bars of the

waves, and stony fields of the purpler spaces." She finds "something incongru-
ous . . . a brown spot in the middle of the bay," which she recognizes as "Mr.
Ramsay's boat" (185). Her imagination continues to work, "and as happens
sometimes when the weather is very fine, the cliffs looked as if they were conscious of the ships, and the ships looked as if they were conscious of the cliffs,
as if they signaled to each other some message to each other" (185). Land and
sea, nature and manmade vessel, communicate, thereby composing themselves. This may even suggest artistic method. Eventually the Ramsay crew
is "swallowed up" in the sea—"they had become part of the nature of things"
(191).

Lily is distressed over her own efforts of composition. She feels she must
balance this seascape with the scene of her painting: "For whatever reason
she could not achieve that razor edge of balance between two opposite forces;
Mr. Ramsay and the picture; which was necessary." She sees "the human ap-
paratus for painting or for feeling" as "a miserable machine" (196), thus entertaining a natural/technological divide. The scene of the picture also alters, as
someone occupies a chair and throws "an odd-shaped triangular shadow over
the step" (204), restoring briefly a presence of Mrs. Ramsay. Lily must share
this, perhaps with Mr. Ramsay, and turns again to the seascape. This suggests
that relations of persons underlie her work. At this point Lily realizes that Mr.
Ramsay must have reached the lighthouse; the lighthouse "is melted away
into a blue haze" (210). The steps are empty. We see very little of Lily's final
painting: "greens and blues" perhaps represent the two juxtaposed scenes.
Balance remains important to Lily's "vision," as she finishes with "a line there,
in the center" (211).[22] Woolf's own composition places Lily's picture, and her
effort at balancing memories, and persons, and shapes, within a larger picture, where Mr. Ramsay, James, and Cam have perspectives of their own.

Masculine Command of Landscape

Like the artists we have just been considering, the explorer, the agent of empire, and even the recreational traveler takes control of landscape, betraying
a politics of vision frequently inflected by gender. In studying Victorian male
discourses in her landmark study, *Imperial Eyes*, Mary Louise Pratt identifies
the masculine, imperial gaze with a vista seen from a mountaintop. This commanding view allowed explorers and military men to feel dominion over all
they surveyed. Sara Mills reminds us that women were complicit in imperial

enterprises and encourages us to consider their controlling views. Modernists resisted much that was Victorian, aware that the political ground had
shifted beneath them. The Boer War and World War I shattered assumptions
about imperial order. The trenches and "no man's land" denied young men of
Woolf's generation access to commanding heights. Recreational travel was
one of the commodities of modernity enjoyed by women as well as men.
Their more global access to landscapes bore its own politics of class privilege
and "Englishness," used as a standard of comfort or contrast, and still teth-
ered to imperialist attitudes.[23] Women traveled on different terms from men,
and it is useful to compare the sorts of control (or lack of it) they exerted on
their experiences of landscape.

Woolf's travel abroad began only after the death of her father, who had
his own vision of landscape. Leslie Stephen would likely have provided
his daughter's first model of masculine command of landscape. Much like
Carlyle, working in the attic of his famous house on Cheyne Row while the
women of the house struggled with primitive plumbing in the basement,[24]
Leslie claimed the top of the house at Hyde Park Gate for his study. The Alpine walking sticks stored there served as a reminder that he had explored
mountain heights. Noel Annan computes at least twenty-five Alpine visits
over Stephen's lifetime, many involving first ascents or first-time routes up
peaks.[25] Stephen was an early member and president of the Alpine Club
(1865) and editor of its *Alpine Journal* (1868–72). Comprised predominantly
of members of the upper-middle class and a few aristocrats, members of the
Alpine Club considered themselves "a caste apart, a Spartan phalanx, tough
with muscular virtue, spare with speech, seeking the chill clarity of the mountains just because, as Leslie Stephen . . . put it, 'there we can breathe air that
has not passed through a million pairs of lungs.'" They were in effect "a *natural* aristocracy" (Schama 502). The Alpine clubmen placed a premium upon
what could be described as a masculine value—the physical experience of
the climb. "Only traversing the rock face, inching his way up ice steps, en-
abled the climber . . . to see the mountain as it truly was" (Schama 504). The
ideal is complicit with what would be termed "deep ecology," which idealized becoming a part of the mountain in the mid-twentieth century. Muscular ascent distinguished them from mystical observers such as John Ruskin.
As if to demonstrate the difference, Ruskin in *Sesame and Lilies* unleashes
a tirade against the climbers and tourists for despising "all the deep and sacred sensations of natural scenery" (qtd. in Schama 506). Likewise, Annan

distinguishes between Stephen's vigorous, competitive ascent of the Alps and the sedentary, valley-based sketches of Ruskin. Woolf expressed considerable respect for Ruskin in "Ruskin Looks Back on Life," a review of *Praeterita:* "He is opulent in his eloquence, and at the same time meticulous in his accuracy. He revels in the description of changing clouds and falling waters, and yet fastens his eye to the petals of a daisy with the minute tenacity of a microscope. He combined—or at least they fought in him—the austerity of the puritan, and the sensuous susceptibility of the artist (*E* 4:504).[26]

Among Septimus Smith's collection of disturbing papers in *Mrs. Dalloway* is a drawing of "zigzagging precipices with mountaineers ascending roped together, exactly like knives and forks" (*MD* 144). The idea for this drawing could have come from Edward Whymper's lithograph *The Accident on the Matterhorn,* depicting a fatal fall of members of the Alpine Club, with arms and legs sprawled, but still roped firmly together.[27] This may be a satirical response to his physicians' demand that Septimus measure up to the model of English masculinity.

Though there is much that would assign Leslie Stephen to a muscular, masculine category of mountaineer, this deserves some qualification. Though credited with being the first to climb the Schreckhorn, he credits his guides and evades at least some portion of the masculine heroic tradition: "I utterly repudiate the doctrine that Alpine travelers are or ought to be the heroes of Alpine adventures. The true way at least to describe all Alpine ascents is that Michael or Anderess or Lauener succceded in performing a feat requiring skill, strength, and courage, the difficulty of which was much increased by the difficulty of taking his knapsack and his employer" ("Ascent of the Schreckhorn," *Playground* 13–14; figure 27). Stephen collected his Alpine writing in *Playgrounds of Europe*—a title that detracts from accomplishments and admits to privilege. In collecting a set of Stephen's essays in *Men, Books and Mountains,* S. O. A. Ullmann found the mountaineering essays his "most consistently entertaining," their attributes including a capacity for the ironic and the whimsical, which we might associate with Woolf's satires of human nature (9). Though he asserts aesthetic control in his essay "Round Mont Blanc," Stephen seeks the best view of Mont Blanc, and not a dominating perspective from the top (201). "Sunset on Mont Blanc" does identify masculinity with the peak, where only bold climbers linger at sunset. The mountain is a "he" and a "Monarch." There is also a test of wills, given that the mountain "is a part of the great machinery in which my physical frame is

FIGURE 27. Leslie Stephen with his Alpine guide. (Leslie Stephen Photo Album, Mortimer Rare Book Room, Smith College)

inextricably involved, and not the less interesting because a part which I am unable to subdue to my purposes" (180). While Stephen may not be in a position to command, he respects the mountain's ability to do so. There is also a holistic aspect to the experience: "Does not science teach us more and more emphatically that nothing which is natural can be alien to us who are part of Nature? Where does Mont Blanc end, where do I begin?" (180).

Stephen visited the Alps with both of his wives. Surviving photos depict him with Minny as a bride posed in a landscape of firs and distant mountains. He and a frail Julia are depicted in a churchyard scene where tombstones (some recording Alpine mishaps) claim the center ground (figure 28). For a combination of possible reasons—his increasing age, the expense, or the belief that tourism was destroying the experience—Stephen did not share the Alpine setting with his younger children. They could, however, read his accounts and peruse his photo album. The Alps, no doubt, entered their imaginary. Woolf took up her father's walking on her own terrain and schedule. She compares a rugged part of her beloved Sussex Downs with his prized Alps. The Ramsays' young Swiss nursemaid in To the Lighthouse thinks of her native mountains, even as she grieves that her father is dying there—a significant detail since the novel was one in which Woolf put her father's ghost to rest.

In her final months, Woolf drafted a story, "The Symbol," set in an Alpine village on the day of a fatal climbing accident. The event is witnessed by a lady writing to her sister in Birmingham. She sits on a balcony overlooking the symbolic mountain, her view of the details of landscape assisted by binoculars. Her representation of a crater high on the mountain, as exposed in various lights, might reflect Woolf's Post-Impressionist tendencies and her fascination with hollows. She is troubled by other problems that Woolf struggled with as an aspiring modernist writer, such as falling into cliché. The lady resists a trite, symbolic aspiration to the heights and typical tourists' remarks about the persistent sight of the mountain in various weathers. She is disappointed in her own life, harboring a desire to have been more of an explorer. She also focuses on death. She thinks about the impossibility of surviving at that height, of fallen climbers' graves in the churchyard, and of previous fatal accidents. She regrets her reactions to her mother's slow death by cancer, echoing the Stephen children's restiveness over the protracted death of Leslie Stephen. Her pondering ends in an ellipsis. The climbers fall from her view, and "the pen fell from her hand, and the drop of ink straggled in a zig zag line

FIGURE 28. Leslie and Julia Stephen in Grindelwald
churchyard. (Leslie Stephen Photo Album, Mortimer Rare
Book Room, Smith College)

down the page" (*CSF* 290). It is a figure of fragmentation that mimics the
climbers' ropes on the jagged mountain and that suits modernism and the
breakup of Europe at the time of Woolf's writing, 1941.[28]

In later life Leslie Stephen took day hikes through the English countryside with an all-male group, the "Sunday Tramps," among them Fred Maitland, later his biographer. They were hardly "tramps," but the choice of name
suggests a Romantic attraction to the vagabond, shared by the poet Edward
Thomas. As a "tramp," Stephen was briefly devoid of responsibility, free to

roam, and did so even in periods of family duress. He could cast off class pretensions, making no actual concession to the inequities involved.[29] Stephen's closest representative in Woolf's fiction, Mr. Ramsay in *To the Lighthouse*, plays the explorer along similar lines. He reminisces about his endurance, walking all day with only a biscuit in his pocket in "the country he liked best, over there; those sandhills dwindling away into darkness. One could walk all day without meeting a soul . . . there were little sandy beaches where no one had been since the beginning of time. The seals sat up and looked at you" (71–72). He is disappointed with his progress along a stereotypically male, linear trajectory ranging from A to Z in his profession of philosophy. Ramsay clings to a heroic image of the polar explorer who "now that the snow has begun to fall and the mountain top is covered in mist, knows that he must lay himself down and die before morning comes. . . . Yet he would not die lying down; he would find some crag of rock, and there, his eyes fixed on the storm, trying to the end to pierce the darkness, he would die standing" (38). In another fantasy landscape, he takes as his fate "to come out thus on a spit of land which the sea is slowly eating away, and there to stand, like a desolate sea-bird, alone . . . facing the dark of human ignorance" (47). He has the remote hope that his offspring will somehow "staunch the flood." Thus, he approves James's taking over the helm of the sailboat in the final scene of the novel. Similarly, his lecture to the young men at Cardiff will assert the imperialist values of preparing his own to fight against the alien hordes. Though his fantasy landscapes have polar obscurities, there is rational clarity to Ramsay's late apprehension of a crystal-clear lighthouse. He completes the journey and springs "lightly, like a young man . . . on to the rock" (210). Though he fulfills his wife's idea of taking things to the people at the lighthouse, and brings James to his desired destination, Ramsay only manages these with considerable bullying. Nancy, probably the most rebellious of the daughters as portrayed in the first segment of the novel, must prepare the parcels, and they are "badly packed" (209). After a decade's delay, Cam and James are unenthusiastic about the voyage. This next generation will travel differently. James will entertain his mother's hazy lighthouse, as well as his father's crisply defined one, and Cam will follow a layered rather than a linear habit of thought, which we will chart further in chapter 6.

Mounting the heights, even of a single rock, does indeed figure in Woolf's landscape of heroic masculinity. We first meet the protagonist of *Jacob's Room* as a toddler, scaling a large rock: "Rough with crinkled limpet shells and sparsely strewn with locks of dry seaweed, a small boy has to stretch his legs far apart, and indeed to feel rather heroic before he gets to the top" (9). Jacob's success as an explorer is greatly qualified as he proceeds, however. Jacob's confidence at scaling the rock lapses when he comes across lovers, realizes that he is lost, and suddenly finds himself in need of his nanny. He rallies again over the discovery of a sheep's jawbone, but this may only be a harbinger of his own death, hinting at the generation that would perish in World War I. His captured crab is left to struggle through a stormy night in the child's bucket, most likely to die. Septimus Smith, who does return (though shell shocked) from war in *Mrs. Dalloway,* takes no delight in heights. He feels as if he is "exposed on this bleak eminence" when he is merely resting on Mrs. Filmer's sitting-room sofa (*MD* 142). Perhaps his greatest act of courage is to leap to his death from the heights of the boardinghouse window.

Imperial and "Other" Landscapes

Virginia Woolf's travels abroad, like the move of her generation to Blooms-bury after Leslie Stephen's death, was a move toward modernity, though a limited one. Woolf visited many of the classical sites to which she would later send young Jacob and Bernard in *The Waves.* Unlike these young men, Woolf rarely traveled alone. As her siblings and intimate friends accompanied Woolf, various arrangements of women together, male role-play, and couples add complexity to the experience and the vision available to her.[30] Woolf would draw from a steamer cruise, a donkey ride up a mountain, an encounter with shepherds, and a view down at Constantinople for numerous novels. Though she encountered the British traveler abroad, with the late exception of Ireland, Woolf never voyaged out into the geography of the waning British Empire. Britain was moving increasingly into the business of commercial influence, rather than outright colonial control. In 1908 the first oil well was drilled in Iran by the Anglo-Iranian Oil Company—an antecedent of BP, the company now infamous for the disastrous spill from its deep-water well in the Gulf of Mexico. Harold Nicholson's experience in the diplomatic service in Teheran gave Woolf insight into this newer form of British influence abroad. Vita Sackville-West offered vivid descriptions of her journeys to and from Teheran, in letters written at the height of Woolf's affection for her—views preserved in *A Passenger to Teheran* (1926).

Woolf's travel writing varies in its intensity. As with her early landscape writing, she displays distrust in the genre and uneasiness with whatever Bae-deker she is carrying. The dangers of descriptive writing strike her in 1919 during a visit to Florence: "Walking on San Miniato the other evening, it occurred to me the thing was running into classic prose before my eyes. I positively saw the long smooth sentence running like a ribbon along the road—casting graceful loops round the beggar woman & the dusky child—& curving freely over the bare slopes of the hills" (*PA* 396–97). Must she get back to London to trust herself? Is she gracefully looping round the potentially racist issues of the "dusky child"? By far her best diary record is of the family's 1906 trip to Greece and Turkey. This was her last travel with Thoby, who succumbed to typhoid on his return. She records the view from the train approaching Olympia: "Now it was evening, & the bloom on was the hills shone purple, & the sea turned its innermost heart to the light; it was a heart of the deepest blue. On the other side of us was a screen of hills, sudden & steep & incessant, as though the earth had nothing better to do than throw up impatient little mounds. The look of the place thus is fiery & somewhat fragile, for the lines are all very spare & emphatic. No fat pastures & woods cushion the surface: but on the plain the earth was thick with dwarf vines, stooping with pyramids of fruit" (318). There is an implied comparison to softer English landscapes, but also the acknowledgment that this landscape offers an abundant vinery. In Constantinople, Woolf recorded "the verdict of a three day old tourist" that would serve her writing for years: "In the morning a mist lies like a veil that muffles treasures across all the houses & all the mosques; then as the sun rises, you catch hints of the heaped mass within; then a pinnacle of gold pierces the soft mesh, & you see shapes of precious stuff lumped together. And slowly the mist withdraws, & and all the wealth of gleaming houses & rounded mosques lies clear on the solid earth, & the broad waters run bright as daylight through their midst. . . . Nature & art & the air of Heaven are all equably mixed" (351). It is intriguing to follow gender play in this description, written among female companions. It offers a view from above, but not one of masculine discovery or conquest. The observer enjoys the mystery of the mist, described in orientalist, gendered discourse as a veil. This garment obscures treasures that might be bodily ones, their revelation an erotic enjoyment. There is a masculine piercing of the veil by "a pinnacle of gold," and a later revelation of "rounded mosques," as if to offer both male and female attributes for bisexual delight. Woolf presents a possibility of economic interest in wealth and "precious stuff" that motivated imperial conquest. She ends on a balanced aesthetic composition: solid earth balanced against the earlier mist, and an equal mix of elements from nature, art, and perhaps heaven.

Woolf's distrust of the scenes got up by travelers is obvious in *Jacob's Room,* where Jacob composes a description of Italy for an essay: "It is not a country in which one walks after tea. For one thing there is no grass. A whole hillside will be ruled with olive trees. Already in April the earth is clotted into dry dust between them. And there are neither stiles nor footpaths, nor lanes chequered with the shadows of leaves, nor eighteenth-century inns with bow-windows, where one eats ham and eggs. Oh no, Italy is all fierceness, bareness, exposure, and black priests shuffling along the roads" (*JR* 135). This description fails to impress even Jacob's loving friend, Bonamy. The colonial landscape of heat and dust dominates Jacob's view of Italy and, in his longing for tea and stiles, Jacob offers all the symptoms of "Englishness."

The Voyage Out takes us into a colony of British tourists, placed somewhere on the east coast of South America. Like Conrad, writing for a British audience, Woolf avoids a British colonial setting, though she invites reflections on imperialism and offers characters whose personal histories intertwine with empire. Mr. Pepper, whom we have seen in chapter 2 as a figure of satire for women in the novel, offers a rapid imperial history as they prepare to land. We learn that the fictional place of Santa Marina was briefly an English colony, where "all seemed to favor the expansion of the British Empire." Lacking support, the British were displaced by "Indians with subtle poisons, naked bodies, and painted idols," as well as "vengeful Spaniards and rapacious Portuguese" (*VO* 89). There are sufficient ironic clues here for us to suspect further satire on Woolf's part. The young men of the novel, Terence Hewet and St. John Hirst, are hardly of the conquering sort—Terence is overweight and aspires to writing a novel on silence; St. John seems barely capable of stirring from his books. They do, however, set up an expedition to the top of a nearby mountain. The tourist who glories most in getting to the top is Evelyn Mergatroyd, who might have been "leading royalist troops into action" (128). She would have liked to be "Garibaldi's bride," or one of a band of patriots, shooting from on high (130). Though a good measure of imperial masculine ambition enters into this fantasy, so does gender confusion. Terence turns around to look at the group he has brought with him, rather than the distant vista. The age of conquest is over, though there are still fascinating things to be learned from characters' reactions to present prospects.

The vast landscape of South America repeatedly leaves Rachel Vinrace in distress. On this same expedition, walking with Terence, "It became painful to look any longer, the great size of the view seeming to enlarge her eyes beyond their natural limit." She shifts her attention "to scrutinize this inch of the soil of South America so minutely that she noticed every grain of earth and made it into a world where she was endowed with the supreme power" (141). Some days later, she and Terence are again overwhelmed: "The vast expanse of land gave them a sensation which is given by no view, however extended in England . . . infinite sun-dried earth, earth pointed in pinnacles, heaped in vast barriers, earth widening and spreading away and away . . . partitioned into different lands, where famous cities were founded, and the races of men changed from dark savages to white civilized men, and back to dark savages again. Perhaps their English blood made this prospect uncomfortably impersonal and hostile to them." Instead they look at the sea, comforted that it "flowed up to the mouth of the Thames" (210). With its "infinite sun-dried earth," and remarks on progress and regress of the "races of men," this is the sort of colonial landscape representation Homi Bhabha must have had in mind in describing Englishness. Have they come this far only to retreat to Thames-side Englishness? Rachel's subsequent gazing into the sea is also troubled. Having looked to the bottom of its clear depths, Rachel finds herself throwing large rocks down to disturb its calm. "So it had been at the birth of the world" (211). While hardly engaging in an ecologically sanctioned practiced, Rachel's action suggests some form of resistance. Does she want to draw attention to the violence of birth, whether at the origin of the world or in the reproductive role expected of her? Is she trying to stir thought in order to engage more substantially with the young man at her side?

Thames moments, such as in the passage above, recur in the novel. Mrs. Paley opines that the landscapes of Kent and Dorset are essential to Englishness. Writing home as a tourist, Helen extols the exotic beauty of the trees as superior to the blooms of an English spring—a staple of landscape writing that Woolf too had wished to avoid (96). When a group explores the inland jungle upriver, they compare the landscape to Arundel and Windsor. Onshore, the entrance to the jungle resembles "a drive in an English forest" (270). Looking at the riverside growth, Terence is aware of ways that Renaissance decorative art had its source in the landscape before him: "'That's where the Elizabethans got their style,' he mused, staring into the profusion of leaves and blossoms and prodigious fruits" (268). This complicates Englishness, hybridizing it. Woolf had little idea of Amazonian flora, and so may have found the comparative mode more workable than the detailed descriptions she easily imparts to familiar plants.

The voyage into the Amazonian interior opens with the Flushings' assurances that it has become quite customary for English tourists to steam up the river a short way, visit a native village, make purchases, and return "without damage done to mind or body" (264). A more historical voice follows, claiming that this stretch of river had been left relatively unchanged since the days of the Elizabethans. Pratt assigns the Elizabethan travelers to a "marine phase" of exploration—a period that fascinated young Virginia Stephen, who read her way through Hakluyt's Elizabethan travel narratives. The early twentieth-century tourists of *The Voyage Out* may reenact what Pratt identifies as the eighteenth-century phase of exploration, which took naturalists and traders of raw materials inland. Rachel's father, with his commerce in goats, sustains the latter tradition, as does Mr. Flushing, by dealing in native artifacts. They also look forward to the global commerce of modernity and its environmental depredation, particularly of the global south. Introductions of goats and cattle have contributed greatly to the loss of the Amazon rain forest and the depletion of the diverse species of flora and fauna.

Flushing takes on the role of tour guide on this Amazonian adventure, steering the gaze of the group to a clearing on the left bank where they could glimpse "the hut where Mackenzie, the famous explorer[,] died of fever some ten years ago, almost within reach of civilization." Though "their eyes turned that way obediently," Rachel resists, and her eyes "saw nothing" (277). The whole scenario of the directed gaze irritates her. Flushing's tale of the explorer sounds a bit like the accounts of Mungo Park, who barely got out of the African interior, and survived to craft a sentimental tale (see Pratt). In the contact zone of the native village, the group also reproduces a staple of these inland accounts—the return of the female gaze (Pratt 81). In Woolf's text "the stare followed them, passing over their legs, their bodies, their heads, curiously, not without hostility, like the crawl of a winter fly" (*VO* 285). Despite this denigrating comparison, the visitors feel uncomfortably their own likeness to "soldiers among these soft instinctive people." Rather than conquering, they feel "absorbed" into the village. A woman exposes her breast to feed her child, another child is beaten. Terence sighs, saying, "It makes us seem insignificant, doesn't it" (285). The scene is framed to set up the visitors as passive observers, along the lines of Pratt's second wave of inland explorers. They remain intruders, and crafters of difference. Their anxieties of contagion and absorption suggest new problems arising in the landscape of racial and cultural difference. Carol Cantrell dismisses the landscapes of Woolf's first novel as symbolic backdrops to the characters, lacking the dialogical relation that Woolf would attain in later, more environmentally engaged writing (41). Still, the intersectional politics of gender and race is undeniable in this place.

Orlando has its share of both domestic and foreign landscapes. Its long historical sweep allows Woolf to note the subjectivity of representation, as in different eras it affects descriptions of sunsets and vegetation. Orlando, in his initial identity as an aristocratic Renaissance male, jousts with a shrunken head that is a token of ancestral males' assaults on other lands. His favorite place is high on a hill, where he has extraordinary range, seeing "nineteen English counties," the "spires of London," and, under the right weather conditions, the English Channel and "the craggy top and serrated edges of Snowden herself" (18). Near his father's house, which he will inherit, are those of his aunt and uncle: "The heath was theirs and the forest; the pheasant and the deer, the fox, the badger, and the butterfly" (19). They own not just land but also nonhuman creatures used for sport, even butterflies.

Transported as an ambassador to Turkey, Orlando entertains the same view of mists lifting off Constantinople that Woolf describes in her 1906 diary. Orlando has a greater eye for people and animals astir in the city. His observations come to a jarring close as the spice in the air he breathed "seemed the very breath of the strident and multicoloured and barbaric population" (120). Orlando also distances himself from the landscape of "inhospitable Asian mountains," which lack treasured traits of Englishness: "parsonage there was none, nor manor house, nor cottage, nor oak, elm, violet, ivy or wild eglantine." Still, Orlando would exult "to the depths of his heart in this wild panorama, and gaze and gaze at those passes and far heights, planning journeys there alone on foot where only the goat and shepherd had gone before" (120–21). His plans are typical of the imperial British as they turned to interior exploration.

Orlando does eventually get to the remote landscape he had admired from Constantinople, settling among the gypsies as a female fugitive from a Turkish uprising. Orlando's perception of this place provides evidence that nature is largely a cultural construction—here expressed as a British Romantic inheritance that nearly proves fatal: "The English disease, the love of nature, was inborn in her" (143). To the gypsies, Orlando's devotion to nature makes *her* the representative of a barbarous race. In describing Orlando's love of nature, Woolf is able to parody the very patterns she may have feared in her early landscape writing, applying to them the trope of a disease: "The malady is too well known, and has been, alas, too often described to need describing afresh. . . . She likened the hill to ramparts, and the plains to the flanks of kine. She compared the flowers to enamel and the turf to Turkey rugs, worn thin. Trees were withered hags, and sheep were grey boulders. Everything, in fact, was something else" (143).

At this stage in the survey of centuries, Orlando has a Romantic sensibility toward nature: "Raising her eyes again, she beheld the eagle soaring, and imagined its raptures and made them her own" (144). She uses the margins of her old poem "The Oak Tree" to write about Beauty and Truth (145).

Nostalgia displaces adventure after Orlando's encounter with the gypsies, and she must return to England in full-fledged "Englishness." Gazing one more time at the Turkish mountains, she sees a strange projection of her home ground: "She could see an undulating and grassy lawn; she could see oak trees dotted here and there; she could see the thrushes hopping among the branches. She could see the deer stepping delicately from shade to shade, and could even hear the hum of insects and the gentle sighs and shivers of a summer's day in England" (150–51).

Rather than ascend a mountain or even a respectable hill, as would a Victorian male, the lady Orlando enters the moorlands, her spirits lifted and moved by feathers falling from rooks "flaunting in the sky" (247). This, as many have noted, is *Jane Eyre* territory—the place Jane fled to when avoiding an impossible marriage. Tripping over a bit of heather, Orlando falls and lies content to die in a hollow, by a pool, among the bog myrtle. Wedded thus to the moors, she declares herself "Nature's bride" (248). Conveniently shaped clouds, such as the young Virginia had admired in the fenlands, allow her to replay her earlier adventures. Then her eyes move to one of Woolf's favorite landscapes, the South Downs, where they meet the sea.

Although *Orlando* ends nearly where it began, on a hill presided over by a now ancient oak tree, we get there through a palimpsestic landscape worthy of both of modernism and Orlando's long sequence of experiences. "The ferny path up the hill along which she was walking became not entirely a path, but partly the Serpentine; the hawthorn bushes were partly ladies and gentlemen sitting with card cases and gold-mounted canes; the sheep were partly tall Mayfair houses; everything was partly something else, and each gained an odd moving power from this union of itself and something not itself so that with this mixture of truth and falsehood her mind became like a forest in which things moved" (323). The land she surveys "was my land once," but that view is canceled out in part by property law regarding married women.[31] In a reversal of the imagined English landscape that brought her home, she now watches the landscape heap itself into the hills of Turkey, only to have the English scene reappear with the chiming of a church clock. Perhaps because of the person it honors, *Orlando* is steeped in Englishness, but Orlando's perceptions are fluid and flexible, and reach toward a global imagination.

The men Woolf sends to India in her novels also fail to retain heights of imperial command. Peter's career there fails to elicit even the mildest form of interest from Clarissa in *Mrs. Dalloway,* despite some twenty years of effort. Vastness of landscape and his own loneliness emerge from his memory: "All India lay behind him; plains, mountains; epidemics of cholera; a district twice as big as Ireland; decisions he had come to alone" (47). He "had invented a plough in his district, had ordered wheel-barrows from England, but the coolies wouldn't use them (48). But far from seeking recognition for imperial success, he seems more in need of Clarissa's sympathy (a no less common male demand of women).

In *The Waves,* Bernard and Rhoda exercise their imperial imaginations to see Percival in India and in charge of the natives. Bernard finds nothing elevated except Percival: "'I see India,' said Bernard. 'I see the low, long shore; I see the tortuous lanes of stamped mud that lead in and out among ramshackle pagodas; I see the gilt and crenellated buildings which have an air of fragility and decay as if they were temporarily run up buildings in some Oriental exhibition.[32] I see a pair of bullocks who drag a low cart along the sunbaked road.'" When the car gets stuck in a rut, Percival corrects the situation "by applying the standards of the West, by using the violent language that is natural to him," and thus "the Oriental problem is solved. . . . The multitude cluster round him, regarding him as if he were—what indeed he is—a god" (98). Rhoda has a more mixed report, "muddy roads, twisted jungle, swarms of men, and the vulture that feeds on some bloated carcass is within our scope, part of our proud and splendid province, since Percival, riding alone on a flea-bitten mare, advances down a solitary path, has his camp pitched among desolate trees, and sits alone, looking at the enormous mountains" (99). Percival "advances," as if in the name of progress, but his steed is unimpressive, as is the spot where he only regards the mountains. I read these descriptions, and indeed the construction of the godlike hero, ironically. He may have commanded the hearts of his contemporaries, lounging about on the athletic fields of England, but he fails to stay atop his even his horse, and he falls to his death.[33]

In his dreams Bart Oliver of *Between the Acts* holds tenuously to a career in India, "drowsily, seeing as in a glass, its luster spotted, himself, a young man helmeted; and a cascade falling. But no water; and the hills, like grey stuff pleated; and in the sand a hoop of ribs; a bullock maggot-eaten in the sun; and in the shadow of the rock, savages; and in his hand a gun" (*BA* 13). The landscape is dry and deadly, with one beast being eaten by others, and the native "other," basely labeled, threatened by Bart's gun. As a patriarch, Bart is pleased to have his line carried on through his grandson George. But he bullies the toddler with an imitation bird's beak fashioned from newspaper, and the onslaught of his large, slobbering, alien Afghan hound, Sohrab. Bart's country home brims with Englishness, chosen and framed by Bart himself. Over the edge of his financial paper "he surveyed the landscape—flowing fields, heath and woods. . . . Had he been a painter, he would have fixed his easel here, where the country, barred by trees, looked like a picture" (10). Bart has purchased a picture of a woman in a yellow dress who "led the eye up, down, from the curve to the straight, through glades of greenery and shades of silver, dun and rose into silence" (26). This pastoral bower might offer a more feminine retreat into Englishness, led on by a goddess figure bearing a silver bow.

Feminine Depths of Woodlands, Waters, and Moors

Rachael Vinrace, the central figure in the failed marriage plot of *The Voyage Out,* habitually seeks a change of view. We have noted how, on an anxious walk with her future fiancé, she moves from a vast view to a nearby, more detailed one, where she can achieve the satisfying observation of an insect. Later, when trying to digest the vast sweep of history offered in the volume of Gibbon that St. John Hirst has imposed on her, Rachel starts on a walk by the river. Indistinct views of the landscape interweave with the excitement of a dance the evening before, where Rachel's spontaneous piano accompaniment was a great success: "Filled with one of those unreasonable exultations which start generally from an unknown cause, and sweep whole countries and skies into their embrace, she walked without seeing. . . . She did not see distinctly where she was going, the trees and the landscape appearing only as masses of green and blue, with an occasional space of differently coloured sky." This exultant moment of "doing exactly as she liked" is fixed by "the interruption of a tree." It is an abstract modernist, defamiliarized tree: "Dark was the trunk in the middle, and the branches sprang here and there, leaving jagged intervals of light between them as distinctly as if it had but that second risen from the ground. Having seen a sight that would last her for a lifetime, and for a lifetime would preserve that second, the tree once more sank into the ordinary ranks of trees" (174).

Rachel's tree is comparable to works of art produced by the Omega Workshop. Trees repeatedly stand out from broader landscapes to move Woolf's characters to definitional moments, as demonstrated above in *Orlando,* and in Lily's balancing of aspects of her painting in *To the Lighthouse.*

Rachel's interval of independent wandering, stirred to acute perception by a tree, is more lively and pleasing than the better-known but stultifying jungle scene, where she and Terence, as if mesmerized, exchange vows of love. Having left their party at the borders of the jungle, which "resembled a drive in an English forest," they hear "sighing sounds which suggest to the traveller in a forest that he is waking at the bottom of the sea." Their narrowing path becomes "hedged in by dense creepers which knotted tree to tree. . . . The sighing and creaking up above were broken every now and then by the jarring cry of some startled animal. The atmosphere was close and the air came at them in languid puffs of scent" (270). Their embrace strikes Rachel as "terrible—terrible . . . but in saying this she was thinking as much of the persistent churning of the water as of her own feeling" (271–72). The humid, scented air, tangled vegetation, animal sounds, and churning water assert an uncomfortable sensuality. Terence and Rachel plumb the watery depths of origins and otherness, associated with a primordial mother and nature stereotyped as feminine. Equally terrible is the repeated aqueous nightmare of a slimy tunnel beneath the Thames that first comes to Rachel after Mr. Dalloway forcibly kisses her, having intruded into her music room onboard ship. More puzzling is Helen's queer assault upon Rachel as the group crosses wild grasslands, approaching the native village:

> Voices crying behind them never reached through the waters in which they were now sunk. The repetition of Hewet's name in short, dissevered syllables was to them the crack of a dry branch or the laughter

of a bird.... They never noticed that the swishing of the grasses grew louder and louder, and did not cease with the lapse of the breeze. A hand dropped abrupt as iron on Rachel's shoulder; it might have been a bolt from heaven. She fell beneath it and the grass whipped across her eyes and filled her mouth and ears. Through the waving stems she saw a figure, large and shapeless against the sky. Helen was upon her. Rolled this way and that, now seeing only forests of green, and now the high blue heaven, she was speechless and almost without sense. At last she lay still, all the grasses shaken round her and before her by her panting. (283)

The couple's immersion in the forces of nature is so great that human voices, Hewet's own name, and the sound of people's approach were lost. After she is tackled by Helen, Rachel's eyes, mouth, and ears are engulfed surrealistically in wild grasses, whose green tumbles kaleidoscopically with the blue of the sky. Rachel is speechless and pants, sharing qualities of nonhuman others. Though Helen's "dissevered" words and "iron" touch seem initially mechanical and inhuman, Rachel makes more sense of things as "over her loomed two great heads, the heads of a man and a woman, of Terence and Helen" (283). She realizes that they have kissed and spoken to one another of the impending marriage. In emerging from her tumble, Rachel attaches as an infant might to a maternal figure: "Raising herself and sitting up, she too realized Helen's soft body, the strong and hospitable arms, and happiness swelling and breaking in one vast wave" (284). The vast wave of the female embrace is an improvement over the churning, undersea, and deep jungle metaphors, also selected from nature, for Rachel's heterosexual coupling with Terence.

As Rachel lies dying of fever, perhaps contracted on the expedition upriver, she plays a series of hallucinatory landscapes through her mind, unable to progress in thought, and repeatedly needing to begin again. "She fell into a deep pool of sticky water, which eventually closed over her head. She saw nothing and heard nothing but a faint booming sound, which was the sound of the sea rolling over her head. While all her tormentors thought that she was dead, she was not dead, but curled up at the bottom of the sea. There she lay, sometimes seeing darkness, sometimes light, while every now and then some one turned her over at the bottom of the sea" (341). She surfaces once, again experiencing a sequence of landscapes: "She lay on the top of the wave conscious of some pain, but chiefly of weakness. The wave was replaced by the side of a mountain. Her body became a drift of melting snow, above which her knees rose in huge peaked mountains of bare bone" (346). Her perspective of the room and of Helen expands and falls upon her in a threatening way, reminiscent of Helen's tumbling upon her in the grass. "She wished for nothing else in the world" (347). The play of landscapes is no longer needed.

The characters of *The Waves* are developed largely through their selection of natural imagery, occasionally expanding into a personal landscape. Susan, the character most closely associated with female essentialism and with country origins, has a strong bond with the flat farming land of Lincolnshire, where she cultivates her orchards and rears her cows and her children. She flees to the ringed beech wood, followed by a compassionate Bernard, in the first chapter of the novel. There, amid primeval ferns, she keeps her eyes close to the ground, using a defense familiar to Rachel in *The Voyage Out*. As a woman, she takes material pleasure in all that she has grown and possessed, but admits, "Sometimes I am sick of natural happiness, and fruit growing, and children scattering the house with oars, guns, skulls, books won for prizes and other trophies. I am sick of the body, I am sick of my own craft, industry and cunning, of the unscrupulous ways of the mother who protects, who collects under her jealous eyes at one long table her own children, always her own" (*W* 139). On a visit to Susan, Bernard had shared this scene and found farm carts, the "gabble of rooks and doves," netted fruit trees, and the rhythmically digging gardener "hateful, like a net folding one's limbs in its meshes, cramping" (199).

Rhoda's landscapes are more varied, imaginative, and expressive of threats that she feels on all sides. In an attempt to replace a flimsy dreamscape with something more solid, she goes to the library and lays a book upon the landscape, as suggested in the first epigraph: "Here is a poem about a hedge. I will wander down it and pick flowers, green cowbind and the moonlight coloured may, wild roses and ivy serpentine. I will clasp them in my hands and lay them on the desk's shiny surface. I will sit by the river's trembling edge and look at the water-lilies, broad and bright, which lit the oak that overhung the hedge with moonlight beams of their own watery light" (39–40). She identifies with natural forces, trying to make of them "the whole and indivisible mass that you call life. . . . I am like the foam that races over the beach or the moonlight that falls arrowlike here on a tin can, here on a spike of the mailed sea holly, or a bone or a half-eaten boat. I am whirled down caverns, and flap like paper against endless corridors, and must press my hand against the wall to draw myself back" (94). There is a suicidal episode set in Spain, where she rides a mule up the ridge of a hill that gives a prospect of Africa, and she imagines sharing the prospect of a garland tossed into the sea: "We launch out over the precipice. Beneath us lie the lights of the herring fleet. The cliffs vanish. Rippling small, rippling grey, innumerable waves spread beneath us" (151).

Though he realizes that he is adept at landscapes, and could seize upon any number of details of a Roman cityscape, the mature Bernard decides, "Why impose my arbitrary design?" (137). Merging with other characters in the final segment of the novel, Bernard returns to their landscapes. Woolf expresses Bernard's decisive turn toward selflessness with the image of an elderly man lying in a ditch, admiring the height, indifference, and fury of the clouds (176), and later experiencing moorlands effaced during an eclipse (211). The landscape returns, but to a man "unscheduled" and "without a self" (213). Bernard assumes a more heroic pose at the very end of the novel, imagining waves to be his steed; he thinks of Percival, galloping in India, and flings himself "unvanquished" against death (220).

Women who cannot quite bear their position in patriarchy have their own retreats in nature, and more often than not, Woolf assigns them to the moors. In A Room of One's Own, when Woolf tries to develop a sense of the grievances Charlotte Brontë took into her writing, she takes us with Jane Eyre to the top of Thornfield Hall, overlooking the moors. This landscape evokes Jane's most fervent complaint that women's desires cannot fit into the constrained occupations and travels allowed them. The seclusion of the moors is what allows Rochester to sequester his mad wife. Mrs. Jarvis of Jacob's Room is fond of the moon and "walked on the moor when she was unhappy, going as far as a certain saucer-shaped hollow, though she always meant to go to a more distant ridge" (JR 27). She reads poetry in this sheltered place. She is pronounced "just the sort of woman to lose her faith upon the moors—to confound her God with the universal that is—but she did not lose her faith, did not leave her husband, never read her poem through" (27). Clara, bereft of all prospect of Jacob at the end of the novel, thinks of the moors as well. Isa Oliver, a secretive poet and dissatisfied wife in Between the Acts, murmurs Shelley's lines "The moor is dark beneath the moon, rapid clouds have drunk the last pale beams of even" as she prepares for lunch (BA 18).

In The Years, Kitty has a long-term attraction to the moors of the North of

England, which she associates with her mother's family. As a young woman, she has a fantasy that "the sky, blown into a blue open space, seemed to be looking down not here upon streets and houses, but upon open country, where the wind brushed the moors" (69–70). Even after marriage to an aristocrat, her affections reside in the North, where conveniently her husband has an estate. A dynamic passage chronicles her departure from her party, across London, north by train, and finally up a steep incline by automobile, past "the grey stone house where the mad lady lived alone with her peacocks and her bloodhounds" (259) into the grounds of the estate. She goes in thick-soled shoes through the elegant garden, into the woods, and onto the moors. "The country spread wide all round her. Her body seemed to shrink; her eyes to widen. She threw herself on the ground, and looked over the billowing land that went rising and falling away and away, until somewhere far off it reached the sea. . . . A deep murmur sang in her ears—the land itself, singing to itself, a chorus, alone. She lay there listening. She was happy, completely" (263). Her prospect of the land, like Orlando's, is elevated and comes out of privilege; but also like Orlando, she grounds herself in the earth. Landscape proves more important than real estate in both works. After her son has inherited the estate, Kitty lives content in the mad lady's house.

A Final English Landscape

Between the Acts provides an intense view of English village life, seen on the day of an annual pageant that runs through several centuries of pastoral life. Donations on this occasion will go to the illumination of the church—a central element in the village landscape. Nearby stands an ancient tithe barn, which has seen much of the history represented in the pageant, and which is appropriated by nature as well as man (figure 29). Days before the declaration of World War II, airplanes provide a new perspective on landscape, revealing scars left by Britons, Romans, Elizabethans, and the Napoleonic Wars (*BA* 4). Woolf sets her village away from her preferred seaside location, as if to intensify its Englishness in the light of the encroaching war. One cannot count on fresh fish for luncheon when one is thirty-five miles from the sea. The setting is a considerable commute from cosmopolitan, commercial London—far enough that visitors regularly buy paperback novels to pass the time on the train. Mrs. Manresa, the self-styled "wild child of nature" (31), comes from London to "roll in the grass." Despite possessing "finger nails

FIGURE 29. Tithe barn. (Photograph by the author)

red as roses," "silk pyjamas," and a "loud speaker playing jazz" (28), Manresa strikes Isa as genuine (30). Thanks to Mrs. Manresa's lack of decorum,
"fresh air" is introduced "to follow like leaping dolphins in the wake of an
ice-breaking vessel" (29). Figuratively, she brings creatures of the sea, and
their spirit, inland.

The narrator of *Between the Acts* suggests that man has done poorly with
what nature had to offer in this locale: "It was a pity that the man who had
built Pointz Hall had pitched the house in a hollow, when beyond the flower
garden and the vegetables there was this stretch of high ground" (8).[34] Bart
Oliver opines that the site was chosen "obviously to escape from nature,"
then provides evidence of additional disadvantages—the attraction of moisture and accumulation of heavy snows (6). Low and moist, the setting aligns
with feminine gendering of landscape rather than the masculine quest for
the heights. The hollow for Woolf may indeed be a place of shelter and connection and thus a prized location. The lesbian artist Miss La Trobe, whose
origin is mysterious (the Channel Islands, where the name La Trobe is common, are suspected), surveys the grounds of Pointz Hall in winter as she
plans for her pageant. She is delighted with the terrace "nature had provided"

for her pageant (8). Beyond a nearby pool, she spots a dip "where bushes and brambles had mobbed themselves together. . . . It was the very place for a dressing room" (40). With the pageant under way, nature can merge with artifice, as real swallows are attracted to an artificial lake serving as part of the set, and cows on the hillsides add their voices to the script. It is Miss La Trobe's challenge, through the various acts, to bring the village audience to greater awareness of themselves, seen through history down to the present moment, in a setting that flows into the natural world, its primordial sounds and gestures.

His own family poses a similar challenge to Giles Oliver, who must make a rapid transition from his job in London when he arrives for the weekend. He is infuriated that "old fogies" like his aunt can be so disrespectful of the commercial pressures of the city or, worse, unaware that the carnage of war has already begun, "just over there, across the gulf, in the flat land which divided them from the continent" (46). As they sit in the garden, he observes with disgust, "They looked at the view; they looked at what they knew." He is sure that "at any moment guns would rake that land into furrows; planes splinter Bolney Minster" (32). Giles confesses to himself that he loves the view as much as any of them do, and that he would really have liked to be a farmer. He wants to retain Englishness, then, and returns to the emblematic countryside from the city for something that he holds central to his identity. In the course of the afternoon, Giles finds other threats to Englishness, besides the Germans. "What for did a good sort like the woman Manresa bring these half-breeds in her trail?" (34). From Giles's perspective, Dodge is only half English by virtue of being homosexual, and homosexuality introduces another, a presumably darker, more "primitive," race or species.

Lucy Swithin, who strangely annoys her nephew, conjures up an ancient landscape of rhododendrons and "steaming undergrowth," stretching to the Continent, no channel between (6–7). Her sense of connection is quite the opposite of her nephew's, in which the Continent poses a bristling threat. Lucy also has the naïve faith that the English landscape will go on being beautiful long after they are gone. Miss La Trobe, in the final act of the pageant, uses mirrors to fragment both the view and the audience's images of themselves, wishing to make them more self-critical. Though she despairs of her success with them, she ends the day looking at the landscape. "It was growing dark. Since there were no clouds to trouble the sky, the blue was bluer, the green greener. There was no longer a view—no Folly, no spire of Bolney

Minster. It was land merely, no land in particular. She put down her case and stood looking at the land. Then something rose to the surface" (142). She is already composing her next play out of the mud; the generic scene will have "two figures, half concealed by a rock" (143).

The novel ends inside Pointz Hall, but imagines a landscape that is both primordial and intimate. With deepening nightfall, the view from the window "was all sky without colour. The house had lost its shelter. It was night before roads were made, or houses. It was the night that dwellers in caves had watched from some high place among the rocks" (149). Woolf reconstructs the heart of England as a heart of darkness at this vulnerable moment. The relationship of Giles and Isa is equally vulnerable, a condition she registers, echoing Conrad, in these famous lines: "Before they slept, they must fight; after they had fought they would embrace. From that embrace another life might be born. But first they must fight, as the dog fox fights with the vixen, in the heart of darkness, in the fields of night" (148). Thanks to Miss La Trobe, conjuring up her next play, a similar landscape is perceived from two vantage points at the close of this novel. The suggestion is made that, through art, the curtain can rise on a new environment—something that is to be hoped for in successive crises of culture and (in our own time) nature. The doubling, sharing, and superimposing on landscape seen in this chapter is something that Woolf discovered early in her writing, and it is an insight that leads toward the holistic ecofeminist imagination we will explore in our final chapter. This chapter, however, leaves us with the dog and vixen. Woolf's approach to other nonhuman creatures, addressed in the next chapter, also builds toward that conclusion.

5

Crossing the
Species Barrier

I like to think of the tree itself: first the dry
sensation of being wood; then the grinding
of the storm; then the slow, delicious ooze
of sap. I like to think of it, too, on winter's
nights standing in the empty field with all
leaves close-furled, nothing tender exposed
to the iron bullets of the moon, a naked mast
upon an earth that goes tumbling, tumbling
all night long. The song of birds must sound
very loud and strange in June; and how cold
the feet of insects must feel upon it, as they
make laborious progresses upon the creases
of the bark. . . . One by one the fibres snap
beneath immense cold pressure of the earth,
then the last storm comes and, falling, the
highest branches drive deep into the ground
again. Even so, life isn't done with; there
are a million patient, watchful lives still for
a tree, all over the world, in bedrooms, in
ships, on the pavement, living rooms. . . . It
is full of peaceful thoughts, happy thoughts,
this tree.

~Woolf, "The Mark on the Wall"

On my birthday we walked
among the downs, like the
folded wings of grey birds;
& saw first one fox, very long
with his brush stretched; then
a second; which had been
barking, for the sun was hot
over us; it leapt lightly over a
fence & entered the furze—a
very rare sight. How many foxes
are there in England?

~Woolf, *Diary*

ANIMALS HAVE A PERVASIVE, varied, and versatile presence throughout Virginia Woolf's life and writings, as already suggested by the Stephen family's engagement with natural history, in chapter 2. Julia Stephen's children's stories featured talking and thinking animals (monkeys, goats, pigs, cats, and birds, including a parrot and an owl). They teach that good children are sensitive to kind treatment of animals. A little girl named "Ginia," who has been naughty, misses out on much of the action in "The Monkey on the Moor," located in a beach setting very like St. Ives.

Woolf exchanged animal nicknames through much of her life. Her nurturing half sister Stella was dubbed "cow." Virginia bore the name "goat." This may suggest a creature only partly domesticated, or capable of stubborn independence (Vanessa occasionally preceded the "goat" with the masculine "Billy").[1] Vanessa received Virginia's congratulations on her engagement to Clive Bell in a letter signed by a group of apes and one marsupial: "V's devoted Beasts Bartholomew, Mango & Wombat." The red-headed prospective bridegroom was dubbed a "new Red Ape of a kind not known before who is better than all other apes because he can both talk and marry you."[2] Woolf also exchanged nicknames in affectionate relationships with women, starting with Violet Dickinson. Her "dearest creature," Vita, offered "Potto," a dog persona, for Virginia (Sackville-West, *Letters* 331). Woolf teased Ethel Smyth about her demands, via animal analogy, proclaiming Smyth "without exception the most cross grained, green-eyed, cantankerous, grudging, exacting cat or cassowary I've ever met!" (*L* 5:314).

Leonard Woolf's pet name "Mongoose" makes some sense for a man recently returned from Ceylon, conjuring up the heroic Rikki-Tikki-Tavi, the savior of an Anglo-Indian family from murderous cobras in Rudyard Kipling's *The Jungle Book*. An African native and the largest of all monkeys, "Mandrill" is more difficult to explain for Virginia.[3] A gender-related problem (perhaps a source of humor) is that the posterior of the male flushes a vivid red when aroused for mating. Woolf played with these attributes in a letter to "Immundus Mongoosius Felicissimus," saying that Mandrill "wishes me to inform you delicately that her flanks and rump are now in finest plumage, and invites you to an exhibition" (*L* 2:35, December 1913). Animal identities, reaching well into Woolf's maturity, might comment lightly on regrettable behavior, or work into fantasies that facilitated disclosures about the body and sexual desire—otherwise subjects of reticence and coding for Woolf.[4]

Many of Woolf's characters are described as looking like birds and animals.

Scrope Purvis, for example, sees Mrs. Dalloway resembling a jay, "blue-green, light, vivacious" as she sets forth in the morning (*MD* 4). Woolf's characters, like her own family, regularly have pet dogs, net butterflies and moths, and observe the behavior of birds. The hunt lurks in the cultural background, providing a model for play among children, a pastime for the privileged, and memories for elderly men returned from empire. Hunting, herding, and fishing serve Woolf further as metaphors for mental processes and writing challenges. Woolf uses animals politically to comment upon inequities of class, gender, nation, and perhaps even race. In quiet moments, Woolf's human characters try to read the minds of animals. In troubling ones, animals and even trees prove alarming. Trees gesture commands and birds speak in Latin to Septimus Smith in *Mrs. Dalloway* (the latter echoing Woolf's own experience when mentally ill). A great cat pounces, to Rhoda's distressed imagination, in *The Waves*. Whether influenced by evolutionary or psychological theory, characters such as Clarissa or Louis in *The Waves* may suspect that the animal resides within them, grubbing, stamping, or lurking in a mirror. As in the epigraph above, Woolf may even try to think like a tree, thus crossing over green margins of the species barrier.

There has been a recent burgeoning of interest in such species traversals, particularly where animals are concerned. Participants include renowned postmodernists such as Jacques Derrida, J. M. Coetzee, and Giles Deleuze and Félix Guattari. In a sweeping study that ranges from the thirteenth-century Hebrew Bible to the present, Georgio Agamben studies the persistent cultural work humans have done to separate humanity and animality. The timeliness of the topic is shown in Marianne DeKoven's column in a recent issue of *PMLA*, "Why Animals Now?" Her work colludes with a related injunction of recent theory that culture move on from androcentric humanism to posthumanism.[5] Particularly helpful for this chapter are various ecofeminist approaches to the problem. They include studying ways that humans and animals have been settled into cultural hierarchies, and problematizing ways the animal and the human are differentiated and assigned to discursive categories of species. As noted in the introduction, Donna Haraway offers the term "naturecultures," defying a basic binary of unequal power relations that parallels with binaries of race and gender (culture to nature, white to black, man to woman), as Val Plumwood has argued. In moving toward a post-Cartesian "dialogical interspecies ethics," Plumwood encourages greater recognition that other-than-human beings are intentional, having minds attuned to forgotten ecological knowledges, and with capacities for agency and communication (*Environmental Culture* 175–77). Also useful in assessing Woolf's attempts at interspecies connections are Haraway's studies of reciprocal relationships between dogs and humans, the *Companion Species Manifesto* and *When Species Meet,* as well as Josephine Donovan and Carol J. Adams's promulgation of an "ethic of care" toward animals, premised on Carol Gilligan's feminization of caring behavior and situational, relational thinking, *In a Different Voice.*

Tampering with the Gendered Hierarchy of Animals

The early women writers featured in *A Room of One's Own* have remarkable connections to animals through pastoral traditions, nature writing, and construction of their place in the universe. In her poem "Nocturnal Reveries," Anne Finch finds a comfortable place among the lower animals of "th' inferior world" shared with the nightingale, an owl, glow-worms, and grazing animals "whilst Tyrant-Man do's sleep." Margaret Cavendish contributes a memorable line to *A Room* from her "Female Orations": "Women live like Bats or Owls, labour like Beasts, and die like Worms" (qtd. in *AROO* 61). Aphra Behn's hero hunts for recreation in *Oroonoko,* with mixed results. He fells a great "tyger," but he seems to identify with the beast whose heroism was recorded in bullets long carried in its heart (45–46). A fierce eel would have felled him, were it not for first aid administered by indigenous people knowledgeable of plants with healing qualities.

The cultural ecofeminist Carolyn Merchant suggests that modern science reconceptualized reality "as a machine rather than a living organism," and in doing so it "sanctioned the domination of both nature and women" (*Death of Nature* xviii). As part of a similar shift in power relations, Harriet Ritvo suggests that during the eighteenth and nineteenth centuries "people systematically appropriated power they had previously attributed to animals, and animals became significant primarily as the objects of human manipulation" (2). Such manipulation might take the form of selective breeding of oxen for solid, square bodies set on short, slim legs, or thoroughbred horses for speed. It might involve regulations to curb the spread of diseases such as foot and mouth disease in cattle and rabies in dogs.

Woolf makes playful, satirical reference to biological manipulation of animals throughout her works. An early example is guinea pigs selectively bred for their spots by a friend of Miss Allan in *The Voyage Out*. This fictional breeder feels triumphant when she produces a "black baby" out of a yellow mother. Possibilities here are that black is beautiful and valued, or that miscegenation is to be deliberately pursued (*VO* 256)—a reversal of racism in an era enraptured by eugenics. On the other hand, when Minta Doyle is bored with her husband's breeding of Belgian hares, we sense the couple's own difficulty as mates (*TTL* 177). Woolf was the beneficiary of Vita Sackville-West's breeding of spaniels, receiving as a gift Pinka, who in turn inspired Woolf's playful biography *Flush*—a work that demonstrates that pedigree is not all, as will be elaborated later in the chapter (figure 30).

Woolf gives ample evidence that cultural contexts and historical moments influence relationships between humans and other species. Like their coded language of flowers noted in chapter 3, British Victorians had an ordered hierarchy of value for animals, which Ritvo has reconstructed from popular zoological sources. It corresponded to animals' utility and manageability for human purposes. There was little sense that creatures could be an end in themselves, rather than a means for human satisfaction. In the Victorian system, compliant and useful domesticity accrues high status. Wild creatures, particularly ones existing on the outer fringes of the empire, rank low. Like unruly natives, who are placed lower on the human scale than Europeans, wild cats must be subdued and controlled (Ritvo 2–3). Cultural "others" might be equated with specific species—foreigners with exotic animals; blacks and the Irish with simians; lower classes or Jews with vermin, a pattern sustained with tragic consequences in the Nazi era.[6] Cows, oxen, and even elephants (useful for lifting the burdens of empire) ranked relatively high. At the very top were "livelier animals that nonetheless acknowledged human superiority," a prime example being the horse. Set above the feminine cow, the horse tends to do men's work and lifts men into a commanding position. In a further inflection of hierarchies, the horse may be "nobler than the class of humans generally charged with its care" (Ritvo 19). Indeed, the upper classes depended upon the lower ones for care of both exalted and utilitarian animals.

Victorians esteemed dogs for loyal service and capacity to love (Ritvo 21). Woolf's dogs have these qualities in abundance, though they go beyond the Victorian model once Woolf (who does assume that animals are mindful) represents their thoughts. The cat, usually gendered female, was vilified by the Victorians for failing to subordinate its will to humans. One of the

FIGURE 30. Virginia, Vita, and their spaniels. (Monk's House Album 3, MS Thr 560, Harvard Theatre Collection, Houghton Library, Harvard University)

male authorities Woolf holds up to ridicule in *A Room of One's Own* has a pronouncement on cats: "That old gentleman, who is dead now, but was a bishop, I think, who declared that it was impossible for any woman, past, present, or to come, to have the genius of Shakespeare ... He also told a lady who applied to him for information that cats do not as a matter of fact go to heaven. . . . How much thinking these old gentlemen used to save one!" (46). Woolf's irony encourages rethinking the supposedly rational assessment of animals.

For deep ecologists such as the venerated Aldo Leopold, wild animals have top priority. To preserve them, he admonishes that we learn to "[Think] Like a Mountain" (129). In feminist response, Karen Davis calls on humans to "[Think] Like a Chicken." One of the founding works of ecofeminism, Susan Griffin's *Woman and Nature,* devotes remarkable sections to men's domestication of cows, mules, and show horses (67–82), before she turns to comparable handling of the female body. Within the animal species, women are seldom compared to wild animals, or ones at the top of the domestic animal hierarchy. They are frequently juxtaposed with creatures easily managed and reared for dairy products or fleece: sheep, cows, and chickens. In a hilarious early diary entry, Woolf confuses these categories, casting sheep as complaining human beings of both genders: "One is clearly exhorting the rest to save their souls from damnation—another, if I mistake him not, denounced some ovine education bill—a third upholds the rights of the sheep to be considered the intellectual equal of the ram." All prefer exhortation and complaint to listening and collaborating. Their prevailing tone of "weariness" or "hopeless regret" makes Woolf "opine that the sheep themselves are aware why they still remain sheep" (PA 197).

Ecofeminist writing refers back to the British "game" tradition in developing a typology of the hunt. In "License to Kill," Marti Kheel describes the "happy hunter" model, the American version of British blood sport practiced by Theodore Roosevelt, Ernest Hemingway, and even Leopold. Gentlemanly, aristocratic values include the cultivation of manliness, coupled with the restraint of aggressive and sexual drives. Happy hunters initially showed little respect for predators, whose incursions on farm animals excused their extermination. Large predators were long ago eliminated from the British Isles, made the subject of massive culling and collecting in Asia and Africa, and greatly reduced in North America. Conservation of habitat and practical or scientific knowledge of species also figure in the sportsman's profile, though usually in order to stock the hunt. The concern for hunting terrain blends into the contemporary type of the "holistic hunter" who is increasingly attuned to the ecosystem. In reviewing a Theodore Roosevelt biography, Woolf is troubled that "towards the end of his life of a lack of balance which destroys his value as a magnified specimen of the human race[.] The slaughter of animals played too large a part in his life" ("Body and Brain," *E* 3:226). The second epigraph above suggests that Woolf cherished the fox as an English native all too rarely glimpsed in her own time.

Equine Exceptions

A horse was among the gifts George Duckworth bestowed on his half sister Vanessa when she came of age to be presented in proper society. In the early morning, she rode down the Ladies' Mile in Hyde Park. Although Vanessa had, no doubt, different reasons for selecting Clive Bell as her husband, George preferred him to other Cambridge men who came calling because "he was better dressed, had a good seat on a horse and was an excellent wing shot" (Quentin Bell, *Virginia Woolf* 103). That well-bred horses were complicit with hunting in Woolf's mind shows in her analogy, "as the foxhunter hunts in order to preserve the breed of horses" ("Street Haunting," *E* 4:480).

Woolf is less careful of the "breed of horses" and more conscious of their burdens. On Stephen family vacations, Virginia limited her equestrian activities to a pony cart. She describes a pathetic, lazy beast, Solomon, who was whipped along by the driver as he hauled family members around Gloucestershire (*PA* 118, 122, 128). The pony cart she drove in 1903 was pulled by a "Lady pony"—a "disappointed woman" with "no ambitions in life" and an objection to hills. As she regaled Violet Dickinson, "I go driving with Father, and when we meet anything else, he seizes the reins, and I drop the whip, and we are landed in the hedge, to the vast amusement of the rustics" (*L* 1:94). During vacations in the New Forest, Woolf's brothers hunted fox on horseback. She and Vanessa walked through bog and forest, where "forest ponies come when you call them" (*L* 1:168).

The male-gendered equine classification is particularly evident in Woolf's deliberately feminist writings. The horse participates in the hunt, transports the colonial administrator, and helps construct edifices that serve male institutions (figure 31). "Teams of horses and oxen . . . must have hauled the stone in wagons from far countries" to erect men's colleges (*AROO* 9). Things do not always work out well between men and horses, however. This same narrator recollects mischievously the old professor who "at the sound of a whistle . . . instantly broke into a gallop" (9). The great expectations for Percival's imperial career in India are dashed when his horse stumbles and he falls to his death in *The Waves*.

Victorian gender associations aside, Woolf does relate positively to this exalted animal. Horses offer an encouraging metaphor for her work in progress, characterized as "taking [her] fences" en route to her goal.[7] While there may be some identification involved in such comparisons, they fall short of what Haraway aspires to in companion species. She gets satisfaction in her dogs' performance in agility exercises, where animal plus human partners participate in a mutually satisfying achievement (*When Species Meet*). An incident approaching such collaboration occurs as a rider merges muscularly with his horse as it takes a jump in *Jacob's Room*: "Then as if your own body ran into the horse's body and it was your own forelegs grown with his that sprang, rushing through the air you go, the ground resilient, bodies a mass of muscles, yet you have command too, upright stillness, eyes accurately judging" (101). Woolf's description includes a simile of the horse's motion to a "monster wave," thus blending diverse aspects of nature. The "ground resilient" may also embody life—all of this symptomatic of the natural holism we turn to in the final chapter. Jacob's merger with his mount, in a rare depiction of his own thought, does not last. He reassumes his "command" and "judgment." Jacob's frequently idealized form, now on horseback, attracts stares from country people as he passes.

In *Between the Acts*, soldiers use the story of a horse with a green tail to lure a young woman into gang rape, doubly degrading any nobility of the steed, while connecting violence to women with the military (15). This novel also explores more humble equine species. Bart Oliver retains the image from his colonial days of a "bullock maggot-eaten in the sun" (13). There is a costume donkey in the pageant whose distracting hind parts, played by "Albert the idiot," divert attention from the patriarchal authority of Mr. Hardcastle (116). Isa's fantasy role as a donkey in the desert, herself loaded down by the "white man's burden," also disrupts the cultural order: "How am I burdened with what they drew from the earth; memories; possessions. . . . 'Kneel down,' said the past. 'Fill your pannier from our tree. Rise up, donkey. Go your way till your heels blister and your hoofs crack'" (106). Isa imagines that lightning comes "from the stone blue sky. The thongs are burst that the dead tied. Loosed are our possessions" (106). "Possessions" here deconstruct

FIGURE 31. Leonard Woolf on horseback in Ceylon. (Monk's House Album 1, MS 557, Harvard Theatre Collection, Houghton Library, Harvard University)

into unwanted accumulation. The desert scene also encourages attention to lands and people appropriated in the empire, the accumulation of imperial white men. But there is more—Isa's refusal to heed "the cries of the leaders who in that they seek to lead desert us." This echoes the refusals of *Three Guineas,* where fascism is brought home and the accoutrements of authority are mocked. Isa takes on social awareness instead. She admonishes her ongoing donkey self, "Hear rather the shepherd, coughing by the farmyard wall; the withered tree that sighs when the Rider gallops; the brawl in the barrack room when they stripped her naked; or the cry which in London when I thrust the window open someone cries" (107). Hers is an ethic of caring for the oppressed animal, resulting in connection and mutual assistance.

Taking Stock of Woolf's Domestic Animals

From an early age, Woolf liked to characterize herself as a "cockney" unaccustomed to farm work and natural landscapes. In "A Cockney's Farming Experience," which appeared as a series in the *Hyde Park Gate News* (1982), Woolf mocks the ineptitude of city people with farm animals. Though comedic, the story lends itself to a number of severe readings.[8] Woolf's city-bred farmer is inept at both milking and feeding his cow, leading to its starvation. This "Paterfamilias" proves equally incompetent at childcare. Though the farmer's wife repeatedly protests her husband's neglect and ineptitude, she has infelicities of her own with domestic animals. She collects only two eggs from her chickens and then cooks them hard as bricks—an episode that may also reflect upon the Stephen family's dependence on cooks and nursery staff as servants.

Mrs. Flanders keeps chickens in *Jacob's Room*. She protects her geese from Johnny, who enjoys chasing them with a stick, though she must also protect herself from a rooster. Much later, after her sons are off at war, Betty thinks of her chickens' safety. Similar mother-hen analogies occur repeatedly in Woolf's works. Rezia Smith resembles a little hen as she fends off the intrusive Dr. Holmes, coming to institutionalize (and in effect kill) Septimus in *Mrs. Dalloway*. In *To the Lighthouse*, Mr. Ramsay's sympathetic viewing of a mother hen with her chicks convinces Mr. Bankes that domesticity will compete with academics in Ramsay's future.

Woolf's most troubling chicken episode occurs in *The Voyage Out*, where Rachel Vinrace feels both fascinated and repelled by the "ugliness" of the chase and slaughter of a chicken outside a hotel kitchen. The captor is an elderly woman, bearing an expression of "furious rage." Swearing in Spanish, she "opened her scanty grey skirts to enclose it, dropped upon it in a bundle, and then, holding it out, cut its head off with an expression of vindictive energy and triumph combined" (252). The woman with this bloody task is distanced from Rachel's privileged society as a racial "other" and a servant—foreign and crude in her speech, more energetic than Rachel, and attributed vindictive motivations. Rachel probably has not thought much about the slaughter of creatures for her own eating—a consideration basic to the ecofeminist "ethic of care." The chicken incident occurs amid a series of dispiriting encounters with hotel guests: Evelyn Murgatroyd, tormented by her ambivalence over conflicting marriage proposals (246–51), and the bitter, manipulative Mrs. Paley, who bars her passage (257–58). The fate of the chicken bears comparison to Rachel's sense of sexual entrapment and cultural self-sacrifice. This is the effect Griffin creates in her depiction of the hunt, by alternating scenarios of a male felling an animal and conquering a woman (*Woman and Nature* 103–5). The old woman, her knife, and the rolling chicken head come back to haunt Rachel in feverish hallucinations at the close of the novel (333, 339). These occur with her fiancé, Terence Hewet, present. In the second instance, the woman cuts off a man's head, suggesting a widening pattern of victimization echoed in Terence's loss of Rachel.

Woolf herds domestic animals past us quickly as metaphors, offering lasting cultural readings. In the first chapter of *A Room of One's Own*, the meal served at the women's college is "beef with its attendant greens and potatoes—a homely trinity, suggesting the rumps of cattle in a muddy market, and sprouts curled and yellowed at the edge, and bargaining and cheapening, and women with string bags on Monday morning" (17). These shoppers, compelled to bargain for sprouts that are past their prime, are as déclassé as the meal itself. Of her research methods at the British Museum, Woolf's narrator says, "The question far from being shepherded to its pen flies like a frightened flock hither and thither, helter-skelter, pursued by a whole pack of hounds" (28). This contrasts with a male Oxbridge student "shepherding his question past all distractions till it runs into its answer as a sheep runs into its pen." The student invites additional metaphors. He sits there "extracting pure nuggets of the essential ore every ten minutes or so" (28). The training and golden diet reflect his privilege, but his periodic "little grunts of satisfaction" are simultaneously mechanical and porcine. Other herdsmen come in for a challenge. In *The Voyage Out*, Rachel worries about the goats that are a commodity in her father's trans-Atlantic trade.[9] These he justifies as part of the system that finances her playing of the piano (23). The marriage plot suggests that Rachel herself is carefully managed family stock.

Cows on the hillside are a basic part of Englishness and the pastoral tradition, dotting the landscape we encountered in chapter 4. Woolf's cows make a profound human connection in *Between the Acts*, perhaps rising in her imagination due to her recent reading of Freud on the herd instinct. The uninvited arrival to lunch of the self-styled "child of nature," Mrs. Manresa, and her minion, William Dodge, is explained as coming from "the very same instinct that caused the sheep and the cows to desire propinquity" (26). Woolf's cows link to the primeval past, one preoccupation of Lucy Swithin throughout the novel. Like Woolf's persistent chickens, they are strongly maternal: "One had lost her calf. In the very nick of time she lifted her great moon-eyed head and bellowed. . . . From cow after cow came the same yearning bellow. The whole world was filled with dumb yearning. It was the primeval voice sounding loud in the ear of the present moment. Then the whole herd caught the infection. . . . The cows annihilated the gap" (96). The cows provide what Miss La Trobe, despairing of her audience, needed at that moment in her pageant. Like the sheep of the early diary, the cows model human behavior, whether bellowing despair, browsing over fodder, or joining one another in their actions. Cows also interrupt the individual human dramas of the novel, asserting something basic and shared.

Companion Species Stories

Woolf's childhood menagerie included a caged bird presented by her god-father, James Russell Lowell; a Persian cat purchased from early writing revenue, as described in "Professions for Women"; and briefly a squirrel, Jacobi, "the most delightful creature that ever was. We pursue each other round the room!" (*PA* 110). Woolf's diaries and letters provide numerous glimpses of the everyday lives of the dogs and an occasional cat. Dogs are a constant presence both before and after her marriage to Leonard Woolf. Her presentation of canines ranges from stories of loyal devotion, worthy of the Victorians, to queries into the morality of having and confining pets; she makes numerous comparisons between dogs and specific human types, as well as endeavors to know their thoughts as they share people's lives. Woolf's treatment of companion animals is rarely hierarchical, and her control of her own pets sufficiently lax to provide amusing tales.[10]

The recent flurry of critical interest in dogs has had some bearing on modernist studies. Geoff Gilbert, for example, uses the "figure of quarantine" as a tool for investigating British modernist abstraction. This takes us back to Wyndham Lewis and T. E. Hulme, as introduced in chapter 1, expressing modernist mechanistic "separation from the world" and especially the organic world. In late nineteenth- and early twentieth-century Britain, dogs were separated from the world in multiple ways, including the insularity of British dog breeding and the effort to eradicate rabies, which like venereal disease occasioned great cultural anxiety. The muzzling of dogs, which Gilbert compares to the muzzling of suffragists and sets in the context of the contagious diseases acts regulating prostitution, applies as well to Woolf's experience and representation of dogs. Even more applicable is Haraway's work on dogs and humans as companion species with mutual perceptions and needs, having come together through coevolution. Her criteria are as follows: "To hold in regard, to respond, to look back reciprocally, to notice, to pay attention, to have courteous regard for, to esteem" (*When Species Meet* 19). Woolf touches upon some of Haraway's desired acts of reciprocity, though not the full list.[11]

Woolf's early essay "On a Faithful Friend" commemorates the passing of Shag—along with Gurth, the most photographed and remembered of the Stephen dogs (figure 32). Gerald Duckworth purchased Shag in 1892, and he lived until 1904, when he was run over in the street. Given this time span, Alison Light sees Shag as the object of Woolf's nostalgia for lost childhood. He is the model for "Rover" in *The Years,* a dog handed over in his dotage to an adoring servant, Crosby—herself set aside as the younger generation moved on. The Stephens' maid, Sophie Farrell, demonstrated loyalty comparable to Shag's, and pleasing Sophie was on Virginia's mind in writing the essay.[12] Indeed, Woolf's animals were often dependent upon servants for care, and so they inhabit the human class system in ways that we may find discomfiting today. Light attends to Sophie and Shag in *Mrs. Woolf and the Servants,* suspecting that for Woolf dogs often appear "as a stand-in for that other dogsbody, the servant—dogs arouse the mixed feelings associated with being a dependent and being closer to one's 'animal nature'" (50).

More is going on in Woolf's eulogy. Shag has pretensions to nobility. Though acquired from "a low-born blacksmith," he is supposed "the sole scion of true Skye blood." Shag proves more a clubman than the hunter of rats the family had hoped for. But by 1899 he was yielding attention to a young sheepdog called Gurth, who joined the bugging expeditions detailed in chapter 2. The essay recounts Shag's reappearance several years after banishment from 22 Hyde Park Gate—a miraculous return worthy of Victorian stories of canine loyalty, and apt to appeal to Sophie. Woolf begins her essay on a more critical and contemporary note concerning human relations with animals, finding it an "impertinence" that "we buy animals for so much gold and silver and call them ours" (*E* 1:12). Woolf then idealizes canines in the wild, assuming that humans have deprived them of original joys by making "these wild creatures forego their nature for ours, which at best they can but imitate? It is one of the refined sins of civilization, for we know not what wild spirit we are taking from its purer atmosphere, who it is—Pan, or Nymph, of Dryad—that we have trained to beg for a lump of sugar at tea" (*E* 1:12). Woolf's argument resonates with animal rights activism, though as Haraway points out, alternate accounts suggest that wolves may have initiated coevolution by approaching human settlements for food and protection

FIGURE 32. Shag. (Monk's House Album 5, MS 562, Harvard Theatre Collection, Houghton Library, Harvard University)

(*Companion Species* 28). With references to Pan and Dryads, Woolf my-thologizes the wild—a movement away from real dogs that Haraway might question. When imagining the thoughts of a Persian cat, the "critic on the hearthrug," early in this same essay, Woolf's analysis is more cultural than ecological.[13] It becomes a "mystic Persian, whose ancestors were worshipped as gods whilst we, their masters and mistresses, groveled in caves and painted our bodies blue. She . . . smiles, I often think, at our late-born civilization, and remembers the rise and fall of dynasties" (*E* 1:12). Such deflation of Western civilization remained a theme with Woolf, as when the gypsies compare their far longer history to Western civilization in *Orlando.*

At the turn of the twentieth century, dogs in Great Britain were increas-ingly subject to the law, which sought to protect citizens from physical attack and disease and resulted in the elimination of rabies from the British Isles.[14] Virginia and her mother went to court to testify against a dangerous dog in their neighborhood—a story that leads off the first issue of the *Hyde Park Gate News.* Though Woolf does not express fear of dogs, she does report that Vanessa was anxious about meeting unmuzzled dogs in the vicinity of Kens-ington Gardens. Even the noble Shag underwent the indignity of muzzling.

With a mixture of humor and annoyance at the "lower classes," Woolf reports on the jailing of Gurth and Hans during a vacation at Wells.[15] Her dogs had escaped while being walked by the boardinghouse maid, and, lacking an address on his collar, Gurth was in violation of the law (L 1:353, 354–55). What Woolf finds doubly tedious is her landlord's repetitive account, complete with the theory, laced with sexual innuendo and aristocratic titles, that "Miss Hans had run away, and his Lordship (Gurth) followed after," the assessment that "in the eye of the law [Woolf was] a criminal," and his attempt to manage her response to the authorities, suggesting that "a young lady, traveling alone—its very awkward" (L 1:355). Here on the village level was belief in the the co-restraint of young women and dogs.

Gurth became a regular companion for Woolf after the younger generation moved to Bloomsbury following Leslie Stephen's death. They learn together how to negotiate their independent life in a new part of the city. As Gurth accompanies her to and from the London Library, stopping in shops, or purchasing concert tickets, he is sometimes too vocal or elicits a cabman's complaint about his muddy feet. They negotiate when he may acceptably proceed off leash. As Woolf writes, Gurth waits by her side, becoming "a load on my conscience," which is eased with a walk that proves pleasant for both (PA 238). Gurth and his mistress develop a working relationship for cohabitation and a certain amount of common resistance to authority.[16]

Woolf's novels and essays are well stocked with incidental dogs and cats, many of whom invite interpretation as Haraway's natureculture. Woolf's most famous feline creation is the Manx cat, spotted outside the window of a men's college at Oxbridge in A Room of One's One. She decides she and the cat have something in common. The cat pauses on the lawn, "as if it too questioned the universe" (11). She tries to identify what was different, not so much with the tailless cat, but in the present world, which lacks the "humming noise" that existed before the war and the women's movement, and before she started raising questions. She explains away her resulting laughter with a gesture toward her co-conspirator, the Manx cat. In the subsequent conversation come the judgment that the cat "did look a little absurd, poor beast, without a tail," questions about whether the cat was "really born so, or had he lost his tail in an accident," and observations that "it is a queer animal, quaint rather than beautiful. It is strange what a difference a tail makes— you know the sort of things one says as a lunch party breaks up" (13). If an authentic Manx cat, the visitor would be a distinct breed possessing a genetic mutation that altered its spine. On an isolated island, this mutation could dominate the cat population. In their comments, the guests do not go this far into science, but the cat has queered the conversation, taking it beyond considerations of beauty, opening up ideas related to genetics and evolution.[17] "The sort of things one says as a lunch party breaks up" cannot pass as trivial in this modernist text.

Dogs glimpsed as the companions of young women in Woolf's novels seem to work as palliatives for disaffected lives. Clara may rely on dog walking to get her out of the house once she loses the attentions of the young hero of *Jacob's Room*. When he attempts to engage his daughter Cam in conversation as they sail to the lighthouse, Mr. Ramsay grasps as a subject the new puppy she has acquired. In *Mrs. Dalloway*, girls take their "absurd wooly dogs for a run" (5). The confinement of Grizzle (who is heard howling) provides Elizabeth with yet another reason to dislike attending a party.[18] Clarissa, before her, has been equally dedicated to her dog.

Dog selection in *Orlando* is largely dictated by gender, period, and aristocratic preference. In the early seventeenth century, young Orlando turns to his elk hounds when his love life or poetic career are floundering. His mastiff obligingly bites the unappreciative Nick Greene (85). The female Orlando, like her real-life model, Vita Sackville-West, has a spaniel named Pippin. The narrator investigates the variety and meaning of dogs' responsiveness. "They wag their tails; they bow the front part of the body and elevate the hind; they roll, they jump, they paw, the whine, they bark, they slobber; they have all sorts of ceremonies and artifices of their own, but the whole thing is of no avail, since speak they cannot" (195–96). The premium placed on human language falls short of co-species communication envisioned by Haraway, and of Orlano's own needs. By the time she expresses this, Orlando is complaining of the behavior of the aristocrats of Arlington House. She misses time spent with Pippin, clearly a better friend, and one whose messages would bear more careful deciphering.

Coevolution in *Flush*

Like *Orlando*, Woolf's biography of Elizabeth Barrett Browning's dog Flush was a loving gesture toward Vita Sackville-West, who had given her Pinka, the cocker spaniel pictured on the cover of both Hogarth Press and American editions (figure 33). *Flush* sustains Woolf's interests in biography and lives of

FIGURE 33. Cover picture of Pinka as Flush. (Monk's
House Album 3, MS Thr 560, Harvard Theatre Collection,
Houghton Library, Harvard University)

the obscure. Flush and Miss Barrett's loyal maid, Wilson, pose comparable
challenges of depicting marginality to the biographer.[19] Critics have found serious study of the politics of gender in this unlikely place. Robert Browning's
challenge to Flush's relationship with Elizabeth Barrett has been compared to
disruptions in Woolf's relationships with Sackville-West and Vanessa Bell.[20]

The literary playfulness demonstrated in Woolf's previous biographical
experiments continues in *Flush*. Woolf begins with a spoof of etymology,
which merges into evolutionary and even creationist approaches. Woolf

plunges back "many million years ago," going to Spain, as it "seethed uneasily in the ferment of creation. Ages passed; vegetation appeared; where there is vegetation the law of Nature has decreed that there shall be rabbits; where there are rabbits, Providence has ordained there shall be dogs" (11). To serve etymology, Woolf supplies anonymous historians and a romantic scene to establish that Carthaginians, seeing rabbits as they landed in Spain, named it "Span" for rabbit; the dogs chasing said rabbits became spaniels (12).[21] In the name of "truth," and as a dig at theory, she admits two additional derivations, neither of them related to rabbits, and only indirectly concerned with dogs.[22] Pamela Caughie suggests further that Woolf was playing with notions of high and low literature, alongside notions of high and low breeding (*Woolf and Postmodernism* 146–47).

Flush has impressed numerous critics as a study of women's conditioning under patriarchy. Miss Mitford, Flush's first mistress, lives under the grip of a wastrel father (whom Woolf, applying a doggy standard, knows the Spaniel Club would never have permitted to breed). Mitford rewards herself for her day's writing by walking the fields with her dogs (a reward Woolf also gave herself).[23] After Flush relinquishes his pungent, outdoor life with Miss Mitford, he must accommodate to urban confinement with a strange new mistress. He occupies an invalid's bedroom or walks a park that requires dogs to be leashed. Woolf supplies a "chain" as the confining device, suggesting forms of brutality and enslavement (38). Flush also encounters the demanding patriarch, Mr. Barrett, who visits his daughter each evening, enforcing her medical regimen. Flush's reaction is both terrified and modernist: "So a savage crouched in flowers shudders when the thunder growls and he hears the voice of God" (51). On one level Woolf would seem to attribute less evolved behavior to the "savage" for superstitiously associating an ominous natural force with God. Yet creatures intelligently fear thunder for the destructive potential of lightning; it can be equally intelligent to fear patriarchal oppression. Both scenarios bring the concept of a vengeful Judeo-Christian God into question. Flush is transformed in this environment, assuming timorous, hypersensitive traits. Still, he is a co-conspirator against authority, helping Elizabeth dispose of her enforced diet. Woolf, having been assigned bed rest and a cloying diet by medical authority, could well appreciate this assistance.

The exquisitely bred Flush, like Woolf's own Shag, sees himself as an aristocrat, a class that unceasingly fascinated Woolf, if only for satire. She has fun comparing the greater rigors of the Spaniel Club to the standards of the Heralds College, in its "attempt to preserve the purity of the human family" (*F* 15). She seems quite aware of the Victorian programs for controlled breeding described in Ritvo's *Animal Estate.*[24] *Flush* augments Woolf's other mappings of London, ranging from the privileged, imperial enclaves of Wimpole and Oxford streets to the surprisingly nearby squalor of Whitechapel, where lowlife kidnappers hold him for ransom. Only when he arrives in Italy does Flush appreciate a more democratic, mongrelized society, in an extended affair with a "spotted" spaniel.

Flush allows us to consider a coevolution, with mutual receptivity between woman and dog. He comes into Barrett's life at a decisive stage, some years ahead of Mr. Browning's appearance. He finds a serious invalid in a patriarchal household. Flush carries on as a participant observer through courtship, marriage, relocation in Italy, and the birth and babyhood of a son. From his earliest days with Miss Mitford, as befits a Victorian dog, Flush is capable of "excessive appreciation of human emotions." Seeing her taking in fresh air "excited him to gambols whose wildness was half sympathy with her own delight" (19–20).

Woolf sets up a mutual encounter as Barrett and her dog share their first moments together. This begins with exchanged looks, each "surprised" at their similarity in appearance (30). "As they gazed at each other each felt: Here am I—and then each felt: But how different! . . . Broken asunder, yet made in the same mould, could it be that each completed what was dormant in the other?" (31). As in *Orlando,* Woolf here uses language as a basis of profound difference: "Between them lay the widest gulf that can separate one being from another. She spoke. He was dumb" (31). There is something familiar in the juxtaposed positions of Woolf's description—comparable to the reasoning of Woolf's protagonist in *A Room of One's Own* as she recognizes that the beadle is throwing her off the turf of Oxbridge. It repeats received order rather than achieved understanding. Human speech establishes difference in the tradition of Western philosophy (the anthropological machine) traced by Agamben. As the book proceeds, it emerges that Flush has unique abilities, agency, and capacity to adapt.

Remade by what Woolf calls the "bedroom school" (*F* 43), Flush learns "to resign, to control, to suppress the most violent instincts of his nature" (42). We enter Flush's decision-making process: "Between them, Flush felt more and more strongly, as the weeks wore on, was a bond, an uncomfortable yet thrilling tightness; so that if his pleasure was her pain, then his pleasure was pleasure no longer but three parts pain" (43). Miss Barrett comes to her own understanding: "'Flushie,' writes Miss Barrett, 'is my friend—my companion—and loves me better than he loves the sunshine without'" (43). She has a fantasy that he is Pan and she, a nymph, and preserves this vision of mutuality in poetry (46).

Flush can read changes in Miss Barrett's affections, and detects clues about her plans with Browning long before the Barretts do. He must think through his hatred of the rival Mr. Browning, whom he twice goes to the length of biting. Flush gradually surmises, "If he bit Mr. Browning he bit her too. Hatred is not hatred; hatred is also love. . . . Mr. Browning was Miss Barrett—Miss Barrett was Mr. Browning; love is hatred and hatred is love." Flush takes on a doggie performative. He communicates his change in attitude, or so Miss Barrett interprets, first by gazing with rapture on Mr. Browning's armchair, and then by eating cakes brought by his former enemy, even though stale and "bereft of any carnal seduction" (79). Flush becomes leagued with them.

Woolf also sketches out something sensual and primal in Flush that remains accessible in his dream states, and reasserts itself when he pulls away from human kind. Interestingly, humans are very deep down in his unconscious, and he can sometimes hear the early, dark, Carthaginian hunters shouting "Span, span" as dog and human hunt rabbits, experiencing the mutual pleasure Haraway seeks from companion animals. Flush's quintessential activity is to romp through a field, flushing out partridge and hares, smelling the soil and the flowers, and feeling the texture of the soil beneath his feet. When he first enters 50 Wimpole Street, he tries to apply these skills—taking in the meaty smells of the kitchen, the whiff of people, wooden furniture, and curtains, and the texture of carpet. Eau de cologne is a final insult to his system (28). From puppyhood onward, Flush has sexual desire for other dogs, culturally couched in terms of the hunting horn and Venus (21). In this sexual aspect, he is the envy of the woman writer, and in presenting it, she invokes the sorts of veils and camouflages traditionally employed in writing about human sexuality. It is part of the mutual existence of Miss Barrett and Flush, established over time and geographical as well as familial changes, that he can release himself periodically into these basic fantasies and physical recreations.

Fishing for Freedom

Given their contact with families in possession of country homes and estates, the Stephens could observe and participate in the sports of hunting and fishing. Through courtship, these activities found an intimate place in the Stephen family, encouraging a mental association between women and hunted creatures. Julia Stephen's first husband, Herbert Duckworth, posed proudly with his gun in a photo at his family seat. John Waller "Jack" Hills, who courted Stella Duckworth for many years, shared various outdoor recreations with Stella's younger half brothers and sisters.[25] He presented them with Frances Orpen Morris's book on butterflies and moths and taught them the sugaring techniques they applied to their moth hunting—a venture Quentin Bell would jokingly label their "blood-sport" (*Virginia Woolf* 113). Hills provided Virginia the opportunity to study a dedicated angler when, in 1897, the Stephens visited his family home at Corby Castle, Cumberland. The visit came soon after Stella's untimely death, probably from complications of pregnancy. Virginia disliked watching him fish, and may have been inclined thereafter to connect fishing with victimization and troubling sexual entanglements.

Giles Oliver combined courtship with fishing, as Isa recalls in *Between the Acts*. Her story of submission merges with the capture of a salmon, a fish associated with magical powers as well as vigorous sport in Celtic tradition: "They had met first in Scotland, fishing—she from one rock, he from another. Her line had got tangled; she had given over, and had watched him with the stream rushing between his legs, casting, casting—until, like a thick ingot of silver bent in the middle, the salmon had leapt, had been caught, and she had loved him" (33). In her married life, Isa has restricted access to fish, and not very magical fish at that. She orders filleted soles—bottom fish—hoping they will be fresh for luncheon. The elderly Lucy, in contrast, remembers salmon so fresh they still had lice on their scales. A more severe case of a woman lost to fishing occurs in *Mrs. Dalloway*. We learn that "once, long ago [Lady Bradshaw] had caught salmon freely," but that "fifteen years ago she had gone under"; "there had been no scene, no snap; only the slow sinking, water-logged, of her will" into that of the domineering Dr. Bradshaw (98).

Leslie Stephen reportedly had great respect for the resident fishermen of Cornwall and regularly conversed with them. There was perhaps a manly bond, founded on respect for laborers. Stephen includes a photo of their netting operations in his photo album (figure 34). He did not like his children to fish, though he did not prevent them. The family heard local lore of great schools of pilchards captured at St. Ives, and they were disappointed never to have seen a good run of these small fish. There may have been a feeling that something of nature had been lost, or that the coming of the pilchards was beyond human command. A related phenomenon (though not strictly with a fish) is the mystical communion afforded by the fin of the porpoise spotted by Virginia Stephen off Cornwall, when she and her siblings returned there in 1905. In *The Waves*, Bernard records a similar observation in his notebook: "I see far out a waste of water. A fin turns. This bare visual impression is unattached to any line of reason, it springs up as one might see the fin of a porpoise on the horizon" (137–38). Today, in the wake of the worst oil spill in history in the Gulf of Mexico, a fin in a "waste of water" accrues new, deadly meaning.

Perhaps recalled from Woolf's childhood, there is a troubling experience of fishing in the final part of *To the Lighthouse*. As the boat bearing Mr. Ramsay, James, and Cam approaches the lighthouse, "Macalister's boy" is engaged in fishing: "[Macalister's boy took one of the fish and cut a square out of its side to bait his hook with. The mutilated body (it was alive still) was thrown back into the sea]" (183). This brief passage stands as section 6 in the narrative, and its square brackets are reminiscent of the device used to report human fatalities in the middle section of the novel. That the fish was "mutilated" while still alive suggests vivisection. Vivisection was protested by Woolf's contemporaries, including Charlotte Perkins Gilman, and serves as a pretext for the present-day ecofeminist ethic of care (Donovan, "Attention to Suffering"). We do not know who observes this act, if indeed anyone does. The report could manifest Woolf's cosmic register, which regularly takes on a broad, detached view of a scene in which humans are relatively small players. The passive construction, in which the fish "was thrown back," subtracts human agency from inhumane treatment of a creature, much as "objective" scientific discourse of methodology does, as Lynda Birke has argued. Cam is the character most likely to have seen this desecration. We share her perceptions at the start of section 8. Mr. Ramsay's gaze is fastened to his book; James's, to the sail. Cam's first thought, "They don't feel a thing there" (186), comes as she looks to the shore. Cam feels pressured by both her father and her brother to cave in to their wishes. Her mental note could betray, coincidentally, empathetic feelings for the fish.

FIGURE 34. St. Ives fishing fleet. (Leslie Stephen Photo Album, Mortimer Rare Book Room, Smith College)

Lucy Swithin bears into old age unpleasant childhood associations with her brother's fishing—a bloody, coercive, precise activity that contrasts with her self-affirming collection of meadow flowers, bound into "tight little bunches." His "growling" of her childhood nickname, "Cindy," brings back the scene: "Once, she remembered, he had made her take the fish off the hook herself. The blood had shocked her—'Oh!' she had cried—for the gills were full of blood" (*BA* 15). Lucy maintains her spirit in the face of her brother's lifelong despotism, and she has Isa's silent endorsement for her resistance. Lucy's faith is rewarded when, toward the end of the novel, the fish in the lily pond surface: first "her favorite fantail. The golden orfe followed. Then she had a glimpse of silver—the great carp himself, who came to the surface so very seldom" (139). Although she goes to get them crumbs, the fish aren't necessarily lured to the surface by the behaviorist rewards system old Bart believes in. Lucy's is a different form of fishing, one in which woman and fish merge as "ourselves" (139). Her conduct resonates with female primatologists such as Barbara Hardy, Jane Goodall, and Dian Fossey, with their mode of passive viewing. Hers is more devotional, less voyeuristic.

Woolf's 1928 essay "The Sun and the Fish" brings together her experiences of a solar eclipse in Yorkshire and a visit to the new aquarium at the Regent's Park Zoo. Metaphorically, fish are wedded to depths of water, which serves often as a figure of the mind to Woolf. Nearly contemporaneous with the fish viewed at the aquarium is the metaphorical fish, representing a lost idea, in *A Room of One's Own*—its loss occasioned by the narrator's ejection from the lawn of the men's college. Woolf experiences the long rows of fish tanks as "squares of immortality, worlds of settled sunshine, where there is neither rain nor cloud" (*E* 4:523), striking a contrast to the diminishing color and fading light of the eclipse.

As she would write of Lucy Swithin's reception of fish in *Between the Acts*, reason has little to do with her apprehension. "Blue and silver armies, keeping a perfect distance for all their arrowlike quickness, shoot first this way, then that. The discipline is perfect, the control absolute; reason there is none. The most majestic of human evolutions seems feeble and fluctuating compared with theirs" (*E* 4:523). There are a lot of contrasts to human existence here, including her unusual use of the word "evolution" to remind us of the theory that would place humans and their reason as most evolved of creatures. She insists instead that fish evolve more remarkably, and she finds original analogies to describe their physical beauty and variety. Humans' idea of purpose is irrelevant here: "The fish themselves seem to have been shaped deliberately and slipped into the world only to be themselves. They neither work nor weep. In their shape is their reason" (*E* 4:523). In sum, "more care has been spent upon half a dozen fish than upon all the races of men." Humans having only "a monotony of pink nakedness," we emerge from the essay grateful not "to be turned naked into an aquarium" (*E* 4:524).[26]

Privileges and Oppressions of Hunting

Virginia Woolf had an excellent capacity to detect the hunt beneath the social fabric of British male privilege. She notes that the typical cause for letter writing by members of the great House of Lyme was "generally provided by some cock-fight or horse-race or business connected with the famous herd of red deer," or happiness over having killed a fox ("The House of Lyme," *E* 2:99–100). Elsewhere, she characterizes the "nobleman happy among his collection of antlers" (*E* 3:90). It is very important to an ancestor of the Olivers in *Between the Acts* that he be depicted with his horse and hound, or so one observer tells the story of the painting still displayed at Pointz Hall.

Woolf's 1938 story "The Shooting Party" presents a particularly brutal old country squire, the last surviving male of an ancient family that once explored the Amazon and went "nosing round the islands" taking emeralds and captive maidens (*CSF* 255). We view a cartload of newly shot birds, "with soft warm bodies, with limp claws, and still lustrous eyes" (255). These are taken "by the neck and flung . . . on the slate floor of the game larder," which "became smeared and spotted with blood" (257). When he enters the room where his two elderly sisters and their spaniel have been consuming a pheasant, the squire's hounds assault the spaniel, and he whips both the dogs and his sisters (their cheeks were already scarred). One stroke brings the family arms and spears hung above the mantle smashing down on Miss Rashleigh. In the frame of the tale, the surviving sister transports a brace of pheasants by train. She both suffers from and lives off the culture of the hunt.[27]

In his letters, Thoby Stephen reports hunting both stag and fox, though often with some reservations. He confides to Clive Bell that he didn't consider himself a good enough shot to participate in a proposed "big shoot."[28] Thoby tells his friend about various attempts to track down some of England's remaining wild creatures—badgers and otters—and proposes that they take out otter hounds in Devon or Wales. While courting Vanessa in 1902, Bell presented the family with braces of partridges and quail. He "came from a society which hunted birds, animals, and, in his case, girls," as his son Quentin quips (*Virginia Woolf* 103). In his jocularity, Quentin confirms the connection, suggested above, between women and animals sought in the hunt. He goes on to describe the Bell family home, Cleeve House in Wiltshire: "The place was populated by stuffed animals and to a large extent by living ones; animals dominated the conversation, yielding only occasionally to lawn tennis, hockey, and the weather. The human inhabitants had something of the bucolic health of brutes, something of their ferocity, something of their niceness and a good deal of their intellectual limitations" (113). Staying at Cleeve House some years later, Virginia was amazed to be using an inkwell fashioned from a cherished mount's hoof.

Leonard Woolf figures uniquely among Bloomsbury sportsmen. When he departed for Ceylon as a colonial administrator, Woolf brought a favorite dog from home; he acquired others while there. Leonard and a friend kept a small menagerie in their compound, including a leopard obtained as a cub, a monkey they chained to the roof, and a deer. The advisability of keeping such stock becomes questionable when we learn that each of them, in turn, met with accidental deaths, or in the case of the monkey, probable assassination by servants. Leonard's diary confides that he shot hare, birds, and stags for sport, and he pursued both bear and leopard, sitting up all night at a waterhole, on one occasion.[29] Though, like Thoby, Leonard modestly claims to have been a poor shot, he did bring down at least one leopard, which he pursued for humane reasons after another hunter had wounded it.

Leonard Woolf's biography presents an increasingly reluctant hunter. Part of his job was to issue hunting licenses, a responsibility that made him skeptical of visiting European hunters. Applicants included Baron Blixen, husband of Isak Dinesen, who failed to convince Leonard of his ability to shoot anything without the help of a big game guide. Woolf remarks cynically, "A great deal of this big-business, organized safari or whatever they called the thing in Colombo was despicable butchery" (*Growing* 221). Leonard's own hunting expeditions are usually explained as necessary for amusing visitors or for eliminating a creature endangering the native population. He describes stalking a leopard that had been troubling villagers: "Suddenly with no warning, without my seeing a movement of his approach, there was the leopard standing upright a few yards from me, staring straight into my eyes. I looked straight into his eyes, fascinated, so fascinated by his ferocious eyes and his magnificent beauty that I could not shoot, did not think of shooting" (*Growing* 196). Back in Britain courting Virginia Stephen, Leonard recalls a conversation with Clive Bell and Virginia concerning shooting. They posed the question, "Does one take pleasure in the killing?" I have found no evidence that Leonard was a hunter later in life.

Quentin Bell found Leonard "extremely unsentimental" in regard to animals: "He was gruff, abrupt, a systematic disciplinarian, extremely good at seeing that his dogs were obedient, healthy, and happy" (*Virginia Woolf* 175). Leonard himself can be expansive in expressing his relationship to animals: "I do not know why I am so fond of animals. They give me the greatest pleasure both emotionally and intellectually. I get deep affection for cats and dogs, and indeed for almost every kind of animal which I have kept. But I also derive very great pleasure from understanding them, *their* emotions and *their* minds. They are, too, as I have said, usually amazingly beautiful." Accused by Lytton Strachey of being sentimental, he responds, "There grows up between you affection of a purity and simplicity which seems to me peculiarly satisfactory. There is also a cosmic strangeness about animals which always fascinates me and gives to my affection for them a mysterious depth or background" (*Growing* 100). He concludes that animals "make nonsense of all philosophies and religions" (101). Perhaps as a vestige of his colonial past, Leonard kept a tiny marmoset, Mitzi, who gained a reputation as an excessively messy creature, to be avoided by the Woolfs' guests (figure 35).[30]

The hunt and big game animals make occasional appearances in Woolf's novels. We have already found Jacob on his fox hunt in the New Forest. His father died absurdly and prematurely of wet feet following a duck hunt. Bernard also hunts at a country house in *The Waves* as one of his male rites of passage.

In the opening of *Orlando*, a heraldic leopard in stained glass casts its colors on young Orlando as he thrusts his sword at a shrunken head. His actions are tinted by the imperial conquests of his male ancestors over native men and big cats. Regendered Lady Orlando, our heroine expresses boredom at Archduke Harry's hunting stories: "The Archduke would bethink him how he had shot an elk in Sweden, and Orlando would ask, was it a very big elk, and the Archduke would say that it was not as big as the reindeer which he had shot in Norway; and Orlando would ask, had he ever shot a tiger, and the Archduke would say he had shot an albatross, and Orlando would say (half hiding her yawn) was an albatross as big as an elephant, and the Archduke would say—something very sensible, no doubt, but Orlando heard it not, for she was looking at her writing table, out of the window, at the door" (181).

The pursuit of big game and his fear of the pouncing panther or leopard haunt the memory of Bart Oliver in *Between the Acts,* one of Woolf's elderly men back from India. At the conclusion of the novel, the wild fox and vixen are imagined fighting before they mate. They escape for the moment the violence of the hunt, but Woolf does not romanticize their relations in a place beyond the boundary of civilization; she shows them sharing human behaviors.

Sharing Life and Death with Insects

Woolf's mock-heroic description of the scientific moth hunt, in which Thoby takes on the role of great white hunter, has already claimed our attention in chapter 2. In this sketch Woolf admits her own complicity. In "Butterflies and Moths: Insects in September," a 1916 article in the *Times* signed "From a Correspondent," Woolf reminisces about a child's hunt over the moors after a Clouded Yellow and beautifully describes the visit of a Death's Head Hawk

FIGURE 35. Mitz. (Monk's House Album 3, MS Thr 560, Harvard Theatre
Collection, Houghton Library, Harvard University)

moth to Asham House (*E* 6:382). Insects, especially the moth and the butterfly, have aesthetic importance in many of her works. In *To the Lighthouse,*
the butterfly provides Lily Briscoe with structural help as she makes a second
attempt at her painting. Sensitive to the "down" on the butterfly's wing, Lily
develops an artistic analogy—a metaphor for her painting's requirements:
"Beautiful and bright it should be on the surface, feathery and evanescent,
one colour melting into another like the colours on a butterfly's wing; but
beneath the fabric must be clamped together with bolts of iron" (174). Nature
and culture are firmly connected in this concept.

Insects frequently move in on Woolf and her characters, providing not
just aesthetic appeal, but an alternative to rational thinking and guidance in
comprehending the place of death in nature.[31] Rachel Vinrace of *The Voyage Out* is the first of Woolf's characters to be associated with butterflies and
moths. She observes "a great yellow butterfly, which was opening and closing
its wings very slowly on a little flat stone" and spends some time "hypno-
tized" by its wings. When it parts, she rises, prepared to take on the "terrible
possibility" of love (173–74). A more symbolic moth joins the hotel visitors

as they wait out a violent storm, following Rachel's death. The moth is aged and dull, "grey of wing and shiny of thorax." As it flies into various lamps, a young woman thinks "it would be kinder to kill it" (370). Its survival suggests that Rachel can both haunt and flee the culture that claimed her.

No other character in Woolf's writing is more closely associated with moths than Jacob, the character who most closely resembles Thoby as the great moth hunter. Jacob's butterfly box provides a useful pivot to all the places he goes to collect specimens, and by extension, it offers a route into his powers of observation, memory, and allied interests: "The pale clouded yellows had pelted over the moor; they had zigzagged across the purple clover. The fritillaries flaunted along the hedgerows. The blues settled on little bones lying on the turf with the sun beating on them, and the painted ladies and peacocks feasted upon bloody entrails dropped by a hawk. Miles away from home, in a hollow among teasles beneath a ruin, he had found the commas. He had seen a white admiral circling higher and higher round an oak tree, but he had never caught it" (24). Later in the novel, Woolf behaves like a moth to observe what she needs for her story, including sexually charged scenes between Jacob and Bonamy: "Something is always impelling one to hum vibrating, like the hawk moth, at the mouth of the cavern of mystery" (73). Jacob, like Thoby, gravitates toward a complex of creatures—foxes and badgers sharing the territories of butterflies and moths. His lantern in the forest attracts not just moths but a large toad. He decides "something senseless inspires them" (32)—the "senseless" betraying the limits of his own reason. This vivid memory, which ends with the death of a tree in the forest, cracking like a volley of pistol shots, diverts his attention from a service in King's College Chapel, and his irritation that women should be present. It is clearly of a different order.

A working title for *The Waves* was *The Moths*. To Susan, Rhoda's eyes resemble the flowers moths come to (16). Struggling with mathematical figures on the blackboard, Rhoda resembles a butterfly to Louis: "Her shoulder-blades meet across her back like the wings of a small butterfly" and "her mind lodges in those white circles; it steps through those white loops into emptiness, alone" (22). Rhoda and Louis are the only children who do not net butterflies in play, and Louis characterizes the "boasting boys" as the ones who "leave butterflies trembling with their wings pinched off" (47).

For Woolf, cocoon and chrysalis—the caterpillar's protective casings as it transforms to moth or butterfly—are typical metaphors for female withdrawal and emergence into a different world. In *The Waves,* Susan spots a caterpillar and has her own cocoon for retreat. Rachel of *The Voyage Out* and Sara of *The Years* possess the chrysalis.[32] Harvena Richter associates this chrysalis stage with Woolf's illnesses and a period of withdrawal that could be creatively productive.

One of Woolf's most contemplative essays is "The Death of the Moth," in which she observes the gradually lessening activities of a day-flying moth. Like a naturalist, she places it among similar species, though in her own system this is further defined by the attitudes of the human observer: "They are hybrid creatures, neither gay like butterflies nor somber like their own species." Somber night-flying moths "excite" in her "that pleasant sense of dark autumn nights and ivy-blossom." The initial mood of this humble moth is that it "seemed to be content with life." It shared the same energy expressed by other creatures (rooks, ploughmen, horses) on a mild mid-September morning. This construct suggests the Gaia concept of the globe as a united, living thing, a holistic concept we will return to in the next chapter. The mood of the essay alters as Woolf pities the self-imposed limits of the moth, banging around on a single pane of glass, when the wide expanse of the downs lies just beyond the house. Slowly she recognizes that this relatively plain, obscure creature, of limited range, is struggling with the enormous question of death. It falls on its back, but Woolf resists using her pencil to right it, opting to be a passive observer. The moth wins her respect by deliberately righting itself, achieving what the woman writer constructs as composure.[33] With her sense of shared energy, respect for composure, and common yielding to death, Woolf develops unity and solidarity across distant species.

The Society of Birds

Virginia Woolf's uses of birds in her works are probably more various and hence more interesting than her interactions with any other creature. Her precise recording of their movements could have come from observations shared by Thoby, whose early enthusiasm for collecting insects gradually yielded to watching birds and representing their habits scrupulously in a notebook.[34] All is not admiration. At fifteen, Woolf has harsh words for sparrows that move in on grass seed she has planted in the back garden, twittering to one another as if in communication: "the horrid little creatures swooped down twittering & made off with the oats" (*PA* 96). Starting with "Kew Gardens" and culminating with the intervals of *The Waves,* Woolf follows birds about the business of survival, and describes their habits of hunting and consuming prey precisely and realistically. Woolf makes use of birds in mental as well as physical descriptions of characters. One of the best-known symptoms of her own mental illness is the hallucination of birds saying nasty things in Greek—a symptom extended to Septimus Smith in *Mrs. Dalloway.*[35] A "beak of brass" is attached to Mr. Ramsay in order to show him as a demanding father and husband in *To the Lighthouse;* his attack with metallic beak suggests a mechanical bird, or the Stymphalian Birds setting upon Hercules in one of his twelve labors.[36] Reapplying the metaphor to herself as she negotiates the writing of *A Room of One's Own,* Woolf suggests, "I should need claws of steel and beak of brass even to penetrate the husk" (*AROO* 26).[37] Like moths, butterflies, and fish, birds can provide magical, mystical connections and serve libratory functions, but they also have intentions of their own and can model frightening, invasive acts attributable to humans.

Nowhere do birds help more in characterization than they do in *To the Lighthouse.* We have Mr. Ramsay, not just wielding his beak of brass, but also standing like a solitary sea bird on a spit of land, where he feels the paternal duty of protecting his family (47). Mrs. Ramsay may represent a mother hen to Mr. Bankes, but in her moment of satisfaction at the end of the dinner scene, she feels like a hawk suspended (106). Mrs. Ramsay's thoughts and Cam's flight are described as birdlike for their speed, with the text moving in quick succession from Lily's description of Mrs. Ramsay (52) to Mrs. Ramsay's description of Cam (57). Words are the birds that the catlike poet Mr. Carmichael claps his paws to capture (99). Both protagonists in *Mrs. Dalloway* are birdlike to observers. We have noted Mrs. Dalloway's likeness to a jay; Septimus reminds his wife, Rezia, of a young hawk or a crow (145). *Between the Acts* has a host of characters described in terms of birds. As night settles upon the opening page, there is a bird "chuckling over the substance and succulence of the day, over worms, snails, grit, even in sleep" (3). The "goosefaced" Mrs. Haines has "eyes protruding as if they saw something to gobble in the gutter" (3) and she later is expected to attack any possible emotion felt between her husband and Isa "as a thrush plucks the wings off a butterfly" (6). Isa sees herself and Haines as swans, tangled in the duckweed. Miss La Trobe "cast her quick bird's eye over the bushes at the audience," anxious that she might lose them (103).

Woolf offers a day in the life of birds in the opening scenes of the first four interludes of *The Waves*. As light strikes the trees in the first interlude, "one bird chirped high up; there was a pause; another chirped lower down . . . The birds sand their blank melody outside" (3). This seems to invite the artist and her characters to fill in the song. The first to notice birds, Rhoda, picks up on the dynamics of sound: *"cheep, chirp; cheep, chirp; going up and down"* (4). The birds' capacity to sing together in a *"strain"* (19) or a *"chorus"* (52) increases in the second and third interludes. The narrator applies musical terms of human derivation, but uses "as if" cautiously when suggesting motivations appropriate to humans. Birds' activities dominate the third interlude, going on from varieties of song to record motions of flight, and their apprehension of fear *"when the black cat moved among the bushes, when the cook threw cinders on the ash heap."* They chase and peck each other. The narrator follows their *"bright eyes glancing,"* noting a series of vivid objects in the garden. It is a bird/human collaboration, the description enhanced by reference to manmade things. There is *"a snail shell, rising in the grass like a grey cathedral"* and *"a rain drop on the hedge, pendent but not falling, with a whole house bent in it."* The birds are not surface decoration; they obtain what they need to eat *"down the dark avenues into the unlit world where the leaf rots and the flower has fallen. Then one of them, beautifully darting, accurately alighting, spiked the soft, monstrous body of the defenceless worm, pecked again and yet again, and left it to fester"* (52–53). Additional birds *"plunged the tips of their beaks savagely into the sticky mixture"* (53). Their quest for food is just as pitiless and intense in the next interlude, where *"they spied a snail and tapped . . . furiously, methodically, until the shell broke and something slimy oozed from the crack"* (78). Their strident, separate songs at this point are suspiciously like the independent movements of the growing humans in the following chapter.[38] There are additional encounters with birds within chapters of this work. A woodpigeon presides over the woodland reached by Susan and Bernard, fleeing the gardeners at Elvedon. Susan feels less comforted when she realizes that she has lost Bernard to phrase making: "The pigeon beats the air; the pigeon beats the air with wooden wings." Susan responds, "Now you trail away . . . making phrases" (11). In her fantasy of exotic retreat, Rhoda reaches an "island where the parrots chatter" in her petal boat (11). She also has the beautiful vision of the other side of the world where "the swallow dips her wings in dark pools" (75), a winged flight that Neville senses her taking (144). Jenny summons her lovers through various natural devices, including the call of the nightingale (128). Lewis and Neville both have fears they represent through bird images.

For Louis, fear of the past takes form as folded wings of birds (69). He associates himself with one of their victims, the snail. Louis dreads the impaling beak that would be Susan's love (86). Bernard has positive uses for birds— the song of the lark for courtship, that of the nightingale to sing through history (210), and the noise of the sparrows on the plane trees toward the very end of the book, betokening a new dawn (220).

Though she was hardly an expert on birds, Woolf is able to place the right species in the appropriate place. In *The Waves*, parrots chatter on exotic islands and woodpigeons inhabit the woods. Plovers haunt the fields in *The Years*. Doves are a recurrent, even tedious urban element through that novel. They speak the same words to Kitty, Eleanor, and Sara, whether from the eves of an Oxford house or from the trees of London: "Take two coos, Taffy. Take two coos" (70, 108, 178, 411). This is language in Woolf's imagination.

Captive parrots, like pet dogs, are frequently the one compensation of a dull or confined life for women characters. We learn in *To the Lighthouse* that conversation at Minta Doyle's house was "limited to the exploits of the parrot" (60). Woolf hopes that the dull, unappreciated life of Queen Adelaide, the consort of William IV, was enlivened by the "wonderful red and grey parrot" occasionally glimpsed by visitors, and uses this one bright element to frame her essay (*E* 2:19). "The Widow and the Parrot" is a delightful, rarely cited children's story by Woolf, commissioned by her twelve-year-old nephew, Quentin Bell, for his family paper. Set in and around Rodmell, where the widow has come to claim the house and inheritance left to her by a miserly older brother, the story has numerous familiar elements. The widow, Mrs. Gage, leaves at home her faithful dog "Shag." The widow recalls among her brother's childhood cruelties the torturing of insects: "I've known him trim a hairy caterpillar with a pair of scissors before my very eyes." Her principal collaborator is James, a gray seaman's parrot left behind by her brother. The widow's empathy for animals and her concern for James's welfare make her uniquely capable of decoding his messages. The pair secure the treasure, triumphing over both the brother and the bank, to live happily until their nearly simultaneous deaths.

Mystical birds function in several of Woolf's works. There are the swallows that return each year to the great 700-year-old barn of *Between the Acts*. They are cherished by Lucy, the "sister swallow" to her domineering brother: "'They come every year,' she said, 'the same birds'" (71).[39] Starlings pelting a tree for its fruit at the end of the novel trigger the inspiration for Miss La

Trobe's next project in *Between the Acts* (144). Birds also play a role in the resolution of *Orlando*. In Victorian times, Lady Orlando flees to the moors in order to escape expectations placed on her to marry. There, she is showered with the "steel-blue plume" of the rook: "Six feathers had she picked from the grass and drawn between her finger tips and pressed to her lips to feel their smooth, glinting plumage, when she saw, gleaming on the hill-side, a silver pool, mysterious as the lake into which Sir Bedivere flung the sword of Arthur. A single feather quivered in the air and fell into the middle of it" (248). Marmaduke Bonthrop Shelmerdine comes equipped with a "wild, dark-plumed name" and is associated with a succession of birds (250–51). Seafaring gannets roost at his castle in the Hebrides. *Orlando* ends exuberantly with the advent of the kingfisher (reminiscent of the fisher king of the grail myth, whose healing by Percival restores the wasteland) and the wild goose (associated with Thoby after his death). As the kingfisher comes "flashing from bank to bank" down a stream at Kew, it offers Orlando a token of "all fulfillment of natural desire" (294). Shel enters modernity to visit Orlando in his airplane; above his head rises "the wild goose" (329). Orlando has gone through a lifetime of doubting whether nature and writing can ever be mixed, but with the "steel blue plume," s/he may finally have an answer.

Gender versus Environmental Politics

"The Plumage Bill" is probably the most puzzling of Woolf's works in relation to nature and, more specifically, endangered birds. In this essay, written in 1920, Woolf struggles with the environmental movement of her day over issues of female representation in their campaign to save birds killed in the millions for their fashionable plumes. The defense of birds was an issue that engaged Woolf's female contemporaries. The Royal Society for the Protection of Birds, founded in 1899 and chartered as "Royal" in 1904, had women leaders and originally did not admit men to membership. Their tactics included shaming women for their plumed headgear (Gates, *Kindred Nature* 117)—a tactic Woolf disapproved in her essay. The ecofeminist Joni Seager has more recently taken issue with the environmental group Lynx for the gender bias expressed in advertisements that similarly shame women as consumers of fur.[40]

Rather than support "A Wayfarer" (H. W. Massingham) in his promotion of a bill prohibiting the importation of egret plumes, Woolf faults his argument on feminist principles.[41] Her diary suggests that she wrote her essay, which appeared in the *Woman's Leader*, at the urging of its editor, Ray Strachey. Woolf launches into the assignment with drama and gusto. "If I had the money and the time I should, after reading 'Wayfarer' in the *Nation* of 10 July, go to Regent Street, buy an egret plume and stick it—is it in the back or the front of the hat?—and this in spite of a vow taken in childhood, and hitherto religiously observed" (*E* 3:241). With the childhood vow, we are transported to the Stephen children's engagement of natural history, and to a little girl's empathy for an injured bird. In her plan of revenge, Woolf provides the ironic cue that she doesn't even know which way the feather should go into a hat, and we feel confident that she has not the money, nor the time, nor the inclination to carry it out.

Woolf then identifies problems with Massingham's argument, which indicts women for vanity for wanting to display themselves in feathered hats. He essentializes women in connection with childbearing, finding it a betrayal for women to endanger other breeding creatures. Woolf quotes him: "They [the egrets] have to be shot in parenthood for child-bearing women to flaunt the symbols of it" (*E* 3:241). She repeats this statement several times for emphasis and self-incrimination. She counters Massingham's essentialism by balancing "child-bearing women" with reference to "child-begetting men" (243). Woolf then complicates Massingham's argument by providing dramatic contexts for the plumage industry in a pair of imagined scenes. The first joins the woman on Regent Street, explaining the attraction of the plumes; the second exposes the violent deeds of men in commerce.

On Regent Street, Woolf points out the diversity of the women walking there. Most can only afford to window shop, to "steal a look." Woolf does not fault women for finding the plumes "lovely": "For, after all, what can be more ethereally and fantastically lovely? The plumes seem to be the natural adornment of spirited and fastidious life, the very symbols of pride and distinction" (242). Here positive qualities of life span the species: spirit, fastidiousness, pride, and distinction. Next she spots a woman "of a different class altogether," though not necessarily a superior class. Her clothes and posture are "more delightful than any other object in street or window." But she is an "object," she has a "stupid face, and the look she sweeps over the shop windows has something of the greedy petulance of a pug-dog's face at tea-time." Crossing species in a negative way, Woolf casts her as a spoiled and greedy pet. There is something disgusting when her "silver bag disgorges I know not how many notes" (242). We might wonder whose pet she is. Regent Street thus offers different stories about women, display, and consumption.

In her second scene, Woolf takes us to the locus of the hunt in South America, elaborating the violence and inhumanity of the deliberately planned bird capture, but only gradually arriving at the gender of the perpetrator. Her details anticipate Susan Griffin's depiction of Audubon's methods of stalking an eagle, disturbing its nest, shooting it, piercing it with wires to achieve a desired pose, then painting it meticulously (113–14). Woolf leads into the scene through a circling "bird with a beautiful plume," which proves to be a blinded decoy (E 3:242). She mentions wounded birds that "flutter off to droop and falter in the dust" and baby birds left to rot in the nest, when parents, seized in full mating plumage, fail to return. The scene culminates with a return to the decoy birds, revealing the process that blinded them: "But perhaps the most unpleasant sight that we must make ourselves imagine is the sight of the bird tightly held in one hand while another hand pierces the eyeballs with a feather. But these hands—are they the hands of men or of women?" (242).[42] Masculine metonymy reaches the East End traders who import the plumes, and the legislators who are stalling the plumage bill in Parliament. Some years later, in *Three Guineas*, Woolf would write to her male recipient, "Scarcely a human being in the course of history has fallen to a woman's rifle; the vast majority of birds and beasts have been killed by you; not by us" (9).

Woolf admits that her "Plumage Bill" argument is "much embittered by sex antagonism" (E 3:243). She does set up a gender binary, finding that direct blame can be placed more on men for their torture and profit from birds, than on women for the "vicarious" pleasure they take from the plumes. Approaching gender responsibility in another way, she wonders why only the sale of bird plumes on Oxford Street is questioned. "Such an outburst about a fishing-rod would be deemed sentimental in the extreme. Yet I suppose that salmon have their feelings" (243). As discussed above, she went on in *To the Lighthouse* to suggest that a mackerel slashed for bait deserves compassion. Woolf's introduction of feeling as a criterion also anticipates the arguments of ecofeminist ethicists such as Josephine Donovan, which focus upon the concept of "sympathy" that attends to suffering. Donovan finds that "the dominant strain in contemporary ethics reflects a male bias toward rationality" expressed in "the construction of abstract universals that elide not just the personal, the contextual, and the emotional, but also the political components of an ethical issue" (174–76). Turning from Kantian, reason-based ethics, with its assumption that animals are instrumental to human needs, Donovan pursues an alternate tradition of emotionally based ethics. This invites complex imaginative constructions and analysis of nature's own expressive language. The fit with Woolf is a fine one, and we will return to this in the final chapter. As we have seen in chapter 1, a bias against the sentimental figured strongly in early formulations of modernism.

Woolf ends her essay with a question: "Can it be that it is a graver sin to be unjust to women than to torture birds?" This question, by seeming to ask us to privilege humans over birds, poses some difficulty. It stands to make the feminist species-ist. One solution is to read it against the grain, to say that the question should not be asked; it is a false dichotomy playing into the binary system of male dominance decried throughout ecofeminist analysis. Working out her own epistemology in the process of "The Plumage Bill," as she would do later throughout *A Room of One's Own,* Woolf challenges both a biased gendering of animal exploitation, and the epistemologies that might argue that one must choose between animals and women, or between rationality and sympathy. The phrase "graver sin" in this puzzling question can be taken as another ironic cue. Did Woolf, a second-generation agnostic, believe in gradations of sin? Indeed, it emerges that hierarchies of blame, like ones of power, should be challenged.

The essay produced a response from Massingham, and then a counter-response from Woolf. Unable to read her ironic cues, Massingham was confused about her position on the plumage bill. Taking on the mantle of evolutionary science, he directed readers toward the "real and profoundly important common duty of preserving the heritage and continuity of evolution and raising the moral currency of civilised nations" (*E* 3:244n4). Appropriating this grandiloquent statement, Woolf replied that "my way of 'raising the moral currency of civilised nations'" was to "resent such an insult to women as Wayfarer casually lets fall." The harm of such phrases was "disastrous not merely to women's relations with men but to her art and conduct" (245n4). She claims women as a central asset to civilization, belonging to culture as well as nature. Though Massingham had reminded readers of British women's securing of the vote, Woolf sees this as minimal cultural currency. And she keeps her original priorities. Writing as a woman, it seems to her more important to protest Wayfarer's insult "than to protect egrets from extinction." She remains playful, however, assuring us, "I am not writing as a bird," and (on behalf of birds) "with this example of my own ambiguity as a writer before me, it would never do to write another article solely from the bird's point of view" (245).

Woolf refuses finally to make a choice between bird and woman and even contributes the income from the original article to support the Plumage Bill Group.[43] Though her argument did not prove as clear in its own day as it may today, Woolf did model a lasting strategy for ecology—working toward environmental coalition while still challenging hierarchical and gender-biased binary modes of thinking. On a regular basis, Woolf's female characters learn from their animal encounters by framing their own politically informed cultural comparisons. In rare moments, as when they wait patiently upon a great carp, or admire the natural display of a plume, they feel creative merger, a sense of oneness, and a mutual, sustaining spirit of life.[44]

6

Virginia Woolf and Ideas of Environmental Holism

Somehow in the streets of London, on
the ebb and flow of things, here, there,
she survived, Peter survived, lived in each
other, she being part, she was positive, of
the trees at home; of the house there . . .
part of people she had never met; being
laid out like a mist between the people she
knew best, who lifted her on their branches
as she had seen the trees lift the mist, but it
spread ever so far, her life, her self.

~Woolf, *Mrs. Dalloway*

Behind the cotton wool is
hidden a pattern; that we—
I mean human beings—are
connected with this; that the
whole world is a work of art.

~Woolf, "A Sketch of the Past"

THIS BOOK BEGAN BY PLACING WOOLF in the company of her contemporaries, finding that nature has a vigorous if largely unheralded presence in modernist literature and in modernity itself. We have seen Woolf writing about nature in numerous registers—in childhood explorations of natural history, the creative and political challenges of landscapes, cultivation of character in contexts of the garden, and imaginative crossings of the species barrier. This final chapter considers whether an ordering approach to nature is decipherable in Woolf's work, and what her construction of such order might mean in facing trauma and environmental crisis. How do Woolf's uses of nature contribute to or complicate feminist, modernist, and environmentalist understandings and agendas? This chapter, like the previous ones, selectively engages the diverse field of ecofeminist theory, which has struggled with women's passive, essentialist assignment to nature. Early ecofeminists invoked holism, in the form of the Gaia principle, as a model for environmental order. Though interest in the goddess can be dismissed as an early phase of cultural ecofeminism, it is worth noting that Woolf was frequently cited by these ecofeminist forerunners, and that Woolf's rewriting of myths resonates both with natural processes and modernist feminist experimentalism. Our knowledge and appreciation of this aspect of modernism is far from complete, as shown, for example, in a recent burgeoning of interest in modernist dance, which often evokes mythic situations and affects classical garb. In *Modernism's Mythic Pose*, Carrie Preston analyzes various forms of solo performance, including recitation, dance, and film, implicating Amy Lowell, Isadora Duncan, and H.D. in the pattern. Woolf's interest in science, present in childhood naturalist pursuits, was renewed in the last two decades of her life, as she pondered the new physics of her day and applied it to her perceptions and representations of natural phenomena.

The preceding chapters of this book have explored the politics of Woolf's responses to various ways that science, culture, and the arts have arranged and contained nature, especially in a world dominated by patriarchy. We have repeatedly dealt with nature as discourse, figured in symbols, similes, and metaphors. For this chapter, such figurations take on greater complexity, as related to the marginal identity of selected perceivers, and to tentative, temporary, but hopeful visions of holistic order.

Both chaotic and holistic scenarios have explanatory and even complementary value in twenty-first-century ecological science—a view anticipated by the eighteenth-century naturalist Gilbert White (Heidi Scott 18–23) and Romantic narratives of nature, both familiar to Woolf. Natural balance or equilibrium is regularly punctuated with disturbances on a local and minute scale (the tree that falls in the forest in *Jacob's Room* [32]) or a catastrophic one (the meteor that led to the extinction of dinosaurs). The little ice age represented in Woolf's *Orlando* falls somewhere in between. Environmentalists of various persuasions concur, however, that human cultures have disturbed natural equilibrium through the power of technology, employed in the service of modernity and for purposes of political domination.

For concepts of the contingent and transitory nature of environmental order, Woolf could turn to new understandings of science in her own day. Contemporary physics, inclusive of Einstein's theories of relativity, wave theory, and quantum mechanics, is now widely accepted as an influence on Woolf. Gillian Beer suggests that by the time she was writing *The Waves*, Woolf had access to the popularized accounts of physics and astronomy offered by Arthur Eddington and James Jeans, as well as new evidence and interpretation of evolution by H. G. Wells and Gerald Heard (*Wave, Atom, Dinosaur*). Beer suggests that wave-particle theory helped Woolf explore an alternate concept of reality, assisting her stylistic move away from realism. Like these scientists, Woolf believed that life is transitory and successive and that simultaneity and rhythm were basic physical principals. They further endorsed working outside of closed epistemologies.[1] Ann Banfield encourages us to think of waves of sound and light, not just water, as "unsensed physical causes" (124). She suggests that, in accordance with alternate particle theory, Woolf sees "an alternation of fluid and solid" in the shape of the world (127), synthesized in Woolf's metaphor of "granite and rainbow" (148).

The Post-Impressionist artists discussed in chapter 4 had made Woolf sensitive to variable qualities of light, particularly as it played upon elements of natural landscape. In 1934 she describes the effect of color on an observer of Walter Sickert's paintings. This essay is laced through with naturalist elements, including reference to rare South American insects who are "all eye" and share the colors of cactus flowers they inhabit. "For as the rocks hide fossils, so we hide tigers, baboons, and perhaps insects, under our coats and hats." The gallery reproduces "conditions of the primeval forest" that make it seem "as if we reverted to the insect stage of our long life" (*E* 6:37). Thus she invokes both evolution and cross-species merger.

According to Janis Birkeland, what singles out ecofeminism from other environmental theories, and what allows it to weave them together, is the targeting of the "power paradigm" that lies beneath exploitation of the environment (16–17).[2] The feminist philosopher Karen J. Warren observes that environmental disturbance has been variously dated by ecofeminists. In *The Chalice and the Blade*, Riane Eisler goes back to the advent of pastoral patriarchs, whose blade introduced a militant society of unequal power relations—an obvious challenge to Woolf's own pacifism. Val Plumwood indicts the rationalist tradition and its harmful dualisms, traceable to Greek tradition, which was both embraced and rewritten by Woolf. Carolyn Merchant looks to the advent of science in Europe in the late sixteenth and early seventeenth centuries, which brought on "the death of nature" (Warren 22–24). Plumwood writes further of the double face of science leading to environmental depredation—one aspect bringing the power of reason to environmental concerns such as climate change, a second employing instrumentally directed knowledges for corporate agricultural or pharmaceutical production, resulting in environmental depredation (*Environmental Culture* 38). Nineteenth-century medical discourses, which modeled heterosexuality as "natural," offered further distortions. We have seen Woolf's engagement in and resistance to the practices of natural history buffs and physicians earlier in this study. Josephine Donovan locates in first-wave feminists such as Margaret Fuller, Emma Goldman, and Charlotte Perkins Gilman "a critique of the atomistic individualism and rationalism of the liberal tradition," finding that they envisioned "collectivity, emotional bonding, and an organic (or holistic) concept of life" ("Animal Rights" 173).

In spiritual and cultural ecofeminisms, which arose and merged in the late 1970s, sacred female figures associated with the earth were recovered and their myths renewed.[3] Mother earth has a presence in the writing of numerous Native Americans, such as Leslie Marmon Silko and Marilou Awiatka, appearing in works that repudiate disrespect for the environment. French feminisms, favored in the 1970s and 1980s, contributed alternate models of environmental order, with *écriture féminine* and maternally based semiotic language. The latter is theorized as precursor to and foundation for the symbolic language of the father. Semiotic language is fluid, evasive of boundaries, and expressive of the female body, its rhythms and sexual gratifications. It persists and can reemerge, according to Julia Kristeva. With Luce Irigaray, the semiotic goes beyond maternal reproductive functions and heterosexual couplings.

Lesbian feminists have in some cases resisted mother earth, among other heterosexual reproductive paradigms, and have called attention to the greater variety in sexuality expressed in nature, or rendered in natural metaphors.[4] Indeed, ecofeminists hold out the hope that discourses of nature may help to establish a different order, based on alternative ethics, permeable boundaries, and democratic principles.

Deep ecology has worked deliberately with holistic concepts. Aldo Leopold's celebrated 1949 essay "The Land Ethic" describes a holistic "biotic community" of which "man is . . . only a member" (204–5)—later a basic premise of deep ecology. In the decentering of "man," Leopold may have had the generic man (men and women, anthropocentrism) in mind, though Plumwood points out that, through much of history, anthropocentrism has meant androcentrism (*Feminism and the Mastery of Nature* 22). Hence the need to apply concerns of gender to various environmental models that arose apart from feminist analysis. Ecofeminists concerned with the "ethic of care" model find that advocates of animal rights such as Peter Singer and Tom Regan preserve masculinist qualities: hierarchical, binary ordering, and a preference for rational, justice-based, individualist thinking over relational and affective values (Clement 301–3). Deep ecology, in striving for holism, traditionally focuses upon and privileges wild over domesticated nature and neglects suffering (Clement 307–8). It is challenging to see how ideas of holism can satisfy ecofeminists equally concerned with domestic and urban settings, affective relations, and globally sustainable naturecultures.

For improved models of sustainable environments, ecofeminists have sought to highlight the roles of women in countering pollution and preserving traditions of indigenous agriculture. Ellen Swallow, the first woman student at MIT, pioneered measuring the purity of water, air, and food, developed the fields of sanitation engineering and home economics, and brought women students into scientific laboratories. Swallow popularized the term "ecology," well aware that, at its Greek root, the term implied "'every man's house' or our universal environment"—a homely form of holism (Breton 59) that embraces domestic discourse for nature. Rachel Carson's work to rebalance nature after abuses with insecticides in the mid-twentieth century remains a model of discourse as well as protest. The grassroots environmental justice movement of today is largely the accomplishment of women of color whose work resonates with that of Zora Neale Hurston, Toni Morrison, and Octavia Butler, as Stacy Alaimo has recognized. Vandana Shiva and Winona LaDuke focus respectively upon Asian Indian and Native American contexts for sustainable agriculture, protesting enduring forms of colonialism in global capitalism.

In literary writing quite generally, nature stocks similes, metaphors, and symbols. Natural images form a strong relation to the primordial, as presumably they have been basic conceptual materials for the mind since the dawn of consciousness. Such images promised fundamental needs of food and shelter, or warned of threatening creatures. Evolutionary psychologists led by Edward O. Wilson suggest that language evolved from mental activities centered on these natural concerns. Nature provides orderly tropes of the human life cycle with images of fecundity, growth, ripening, and decay, and with movement through the seasons. These patterns are visible in the seasonal rites in early Greek drama, as presented by Woolf's friend Jane Ellen Harrison in *Ancient Art and Ritual*.[5] The flowing, recurring rhythms of nature are further suggestive of musical and linguistic forms. More flexible than statements of supposed scientific facts, metaphors provide range for imaginative interpretation and collaboration between reader and writer. Nature seen as systems within a system may provide a model of organic unity that literary forms may aspire to, reject outright, or submit to parody and play. Complex figures of the sacred feminine or earth goddess combine these images and offer early explanatory narratives involving them.

One of the best ways of comprehending Woolf's approach to the environment is to examine the various forms of consciousness to nature that she offers in her works. Who is apprehending nature? If there is gender differentiation, how is this reflected in attitudes toward power and the self? This is important because, as Carol H. Cantrell has noted, modernists' ideas of perception include "involvement of the perceiver within the perceived" (34), and sensitivity to multiple perceivers encourages a sense of a relationship to nature that is dialogic and negotiated on numerous fronts, including across the species barrier. We will have the opportunity to follow the perceptions of nature that enter the thought of a number of characters in this chapter. Among the complex perceivers are Cam, the youngest Ramsay daughter in *To the Lighthouse;* Sara, the younger niece of Abel Pargiter in *The Years;* and Louis and Rhoda in *The Waves.* All of these characters work as outsiders; they see the world and their involvement in it very differently from those who surround them. The orderly natural tropes they entertain are fleeting, compounded of diverse natural elements, and applied to personal discovery and sustainability. As explored in feminist postcolonial thinking,[6] their marginal consciousnesses may even provide cultural alternatives worthy of further exploration.

Woolf's work with nature is very much a part of her fresh take on epistemology, pioneered in *A Room of One's Own,* and her coping with the "damned egotistical self," worked out in her diaries and letters. Her uses of nature may provide a promising move into an order that takes up things of the earth, disperses the self into them, and enters a collective of creatures, in the process deconstructing patriarchal ideas of domination, and even fear of death.[7]

The Gaia, Antigone, and Reframing Patriarchal Myths

Myths—whether told by Greeks, Egyptians, Hindus, Buddhists, Judeo-Christians, the indigenous peoples of the Americas and Australia, or the "pagan" occupants of Britain—may anthropomorphize such elemental objects and forces as the sun, moon, earth, sea, fire, and weather, attributing to them human gender, emotions, motivations, and projects. Their accounts of creation often show gender division and specialization. Myths may work as primordial stories, furnishing the material of literary forms evolved later; they are still evolving. Ecofeminists have since the 1970s cultivated the myth of Gaia, an early Greek earth mother who brought forth the earth and its creatures from a void (Merchant, *Earthcare* 3). As Merchant notes, the Gaia myth was moved into the area of scientific popularization by James Lovelock, who encouraged a view of the earth as a "single living entity, capable of manipulating the earth's atmosphere to suit its overall needs and endowed with faculties and powers far beyond those of its constituent parts" (qtd. in Merchant, *Earthcare* 4).

When T. S. Eliot, faced with assessing Joyce's *Ulysses,* needed to identify its significance to modernist literature, he relied on an androcentric mythic structure, which he found paralleled modern life. Hélène Cixous's essays of the mid-1970s, "The Laugh of Medusa" and "Castration or Decapitation," served as revolutionary texts, forever changing the way second-wave feminists viewed mythology, concepts of the subject, and Freudian family romance, as derived from the Oedipus myth. Feminist scholars have encouraged us to think about the different approaches to myth that women of modernism made available.

The re-centering and re-inscribing of female mythological figures offered by Jane Harrison and H.D. helped set the modernist contexts of chapter 1. The goddess in her triple aspect represents life, death, and rebirth and may be associated with sacred groves of trees, or caves evocative of the womb. Harrison's work on "primitive" rituals attended to people whose rituals heeded the periodicity of nature. Greeks celebrated the annual renewal of spring through Persephone, rising annually from beneath the earth. Forest people created rituals involving the sacred tree, which if paraded through the community brought promise of fruit. Woolf's characters enter these sacred natural spaces. In *Mrs. Dalloway,* Peter Walsh seeks peace as a "solitary traveller" on an imaginary "forest ride" beneath "sky and branches he rapidly endows . . . with womanhood." Peter constructs a mother earth figure "made of sky and branches" that "had risen from the troubled sea . . . to shower down from her magnificent hands compassion, comprehension, absolution" (56). In *To the Lighthouse*, Lily Briscoe associates Mrs. Ramsay with images of a secret treasure chamber, a large jar, or a beehive dome (54–55), images that have been interpreted within lesbian ritual as well as goddess traditions and maternal metaphor.[8] Similarly defiant of heterosexual norms for nature, the contemporary novelist Mary Carmichael lights up "serpentine caves" as she visits two women working in a laboratory who "like" one another (*AROO* 83).

Consistent with her rewriting of history in *A Room of One's Own*, Woolf is much more apt to visit flower fields in the company of mother or daughter figures than battlegrounds contested by male heroes. The cultural power of the hero interests her, but Woolf's study takes in "other," more marginal, migratory members of society that surround the hero, sometimes deconstructing his values, as with Percival in *The Waves*. Woolf is cognizant of the cultural pressures imposed on "others," and she imagines where they may derive their own strength.

From *The Voyage Out* through *The Years*, Woolf had an enduring interest in Sophocles's play *Antigone*, perhaps initially because her first copy was a gift from her brother Thoby.[9] *Antigone* offers a different angle on Greek tragedy, seen by an outsider to patriarchy who holds considerable feminist appeal. Rita Felski asks, "What if we were to reinstate *Antigone* as the exemplary Greek Tragedy," attributing the dominance of the Oedipus myth to "the cultural impact of Freud" (5)? Though Antigone is disruptive, critics do not agree on the character of that disruption, and refer more to the state, kinship, or language and the speech act, than to any rapprochement with nature.[10] As in many Greek dramas, the chorus has passages that redound with natural imagery. Their parts interrupt and re-view the dialogue between principal characters, as do the nature-centered intervals in *To the Lighthouse* and *The Waves*, the chapter openings of *The Years*, and intermissions in the pageant of *Between the Acts*. In *The Years*, Rachel Blau DuPlessis notes movement away from a single protagonist into a "choral" one, and she suggests that women rewrite myth to create a dialogue between marginal and central characters (*Writing beyond the Ending* 162–65).

The first chorus of *Antigone* begins (as does *The Waves*) with a rising sun. The chorus is sensitive to both the city and its surrounding terrain, and uses natural similes to describe the warriors who perpetrate the drama: "Beam of the sun, fairest light that ever dawned on Thebè of the seven gates, thou hast shone forth at last, eye of golden day, arisen above Dircè's streams! The warrior of the white shield . . . , like shrill-screaming eagle, he flew over into our land, in snow-white pinion sheathed" (108).[11] Antigone has the subversive power that would later characterize many of Woolf's cultural others. The daughter of Oedipus and Jocasta, she defies the patriarchal decree of her uncle, Creon, King of Thebes, by twice providing rudimentary funeral rites involving earth and water for her brother Polynices. He is one of two brothers of Antigone who have slain each other, taking opposite sides in war, and deepening the tragedy of Oedipus. Creon had ordered Polynices cast to vultures and dogs for invading Thebes.

Antigone defies the code imposed by Creon in the name of the state—his rationale being that the "higher life of states" takes command over nature. The chorus describes it thus: "The light-hearted race of birds, and the tribes of savage beasts, and the sea-brood of the deep, he snares in the meshes of his woven toils, he leads captive—man excellent in wit! . . . . And speech, and wind-swift thought, and all the moods that mould a state, hath he taught himself; and how to flee the arrows of the frost, when 'tis hard lodging under the clear sky, and the arrows of the rushing rain" (114).

Antigone connects not with the state but with love for her brother, and with the spiritual company of the dead—testament of the final, equalizing power of death in nature. Her cries on finding her brother's body re-exposed by the guards assume the language of nonhuman creatures: "the sharp cry of a bird in its bitterness—even as when, within the empty nest, it sees the bed stripped of its nestlings" (115–16). She returns to cover him again with "thirsty dust" and crown him "with thrice-poured drink-offering" from a "shapely ewer of bronze, held high" (116).

Antigone approaches her own fate, which is to be sealed alive in a tomb, with thoughts of Tantalus's daughter, subdued in stone yet exuding natural liquids from the Sipylian heights: "and the rains fail not, as men tell, from her wasting form, nor fails the snow" (126). Antigone expresses sadness over being denied a bridal bed, but she knows that, had she been a wife and mother, she would not have radically pursued her protest. Entering the tomb, she thinks of Persephone receiving the dead. This suggests resonance with a set of mythic sisters, met in nature, but not necessarily through the maternal role. Eurydice, so brilliantly described in H.D.'s poem by that name, is another of this underground set. Antigone was engaged to marry Creon's son, Haemon, who takes her part against his father. Discovering that she has hanged herself in the tomb, he falls to his death on his sword—further denying patriarchal designs.

Edward Pargiter of *The Years* merges his image of Antigone with Kitty, the young woman he loves in vain. Edward's vision is "a luminous shell formed, a purple fume, from which out stepped a Greek girl; yet she was English. There she stood among the marble and the asphodel, yet there she was among the Morris wall-papers and the cabinets. . . . She was both of them—Antigone and Kitty" (51). As life moves on, Edward becomes a classical scholar and gives a copy of his own translation of *Antigone* to his cousin Sara, who inhabits the classical text in her own manner.

Sara is one of Woolf's outsiders, usually counted among her women-identified characters,[12] and we find her lying in bed at the top of a house, looking out at the garden where people emerge from dancing at a party. Her mental work is deeply enmeshed in nature. Struggling against Cartesian duality and her own fractured mind, she works toward integrating her body with her thought process: "It was easier to act things than to think them. Legs, body, hands, the whole of her must be laid out passively to take part in this universal process of thinking which the man said was the world living." Her feet "seemed separated, very far away. She closed her eyes. Then against her will something in her hardened. It was impossible to act thought. She became something; a root; lying sunk in earth; veins seemed to thread the cold mass; the tree put forth branches; the branches had leaves" (124–25). Her abridged and "inaccurate" reading of *Antigone* focuses upon vultures, come to feed on the dead Polynices, and on Antigone coming out of the dust-cloud to fling sand on his body. In Sara's version, Antigone is seized and bound by the authorities. Next she focuses upon a man sealing the mound where Antigone is buried alive on a "moonlight night. The blades of the cactuses were sharp silver" (128)—details that do not appear in the original but resemble the flora of *To the Lighthouse* (73). Replicating the text while Sara lies on the verge of sleep, "The sound of the dance music became dulled. Her body dropped suddenly; then reached ground. A dark wing brushed her mind, leaving a pause; a blank space" (128). Sara's imaginative sisters in Woolf's work include Cam of *To the Lighthouse*, Rhoda of *The Waves*, and Isa of *Between the Acts*, all of whom are inclined toward ritual gestures involving water, flowers, trees, and creatures. All seek to sustain their scattered or traumatized selves through creative merger with nature.

The girl or the woman in a field of flowers suggests the myth of the great earth mother, Demeter or Ceres (granddaughter of Gaia), and her daughter Persephone. Elizabeth Abel and Madeline Moore, with their work on Woolf, were among the early second-wave feminists who found a strong alternative to the male hero in the great goddess. Moore pointed to Jane Harrison's "Mistress and Maid" chapter in *Prolegomena to the Study of Greek Religion* as a source for Woolf (42). With Woolf, both mothers and independent little girls take their place in fields, collecting flowers, as did Persephone exploring her world when she was abducted to the underworld by Hades. Demeter searches those same fields in a season of loss.

Cam repopulates this myth in *To the Lighthouse,* when she is found collecting Sweet Alice that she does not want to give up to Mr. Bankes. Mrs. Vallance in Woolf's story "Ancestors" thinks back to herself as "that little girl who has to travel so far, picking Sweet Alice" and of her widowed mother sitting "among her flowers by the hour ... more with ghosts than with them all" (*CSF* 182). Toward the end of *To the Lighthouse,* Lily Briscoe, thinking like a painter, constructs a mythic landscape for Prue Ramsay following her death from complications of childbearing: "She let her flowers fall from her basket, scattered and tumbled them on the grass, and, reluctantly and hesitatingly, but without question or complaint ... went down too. Down fields, across valleys, white, flower-strewn—that is how she would have painted it" (204). Though a grown woman and mother, Isa Oliver reenacts Persephone's journey in *Between the Acts:* "Down what draughty tunnels?" she muses. "Where the eyeless wind blows? And there grows nothing for the eye. No rose. To issue where? In some harvestless dim field where no evening lets fall her mantle; nor sun rises" (105–6). Though her real name is Isabella,[13] "Isa" suggests the name of the Egyptian goddess Isis, who traversed the land recovering the body parts of her beloved husband, Osiris, for reassembly following his murder. There is resonance with both Antigone and Persephone in this earlier, more patriarchal myth, in which Osiris plays god of the underworld.

Mature women who walk the fields of death are versions of Demeter. After her husband's suicide, Rezia Smith walks out over fields of corn as the sedative takes effect in *Mrs. Dalloway.* "She put on her hat, and ran through cornfields—where could it have been?—on to some hill, somewhere near the sea, for there were ships, gulls, butterflies." Memories mingle with her present situation: "rain falling, whisperings, stirring among dry corn, the caress of the sea, as it seemed to her, hollowing them in its arched shell and murmuring to her laid on shore, strewn she felt, like flying flowers over some tomb" (147). She is taken up in the waves, protected in a hollow that is part wave, part shell, laid on shore, or, in another simile, strewn like flowers onto a generic tomb that might well go back to the Greeks.

Mrs. Ramsay enters Demeter's territory when Mr. Bankes imagines "the Graces assembling seemed to have joined hands in meadows of asphodel to compose that face" (*TTL* 32–33). Mr. Tansley imagines her "stepping through fields of flowers and taking to her breast buds that had broken and lambs that had fallen" (18). Woolf thinks of Katherine Mansfield "putting on a white wreath & leaving us, called away; made dignified, chosen" (*D* 2:226), an image she recollects years later when visiting Hampstead (*D* 3:50), and one that Lily applies to Mrs. Ramsay after her death, "raising to her forehead a wreath of white flowers with which she went" (*TTL* 184).

The Demeter image circulates further in *The Waves*, when we find Susan in her farmlands, as described in chapter 4, and when Rhoda collects flowers in a commemorative gesture following Percival's death. In a more comic version in *Between the Acts*, Mrs. Manresa "looked, as she crossed the lawn to the strains of the gramophone, goddess-like, buoyant, abundant, her cornucopia running over" (82). But she serves as goddess exclusively to the masculine gender. "Bartholomew, following, blessed the power of the human body to make the earth fruitful. Giles would keep his orbit so long as she weighted him to earth" (82). Also serving as comic goddesses are the maternal cows, derived perhaps from the Egyptian goddess Hathor.

Woolf's occasional crones offer the final aspect of the triple goddess. Examples are the old woman, her song resembling an ancient stream "soaking through the knotted roots of infinite ages" by the tube station in *Mrs. Dalloway* (80), and Lucy Swithin of *Between the Acts*, finding her way back to primordial origins in great rhododendron woods, via her reading. Peter Walsh and Rezia Smith react to the old woman by the tube station with charity or pity—Peter giving her a copper; Rezia worrying about where she will pass the night. It takes the narrative voice to elevate into an eternal presence this "voice of no age or sex," which offers only "a frail quivering sound, a voice bubbling up without direction, vigour, beginning or end, running shrilly and with an absence of all human meaning" (*MD* 78–79). As she sings of a lover, dead for centuries, we find that she has presided over "the pageant of the universe." Far from pristine, this voice nets human artifacts and muddies the urban landscape, "soaking through the knotted roots of infinite ages, and skeletons and treasure, streamed away in rivultets . . . fertilizing, leaving a damp stain" (79–80). Woolf frequently reminds us of oozing loam and remains of prehistoric creatures preceding civilization and, in her last novel, of what might follow when civilization expires. Indeed, the primordial is a stronger category with Woolf than the more familiar modernist trope of the primitive. In selecting it, she escapes racist overtones of modernist primitivism or social Darwinism and merges human with animal, and with earth itself. There is comfort in accepting the continuity of wild grasses and burbling song, as well as the transience of all life.

The myth of the Garden of Eden has long excited feminist interest and skepticism. Carolyn Merchant suggests that Genesis vindicates conquest of land in the new world for the sake of restoring the patriarchal order of the Edenic garden (*Earthcare* 27–29). Woolf rewrites this myth in numerous feminist-inspired ways. Alice Stavely suggests that "Kew Gardens" returns "the woman writer/critic to her Edenic origins" and reexamines how this myth has long supported "conventions that deny cultural authority to women" (47). Maria DiBattista detects the fusion of Oedipus, Demeter/Persephone, and Edenic myth in the garden scene of Mrs. Ramsay with James in *To the Lighthouse,* pronouncing this "a 'naïve' vision of a beneficent, prolific, and artful nature" (75). Christine Froula describes a mythical project that unfolded over twenty-five years, through *The Voyage Out, To the Lighthouse, The Waves,* and *Between the Acts* ("Rewriting Genesis"). In this series Woolf reclaimed the "repressed and silenced name (or word) of the mother" as "a ground for the daughter-artist's authority" (197). More recently, Froula finds that, with *The Waves,* Woolf was "forgetting sexual hierarchy" in a "transfigured Garden and Fall" and providing a "'playpoem' of pure being, where . . . no mother or father, divine or human, walks" (*Bloomsbury Avant-Garde* 202).[14]

Woolf is wary and irreverent toward many of the goddesses that enter her texts, and looks beyond her own time, class, and place to account for them as inventions of patriarchal culture. From a historical perspective, she remarks that, for farmers represented in Hardy's *Far from the Madding Crowd,* "Nature is prolific, splendid, and lustful; not yet malignant and still the Great Mother of labouring men" (*E* 5:565). We can see her reservations about goddess figures as patriarchal pawns, starting in *Jacob's Room* with the "nocturnal women . . . beating great carpets," making a sound like guns in the war Betty Flanders's sons have gone to fight (*JR* 175). Goddesslike in her beauty, Mrs. Ramsay encourages gender inequity in *To the Lighthouse,* inspiring rebellion in her daughters and in Lily Briscoe. The clearly negative Goddess of Conversion, "even now engaged—in the heat and sands of India, the mud and swamp of Africa," enters *Mrs. Dalloway* through both the narrator and Clarissa Dalloway (97). A female figure is associated with the rising and setting sun of *The Waves*—"as if the arm of a woman couched beneath the horizon had raised a lamp" (3), a limb Jane Marcus identifies as the "white arm of imperialism" ("Britannia Rules *The Waves*" 65); the head of this sun goddess, bedecked with "jewels, the topaz, the aquamarine, the water-coloured jewels with sparks of fire in them" (52), is suggestive of extracted natural wealth and privilege, whatever culture might claim her. Another force of nature, the weather, occasionally serves up a challenge to patriarchy. In *A Room of One's Own,* Woolf's narrator remarks on men's omnipresence in the daily newspaper: "With the exception of the fog he seemed to control everything" (34). In "Thunder at Wembley," a sudden rain shower puts an end to the cardboard world of the imperial exhibition.

Woolf's sense of myth was not limited to the classics and the Bible, as she betrays in her essays "Heard on the Downs: The Genesis of Myth" and "Across the Border." She wrote the first of these in August 1916 in response to the sound of the guns of World War I, audible on the Sussex downs. While it might be argued that these essays contribute to "Englishness" at a moment of cultural crisis, I find in them attention to local detail and concern with identifying the indigenous cultural formations that provide her own background. Helen Southworth, citing the work of Joshua Esty, cites "recent arguments for the existence of an 'anthropological turn' in English modernist writing of the late 1930s and 1940s," in which Eliot, Forster and Woolf "sought a means to 'reenchant' England" rather than engage in imperialist or cosmopolitan discourse (197)—a direction she applies to *Between the Acts,* especially its pageant. In "Heard on the Downs," Woolf attributes the strange sounds she hears to the "hollows of the Downside which seem to await the spectators of some Titanic drama" (*E* 2:40). But she also recognizes that these events "must have peopled the villages and the solitary farmhouses in the folds with stories of ghostly riders and unhappy ladies forever seeking their lost treasure" (40). "Across the Border" discusses the enduring appeal of the supernatural, particularly when "so wrought in with the natural that fear is kept from a dangerous exaggeration," as in the novels of Walter Scott and Henry James. The essay closes memorably: "The country is peopled with nymphs and dryads, and Pan, far from being dead, is at his pranks in all the villages of England." Indeed, the Morris dances, still practiced in the area, are likely derived from pagan fertility rituals. Woolf recognizes satire and allegory as reasons for rewriting mythology. But she seems to prefer versions of myth that "may lead to a quickened perception of the relations existing between men and plants, or houses and their inhabitants, or any one of those innumerable alliances which somehow or other we spin between ourselves and other objects in our passage" (E 2:220). The process of telling is thus one of uniting across difference.

Woolf's late, unfinished essay, "Anon," which Brenda Silver appropriately sets in the context of cultural critique, retains Woolf's sense of primordial connection with nature. Woolf holds this attachment in common with various other outsiders found at the sources of English writing, when English itself was a peasants' language. She begins "Anon," with a line from G. M. Trevelyan, identifying a time when "the untamed forest was king." This points to a shift in power from nature to patriarch and suggests that the primordial English were "forest people," as described in Jane Harrison's *Ancient Art and Ritual.* Woolf continues: "On those matted boughs innumerable birds sang; but their song was only heard by a few skin clad hunters in the clearings. Did the desire to sing come to one of those huntsmen because he heard the birds sing, and so rested his axe against the tree for a moment? . . . The voice that broke the silence of the forest was the voice of Anon. . . . Everybody shared in the emotion of Anon['s] song, and supplied the story. . . . Anon is sometimes man; sometimes woman. He is the common voice singing out of doors" (my *Gender of Modernism* 679–80). Anon led pagan celebrants clad in "coats of green leaves" to visit "the haunted tree," the well, and the burial place (681). Although, according to Woolf, the advent of the Caxton's press in 1477 killed Anon, it also "preserved him," in Malory's *Mort d'Arthur,* stories of witches, seasonal performances by minstrels, churchyard pageants, and the legend of Robin Hood. Working out ideas concerning memory and the unconscious, Woolf finds that such survivals from Anon are "the world beneath our consciousness; the anonymous world to which we can still return" (682).[15] One might infer that such a return could be a salvation in 1941. Other values coalescing to Anon include an audience-centered, community form of art, regular lines of communication between the ruling gentry and the common folk, and a sensibility that precedes individuality and (by my extension) the egotistical self of the author. Silver offers as an example of a late survival from Anon the creator of the pageant in *Between the Acts*, Miss La Trobe, called "Whatshername" by the common folk of the village (*Gender of Modernism* 654). Lucy Swithin's interest in reading about the primordial forests in that same novel offers a further connection. Manifested in all of the examples above is that Woolf's uses of nature in various legends and myths has a creative and sustaining connection to the human. Rewritten myths may show what has gone wrong in the classics and in cultures of modernity, and allow us to reconnect with a more egalitarian, more politically and environmentally sustainable form of society.

Troubling Order: Indifference, Aesthetic Unity, and Deconstruction

Nature can display frightening indifference to human concerns in Woolf's writing. She remarked that Thomas Hardy feels in nature "a spirit that can sympathize or mock or remain an indifferent spectator of human fortunes" ("Novels of Thomas Hardy," *E* 5:562–63). When Woolf experienced a total solar eclipse in 1927, she saw nature in both indifferent and ordered aspects, plunging into and emerging from death. One of Woolf's early experiments in point of view involved movement far out into space, such that the narrator views a small boat leaving England in *The Voyage Out*. Katherine Hilbery looks out into celestial and primordial space and time on a winter's night in *Night and Day:* "The stars did their usual work upon the mind, froze to cinders the whole of our short human history and reduced the human body to an ape-like, furry form, crouching amid the brushwood of a barbarous clod of mud" (196). In *Mrs. Dalloway*, Rezia Smith's despair is expressed in terms of "midnight, when all boundaries are lost, the country reverts to its ancient shape, as the Romans saw it . . . and the hills had no names and rivers wound they knew not where—such was her darkness" (23).

Meditating over her place in the scheme of things in the first section of *To the Lighthouse*, Nancy Ramsay leaves her friends on the beach and broods over a tidal pool (see figure 3 on p. 49). Experimenting with shifting power dynamics, at one moment Nancy is the agent of chaos, playing "God himself, to millions of ignorant and innocent creatures," by arbitrarily cutting off their sunlight. However, shortly after this, she is overcome with a sense of her own "nothingness" as she apprehends the tidal "power sweeping savagely in and inevitably withdrawing" (78). Represented apart from the human mind in the "Time Passes" section of *To the Lighthouse*, "The winds and waves disported themselves like the amorphous bulks of leviathans whose brows are pierced by no light of reason, and mounted one on top of another, and lunged and plunged in the darkness or the daylight" (138). Winds and vermin nibble away at the household order Mrs. Ramsay has established, a process not entirely different from the sea's nibbling at the land that Mr. Ramsay imagined resisting in the opening segment of the novel. In a weakened condition, characters expect no mercy. Bernard lies abject in a ditch near the close of *The Waves*, experiencing something akin to a solar eclipse. In their daily cycle, tides strand creatures to die, as in the central inter-chapters of *The Waves*, or might drown walkers on the beach, as Mrs. Ramsay dreads in *To the Lighthouse*. The seasons suggest an objective correlative to the human drama of *The Years*—the cruelest month coming with the deaths of Eugenie and Digby; snow covers England as the family prepares to sell Albercorn Terrace, evicting their servant, Crosby.

As Lily launches into a final version of her painting in the last section of *To the Lighthouse*, a narrative voice (perhaps representative of Lily's current attitudes) registers the contingency of any sense of order: "There might be lovers whose gift it was to choose out the elements of things and place them together and so, giving them a wholeness not theirs in life, make of some scene . . . one of those globed compacted things over which thought lingers, and love plays" (195). Indeed Lily has pursued wholeness as an artist in the first segment of the novel. For her, Mr. and Mrs. Ramsay "became part of that unreal but penetrating and exciting universe which is the world seen through the eyes of love. The sky stuck to them; the birds sang through them . . . James in the window and the cloud moving and the tree bending, how life, from being made up of little separate incidents which one lived one by one, became curled and whole like a wave which bore one up with it and threw one down with it, there, with a dash, on the beach" (50).

Unity was quested and found in much Woolf criticism up through the 1980s. A generation of critics, striving toward the order and balance sought in the poetry favored by the New Critics, found reassuring aesthetic order in Woolf's novels. Alan Wilde suggests that into her middle phase, including *The Waves*, Woolf offered aesthetic closure, leaving behind the phenomenal world (142). James Naremore finds that "in the face of the inevitable tragedy of time and death, she offered the consolation of nature seen from a cosmic perspective, as in the inter-chapters of *The Waves*" (244). However, Madeline Moore presents the temporary sense of order achieved by characters in terms of a cycle of thought "wherein individuals are momentarily united with nature, experience both its exaltation and its nothingness, and, in order to preserve their autonomy, reemerge into the present of human effort" ("Nature and Community" 219). For Moore, the pastoral tradition fails adults. They find unity only symbolically.

Critics working in the tradition of Transcendentalism and Romanticism have found Woolf performing spiritual communion with nature, despite her agnosticism.[16] She admired Henry David Thoreau, appreciating a sense of nature enhanced by the "keenness of his senses" and skill with his hands ("Thoreau," E 2:238). While she commends the honesty of his self-examining egoism, she suggests he fails to communicate with a community.

Woolf was familiar with Bloomsbury philosophers who made their own contributions to ideas of unity. The work of the conscious mind in shaping reality to positive ends was inherent to the philosophy of G. E. Moore. Bertrand Russell saw in the order of science something that went beyond individual consciousness.[17] Numerous scholars have applied to Woolf Henri Bergson's idea of *la durée*, continuous subjective or psychological time, expressed in "moments of being" as an access to a true self, freed from flux.[18] Phenomenology, a favored approach to Woolf since the 1980s, keeps the subjectivity of the perceiver very much in mind. Roger Poole's study of Woolf, as Alan Wilde notes, suggests that in Woolf "phenomenology found its novelist" (198).[19]

Gaston Bachelard's readings of both modern science and poetic imagery can facilitate an understanding of the mental work performed on natural imagery by many of Woolf's characters. Bachelard attributed an "epistemological break" to the new physics of the early twentieth century. This new science decentered human consciousness as the source of knowledge, leaving humans with the feeling of being transcended by something beyond their control, yet also feeling "nourished and sustained by it" (McAllester Jones 4). Bachelard's "new literary mind," working out "approximate knowledge" through "interwoven images," applies well to Woolf's work with natural images (see Jones 107–11). Bachelard's analysis of the image of the tree in Woolf's *Orlando* is a case in point, taken up later in the chapter. Nature offers abundant material for creative mental perception, which serves further in character portrayal. By attending to the observer, Woolf may show us the accumulation of images and ideas that falls well short of unity.

Deconstruction, as anticipated by modernists such as Woolf and revised by second-wave feminists, provides new tools for reading both modernism and the uses of nature within it, even as it threatens previously found unities. Writing about "ecology of language" in Woolf, Elizabeth Waller notes that ecofeminists question "the source of language and the qualifications of speaking subjects" (137).[20] This lends new attention to silences and the alternative languages of beings other than humans, as suggested in chapter 5. As if to dismiss patriarchal, written language, Woolf repeatedly has female characters lose books while out wandering in nature, or use leaves and flowers to mark their place. Woolf sets her readers and writers where they can look out a window and attend to natural events beyond the written page or the domestic space. For example, in the essay "How Should One Read a Book," she positions herself in "a sunny room, with windows open on a garden, so that we can hear the trees rustling, the gardener talking, the donkey braying, the old women gossiping at the pump" (E 4:389). In conceiving generative images for The Waves, Woolf imagined that a central female intelligence would open a window to admit a moth (D 3:229), lending substance to her book.

Feminist deconstruction, as practiced by Hélène Cixous, Julia Kristeva, and Luce Irigaray, encouraged readers to look beyond the visual into multiple senses capable of perceiving nature, including the aural, the tactile, and what lies entombed, beneath the surface. Claudette Sartiliot suggests that with modernisms came a new discourse for flowers that is much more fluid than the floral codes of the Elizabethans and Victorians we encountered in chapter 3. As first noted in the introduction, the deconstructive theories have their own natural metaphors: Derrida's "dissemination," referring to distribution of seeds, and Deleuze and Guattari's rhizomatic metaphor. Sartiliot would have us read flowers as "a nodal point in texts which undermines the hermeneutic enterprise and offers an alternative model of signification." This "takes into account what has been repressed by logocentric systems of thought, namely plurality, the signifier, the unconscious, the feminine" (5). Flowers also allow for slippage of sexuality. They have sufficient sexual dimorphism that Darwin and, by his inspiration, Proust are able to shift flowers toward masculine and homosexual manifestations (Sartilot 51; Darwin's The Various Contrivances by which Orchids Are Fertilized by Insects). James Joyce's river/woman Anna Livia Plurabelle combines flowers and water, creating a "languo of flows" for

Finnegans Wake (621) that she takes into her dissolution at sea. Flower and flow are consistently identified with feminine semiotics, making them ideal materials for ecofeminist literary consideration.

Freud in his *Interpretation of Dreams* may give some fixed meanings for things in nature, but he was aware of the wealth of repressed material that lay behind such images. Marianne Torgovnick adapts the Freudian concept of "oceanic feeling" to explore ideas of unity in modernism. She suggests that the "organic" threatened his ego-based psychology. His solution in *Civilization and Its Discontents* was to attach the "oceanic feeling" to the infant at its mother's breast (*Primitive Passions* 206–7). Though Freud suggested that this primitive stage of development was absorbed into later phases, feminist psychologists such as Melanie Klein and Jessica Benjamin have given greater attention to continuity with the maternal bond, as Torgovnick notes. The name "oceanic," and its association with the "primitive" and the nursing mother, form a strong connection to nature, though they bear the burden of essentialism. "Oceanic" is also useful in describing the perceiving consciousness. Oceanic feeling embraces "a dissolution of boundaries between subject and object and between all conceived and conceivable polarities" (*Primitive Passions* 18).

Holistic Collage

Terms of unity with connections to environmentalism include "organic" as well as "holistic." As noted above, Josephine Donovan attributed to first-wave feminists "an organic (or holistic) concept of life" (173). Aurora Levins Morales proclaims herself a "Certified Organic Intellectual" in describing her preferred form of "home-grown" theory. In her metaphor, one should know the local soil, water, and techniques of cultivation to arrive at nurturing, accessible theory. Such knowing of a place as home may not be available when beings are moved, or environments are disrupted by modernity. In the spirit of an "organic," "holistic," or "oceanic" attitude, characters work through a natural imaginary to perceive a system to which they belong; the sense of connection, participation, and continuation instills purpose and hope.

Woolf's natural images are dazzlingly numerous and range in complexity from simple phrases to intricate associations and holistic formations. Just as flowers and oceans figure recurrently in the theory cited above, image clusters of plants (including flowers, grasses, and trees) and water (a drop, pool, river, waves, or ocean) are pervasive in Woolf. Creatures (mammals, birds, fish, insects, and snails), like humans, become involved holistically with these clusters and with one another. Woolf's most memorable natural images rarely stand alone; they fuse with the identity of the animals or human beings who perceive them, or the birds and insects that move among them, with their own perceptions and uses of nature's offerings.

Among the most memorable, frequently cited examples of unity with nature in Woolf's writing is her "organic" perception from early childhood: "I was looking at a plant with a spread of leaves; and it seemed suddenly plain that the flower itself was part of the earth; that a ring enclosed what was the flower; and that was the real flower; part earth; part flower. It was a thought I put away as being likely to be useful to me later" ("A Sketch of the Past," *MB* 71). In seeing "the flower whole," her consciousness came to sudden awareness, emerging from the "cotton-wool" of everyday experience.

A mature Mrs. Dalloway offers a puzzling flower image that suddenly draws attention to deeper matters of identity: "Then, for that moment, she had seen an illumination; a match burning in a crocus; an inner meaning almost expressed. But the close withdrew; the hard softened. It was over— the moment" (*MD* 31). This perception is paired with Clarissa's memory of having felt what a man might feel for a woman, "a tinge like a blush which one tried to check and then, as it spread, one yielded to its expansion, and rushed to the farthest verge and there quivered and felt the world come close, swollen with some astonishing significance, some pressure of rapture which spit its thin skin and gushed and poured with an extraordinary alleviation over the cracks and sores!" (*MD* 31). Critics have understandably read sexual orgasm in this description. The match may suggest the erect clitoris and the crocus the labia, as in Cramer's reading ("Notes from the Underground" 185). The match, which if carelessly used could burn the delicate bloom, in this case illuminates its sensual interior. Its illumination and heat generate additional sensations. As in Woolf's metaphorical caves, we access a feeling previously unexplored. Judith Roof has pointed out how this image registers only one in a shifting set of identifications Clarissa Dalloway makes to lesbianism (98–99). Still, Woolf's images naturalize lesbian feelings; with this acknowledgment comes a soothing cure.

Leaves, whether growing on plants or trees, or dispersed by human or natural forces, have creative and/or protective significance in many of Woolf's texts, as we have seen in Woolf's evocation of Anon leading a troop of leaf-clad celebrants, or in Peter Walsh's fantasy ride through the forest. Cam trails a leaf when she reluctantly responds to her mother's summons in the first segment of *To the Lighthouse*. Septimus Smith reads beauty in brandishing, sun-dappled leaves he sees in Regent's Park, before the trees part in hallucination to reveal his beloved friend, Evans, dead in the war. Troublingly, he has seen a woman's head in the middle of a fern. However, in his last vision of Rezia, lovingly packing away his notes, she has "all of her petals . . . about her. She was a flowering tree, and through her branches look out the face of a lawgiver, who had reached a sanctuary where she feared no one; not Holmes; not Bradshaw; a miracle, a triumph, the last and greatest" (*MD* 144).

An image Woolf worked with as she started conceiving of *The Waves* was "a perpetual crumbling and renewal of the plant" (*D* 3:229), which survives as a plant on the windowsill. Louis thinks himself into the form of a tree in the first chapter, as he hides in the hedge from the other children: "I am green as a yew tree in the shade of the hedge. My hair is made of leaves. I am rooted in the middle of the earth. My body is a stalk. I press the stalk. A drop oozes from the hole at the mouth and slowly, thickly grows larger and larger." (*W* 6–7). This complex tree is designed to meet his needs. The yew is linked to the death and rebirth of Christ on the cross, an association that serves Louis's solitary suffering. Louis's tree offers camouflage, fixity of place, and even self-stimulation. But this order is shattered, with lifelong repercussions, when Jinny finds Louis and kisses him.

Orlando's lifetime writing project is titled "The Oak Tree," as if this staple of British pastoral tradition could contain all the ages of life, and the stages of the developing artist. Located on the hill, Orlando's favorite oak tree is fluid in gender and holistically attached to him and a wider universe of things. "He loved, beneath all this summer transiency, to feel the earth's spine beneath him; for such he took the hard root of the oak tree to be." This rooted, masculine solidity gradually yields to a different imagery: "He lay so still that by degrees the deer stepped nearer and the rooks wheeled round him and the swallows dipped and circled and the dragon-flies shot past, as if all the fertility and amorphous activity of a summer's evening were woven web-like about his body" (*O* 19). The web can serve as a powerful metaphor for female creativity, as in *A Room of One's Own*: "Fiction is like a spider's web, attached ever so lightly perhaps, but still attached to life at all four corners" (41). Surrounding creatures come to Orlando, involving him in nature's sensual vitality, enveloping and securing him, holistically. Bachelard offers a similar reading of the initial masculinity of this relationship. His Orlando is in "communion of hard objects encircling a core of hardness! The oak tree, the horse, and the ship become one, in spite of their disparity of form" (127). Bachelard notes that Woolf later presents us with "all that the Tree means for her imagination. Orlando feels his heart grow peaceful as he leans against the oak's hard, firm trunk; he shares in the peace-giving qualities of the quiet tree, the tree that brings quiet to the whole landscape. Does not the oak tree still even the passing cloud?" (127). Though he is still seeking after some sort of mastery in the tree stilling the cloud, Bachelard finds in this passage "a model of material psychoanalysis" (128). Not just Orlando but many of Woolf's characters make therapeutic use of nature to repair and reattach the self, often in a peaceful, hopeful holistic state.

As we noted early in this study, Woolf records as her first memory hearing the rhythm of the waves striking the shore. Marianne DeKoven's *Rich and Strange* takes sea-change, and for Woolf, imagery set beneath the ocean or a river, as central figurations for a feminist reading of modernism. Underwater imagery is suggestive of the importance placed on the unconscious in Freudian-inspired modernism. In DeKoven's reading of *The Voyage Out*, one can track Rachel's development as a conscious subject in terms of an underwater imagination. Woolf's characters repeatedly construct underwater worlds: Rachel's final positioning of her body, curled at the bottom of the sea, joins the creatures whose abduction for the purposes of natural history had aroused her sympathy early in the novel. We have joined Nancy presiding over a rock pool in *To the Lighthouse*. Lucy waits like a patient naturalist for the great orb fish to surface in the pond in *Between the Acts*. Treasures, which may represent ideas (the lost fish of *A Room*), lie beneath the surface. As Woolf saunters through London or walks her dog, "the string, which as if it dipped loosely into a wave of treasure brings up pearls sticking to it." She pities a friend who "has no string dipping into the green wave: things don't connect for her; & add up into those entrancing bundles which are happiness" (D 3:11). Jouissance, joy touched with sensuality, exudes from water rising in the bowl or a fountain: "After weeding I had to go in out of the sun, & how the quiet lapped me round . . . & the beauty brimmed over me & steeped my nerves till they quivered, as I have seen a water plant quiver when the water overflowed it" (D 2:301).

Among her most mysterious undersea images is Woolf's repeated evocation of "a fin passing far out," representing what she is left with "on the mystical side" of a period of gloom and solitude. Woolf associates the fin with the childhood feeling that she could not step across a puddle. It is both "frightening & exciting," perhaps the first stirrings of a new novel that proved to be *The Waves* (*D* 3:113). A similar feeling of being "far out to sea and alone" oppresses Clarissa Dalloway as she leaves a park to face the traffic (*MD* 8). Fin and puddle are assigned to Bernard and Rhoda, respectively, in *The Waves*, where the fin is set "in a waste of waters" (138). Waste suggests emptiness and stagnation, a space not easily traversed and lacking the regularity of waves that comforted Woolf in the nursery. When "a fin in a waste of waters" occurs to Bernard, it is a "bare visual impression unattached to any reason." He records it under "F" in his book of memorable phrases (138). Bernard eventually resolves this "fin" into description of a satisfactory conversation with Neville, "as if a fin rose in the wastes of silence; then the fin, the thought, sinks back into the depths spreading round it a little ripple of satisfaction content" (202). Though disembodied, the fin calls attention to what is beneath the surface, to a life worthy of comprehension.

Woolf is attracted to "hollow," sheltering spaces as they occur in nature, protecting butterflies, flowers, mushrooms, birds, rabbits, houses, or vulnerable people, and providing a sense of connection. She selects the word sixty times at important junctures in her novels (Haule and Smith 1428). The image of "the hollow of the wave" featured in the title of this book comes from a brief sequence in the "Time Passes" section of *To the Lighthouse*: "So soon a bird sings, a cock crows, or a faint green quickens, like a turning leaf, in the hollow of the wave" (131). The leaf, part of a complex simile dependent upon a nascent plant or the effect of light on water, makes the wave not quite hollow; the wave bestows motion on the leaf, like a miniature world, briefly whirled. Though birds are audible in this interval of the novel, it is doubtful that any human is present to apprehend this event. Nearby in the text, "Autumn trees . . . take on the flash of tattered flags," reminding us of a war that could doom human life (131). Still, inspiring the leaf/wave simile, "green" life "quickens," begins anew. This set of leaf/wave bird images, though more active, is resonant with a simpler simile from *Mrs. Dalloway*, where Rezia Smith is shown in all her vulnerability "like a bird sheltering under the thin hollow of a leaf" (64). The bird and the human of the simile are equally dependent upon the leaf to sustain them, but the leaf provides a scant, fragile, temporary shelter at best. The house located in the hollow of *Between the Acts* is similarly sheltered and vulnerable.

Mrs. Dalloway is one of Woolf's strongest proponents of the holistic view, seen most obviously in the first epigraph, when she anticipates that the "mesh of grey-blue morning air" will "unwind" into a varied set of people and creatures, all of which will connect with and spread her life, as trees lift the mist. At rare contemplative moments, Mrs. Ramsay identifies with the third stroke of the lighthouse, partnered with the wedge of darkness that falls between the beams of light cast over the sea at night. She "looked out to meet that stroke of the Lighthouse, the long steady stroke, the last of three, which was her stroke; she became the thing she looked at" (*TTL* 66). She generalizes from communion with the stroke of light to holistic union with natural objects: "One leant to inanimate things; trees, streams, flowers; felt they expressed one; felt they became one; felt they knew one, in a sense were one; felt an irrational tenderness thus (she looked at that long steady light) as for oneself.... there curled up of the floor of one's being, a mist, a bride to meet her lover" (66–67). Mrs. Ramsay is a committed bride-maker, as shown earlier in the novel; here she has distance from and compassion for nature's bride. Mrs. Ramsay has a method for rising herself out of solitude "by laying hold of some little odd or end, some sound, some sight" (67). On this day she imagines the waves "as daylight faded, and the blue went out of the sea and it rolled in waves of pure lemon which curved and swelled and broke upon the beach and the ecstasy burst in her eyes and waves of pure delight raced over the floor of her mind and she felt, It is enough! It is enough!" (68). The rapture of this description might suggest mental orgasm; coincidentally, she is again beautiful to Mr. Ramsay, who has been concerned about the sternness and sadness of her meditations.

Lily, who twice attempts to bring her sense of the Ramsays to her painting in *To the Lighthouse*, recalls as she resumes her task in the final segment of the novel that "there had been a little sprig or leaf pattern on the table-cloth, which she had looked at in a moment of revelation.... Move the tree to the middle, she had said" (151). The tree is the point of balance around which she organizes her final vision. This tree is as helpful as the pear tree that had earlier organized her thoughts about Mr. Ramsay (28).

The Ramsays' daughter Cam has been much worried over by the critics, and particularly Louise DeSalvo, who sees her as a victim of maternal neglect and an inhabitant of watery worlds. Cam shares the aqueous imaginary of

Rachel in *The Voyage Out* and Rhoda in *The Waves*, both characters who die in the course of their novels. Early in Cam's life, her mother compares her mind with a deep well with clear but distorting waters: "The words seemed to be dropped into a well, where, if the waters were clear, they were also so extraordinarily distorting that, even as they descended, one saw them twisting about to make Heaven knows what pattern on the floor of the child's mind" (*TTL* 58). She knows that natural objects and forces distract Cam: "It might be a vision—a shell, of a wheelbarrow, or a fairy kingdom on the far side of the hedge; or it might be the glory of speed" (57). Appropriately, later that evening Mrs. Ramsay uses images taken from nature to construct a fairy landscape, distracting Cam from worries over a sheep's skull hanging in the nursery.

Years later, as they sail to the lighthouse, Mr. Ramsay tries to get Cam to identify their house, receding on the shore, and to engage her in discussion about a new puppy. Instead of focusing on such domesticity, Cam draws from an array of images, as she drags her hand through the water. She reaches back to the leaf she had trailed behind her years before and shares Woolf's own youthful amazement at existence:

> From her hand, ice cold, held deep in the sea, there spurted up a fountain of joy at the change, at the escape, at the adventure (that she should be alive, that she should be there). And the drops . . . fell here and there on the dark, the slumberous shapes in her mind; shapes of a world not realized but turning in their darkness, catching here and there, a spark of light; Greece, Rome, Constantinople. Small as it was, and shaped something like a leaf stood on its end with the gold-sprinkled waters flowing in and about it, it had, she supposed, a place in the universe— even that little island? (192)

Cam's looking into the depths, and her image of the "fountain of joy," are shared by other characters. Nancy gazes into the depths, on the small scale of her tidal pool. Mrs. Ramsay is associated with the ability "to pour erect into the air . . . a column of spray" (*TTL* 40). Cam's leaf from the first section of the novel, carried into the imagery of the hollow of the wave in "Time Passes," returns as Lily thinks of a leaf pattern before she repaints her picture. Cam finds her own sense of place in a small whirling universe, and Woolf leaves us to wonder whether she will be able to carry this beautiful mental collage into a realized world.

Many of Woolf's most brilliant natural images occur in such collages of modernist bits and pieces, or a rapid series of apprehensions. These often come to characters in crisis or survivors of trauma—outsiders in search of a survivable system. Such passages also warn readers about the sustainability of culture and the environment. The hallucinations of Septimus Smith in *Mrs. Dalloway*, Rhoda's work with abstract shapes in *The Waves*, and the mental collages of Cam in *To the Lighthouse*, Sara in *The Years*, and Isa in *Between the Acts* all fall into this category. The leaf turning in the hollow of the wave is representative of Cam at the close of *To the Lighthouse*. It involves gesture, performance, recollection, continuation. Like other struggling characters, Cam is sustained by collecting and arranging complex natural images to reconstruct an environment. There is some hope that, by touching back to the primordial, the semiotic, sensual, or material, and by interlacing one character's set of perceptions with another's, a new and different cycle of human nature, or nature with culture, may arise.

There is no reason to think all of Woolf's works (or even parts of those works) are doing the same thing in their uses of nature, or to assume that she moved neatly from one natural approach to another.[21] Some of her formal experiments provide unusual angles: for example, lyrical and dramatic interludes with little human presence, or lives of the obscure humans or creatures, or tunnels carved around characters, making them connect. Woolf overcomes the apprentice writer's anxieties of falling into quaint, rustic, or gender-determined representations of nature. Woolf's variously aged and gendered characters show different expressions and levels of engagement with nature. She shows differences of scope (from cosmic to minute), time scale (evolutionary, primordial, historic, or momentary), sensual and sexual arousal, and balanced versus unbalanced system. By representing the perceptions of a highly diverse outsiders' society, comprising early and anonymous composers of song, the young, the aged,[22] relatively powerless women, and animals, she is in tune with ecofeminism, suggesting alternatives to the imbalances of power that have lately afflicted the environment.

Nature is one of Woolf's most impressive players: reaching into time and space, where humans and their institutions are brief visitors, intimate with the depths of the unconscious and the delights of sexuality, changing with each phase of history, expressive of its own language and imagery, diverting in its beauty, vulnerable to acts of war and commerce, and hopeful of better order than humans have achieved. We can know Woolf better as a writer by comprehending more about her uses of nature. That she was so fully and creatively engaged with the natural world, particularly in an age that so deliberately focused on technical achievements and human competitions, makes her a resource for rethinking the sustained future of nature and culture combined.

Notes

Introduction

1. Haraway began blurring the borders between nature and culture with "Cyborg Manifesto" in *Simians, Cyborgs, and Women,* 149–81. *When Species Meet,* concerning dogs and humans, develops the concept most deliberately.

2. Notable exceptions are Tremper, Goldman, and Alt, whose *Virginia Woolf and the Study of Nature* was published after this study was complete. Alt argues that Woolf resisted the taxonomical methodology of the natural history tradition in favor of other contemporary scientific approaches, attending both to these paradigms and to Woolf's uses of scientific analogy. Recent papers from International Virginia Woolf Conferences also turn toward Woolf in a natural frame. See, for example, Alt; Blyth; Gerrard; Goldman, "'Ce chien est á moi'"; my "Woolf, Ecofeminism, and Breaking Boundaries"; and Sultzbach. Work on the modernist primitive by Torgovnick, especially in *Gone Primitive,* is also applicable.

3. Important works relating modernism to modernity include the journal *Modernism/Modernity,* which began appearing in 1994; Felski, Anderson, Dettmar and Watt's edited collection; and Walkowitz. Important resistance to and reshaping of ideas of modernity has emerged in postcolonial studies.

4. See *Earthcare* 75–90. Merchant first detects this formation in the sixteenth century, particularly in Francis Bacon's scientific discourse. This turned from an organic imagination that revered the earth as a living mother to a mechanical approach that subdued the earth to serve mankind's own inquisitiveness. Another mechanical model in Western thought, "the anthropological machine of humanism," has created, according to Giorgio Agamben, the idea of human superiority over animals by ceaselessly creating distinctions and divisions. His crafters of distinction include Aristotle, St. Thomas Aquinas, Linnaeus, and Haeckel.

5. Leading French feminists include Hélène Cixous, Luce Irigaray, Catherine Clément, Julia Kristeva, and Monique Wittig, all of whom challenged logocentric

partriarchal discourse. Ecofeminist evocations of the mother goddess are a concern in chapter 6.

6. See especially Sturgeon and Gaard, "Toward a Queer Ecofeminism."

7. For a fine summary of "Feminist Theory's Flight from Nature," see Alaimo 3–9.

8. Extended studies include Friedman's *Mappings*, Jane Marcus's *Hearts of Darkness*, and Phillips.

9. "Even oneself has felt it, driving any new idea into the great passive vulva of London, a sensation analogous to the male feeling in copulation." This is from his postscript to Remy de Gourmont's *The Natural Philosophy of Love.*

10. See for example *The Waves*, where Bernard is aware of "shells and bones" beneath London's pavements (82), or "London Revisited," where bones of extinct monsters lie in cellars (*E* 2:50).

11. Leonard Woolf felt that St. Ives had a permanent hold on the Stephen family (*Beginning Again* 163). Woolf's nephew, Quentin Bell, proclaimed Cornwall "the Eden of her youth, an unforgettable paradise" (*Virginia Woolf: A Biography* 32).

12. Like the symbols Freud assigned to dream work, the images associated with abuse are, in my opinion, best studied for multiplicity of connotation and presentation, rather than as one-to-one clinical correspondences.

13. I am grateful to Michelle Garvey for bringing the posthuman into focus as a useful category for this study. James Joyce used "posthuman" in correspondence with his patron, Harriet Shaw Weaver. She had used "prehuman" to describe the "Penelope" episode of *Ulysses*. He responded, "Your description of it . . . coincides with my intention—if the epithet 'post human' were added. . . . In conception and technique I tried to depict the earth which is prehuman and presumably posthuman" (*Selected Letters* 289). This makes the human a brief episode—a form of decentering also found in the cosmic view occasionally afforded by Woolf.

14. Examples of recent ecofeminist interest are Cantrell, Kostkowska, Waller, Walker, and Westling. As we proceed, I will be discussing ways that nature enters the mythic and figurative formulations of Abel; Madeline Moore, "Female Versions of Pastoral"; DeKoven, *Rich and Strange;* and DiBattista.

15. The first panel focused on creatures: Ian Blyth on rooks; Richard Espley on "others at the zoo," and Jane Goldman on "the signifying dog." In the second, Diana Swanson sought an ecofeminist in *Jacob's Room*, Astrid Bracke crossed the "human-nonhuman boundary," and I proposed ecofeminist boundary breaking.

1. Toward a Greening of Modernism

1. The term originated in Wyndham Lewis's *Blasting and Bombardiering* (1937) and has been much used in discussions of modernist history, particularly where gender is concerned. His journal, *Blast,* lasted only two numbers (1914–15). The second was a war number, introducing the event that would provide pervasive modernist images of lost illusions and shattered order.

2. I began this discussion in *Refiguring Modernism*, 1:97–98, 102–6.

3. Ortner does not exempt women from willing participation in a system that defines them as cultural inferiors (86).

4. Monroe urged the U.S. Senate to prevent the construction of the Hetch Hetchy Reservoir, which devastated a scenic valley in Yosemite. Schulze couples Monroe's landscapes with a form of nationalism, demonstrating the importance of understanding ways that nature and nation are conflated. Natural subjects dominate Monroe's selection of her poems for a 1925 volume, including Carolina and the American West as settings. She also presents mechanical aspects of modernity, including the turbine and the power plant.

5. See my *Refiguring Modernism*, 1:111, for a more thorough discussion of the gendered dimensions of Lewis.

6. See Jane Marcus, "Taking the Bull by the Udders," for an interpretation of Woolf's response to Lewis's phrase "taking the cow by the horns" (150). Marcus finds Woolf claiming liberal sexuality, against the grain of the Bloomsbury homosexual literary establishment.

7. Cuddy notes that Charlotte Eliot consistently spoke of "evolution" in her cultural activities, some with the Unitarian Church. In her study of Eliot and evolution, Cuddy suggests that "for the culture in which Eliot and his modernist contemporaries were educated, evolution was the principle that suggested both chaos and comfort, progress and regression, unity and fragmentation" (13).

8. The "Cape Ann" landscape poem provides a litany of birds, showing detailed knowledge of types of warblers, and ends on the gull, a favorite bird that made an early appearance in "Gerontian."

9. See DuPlessis's *Genders, Races, and Religious Cultures*. In *Stalking the Subject*, Rohman reads this poem for "post-Darwinian anxiety about the nature of the human" (32), finding "an easy consonance between animality and debased sexual congress" (34).

10. See my *Refiguring Modernism*, 1:123, for Vivien Eliot's recollections of Eliot at Bosham.

11. Eliot was executor for the Mirrlees estate. Her friendship with him is what makes Mirrlees remarkable to some. "Paris" (1919) has attributes comparable to Eliot's later "The Waste Land," as Julia Briggs has effectively argued. "Paris" blends natural and urban elements as it moves along the metro line to various Paris locations. See Briggs's annotated edition in my *Gender in Modernism*.

12. Volume 2 of *A la recherche du temps perdu* (1919) is titled, significantly, *A l'ombre des jeune filles en fleur* (*In the Shadow of Young Girls in Flower*). This opens with the comparison of young girls to a hedge of Pennsylvania roses and moves to an artist painting a flower. In her innocence and fidelity, the character Albertine is frequently described as a flower. Proust's famous madeleine, described in *Swann's Way*, is dipped in linden-flower tea, creating a smell and taste memorable from distant childhood.

13. This attitude was among the reasons Woolf gave for Hogarth Press's declining to publish *Ulysses*.

14. As F. W. Dupee notes in his "General Introduction" to *Selected Writings of*

Gertrude Stein, these two phrases from "Sacred Emily" (1913; published 1922) and *Four Saints in Three Acts* (1929) rapidly joined popular culture (ix). Stein did numerous reprises of "a rose is a rose is a rose is a rose."

15. The year before, they opted not to publish *The Making of Americans* and "Poetry and Criticism."

16. Stein offered an explanation that this "button" described what a donkey looks like going uphill ("Transatlantic Interview" 508). In a paper presented at the 2009 Modernist Studies Association meeting, "Flush and Basket: Woolf and Stein as Dogs," DeKoven suggests that both Woolf and Stein may have used their dogs to work out a relation between identity and writing. She focuses on Stein's *Geographical History of America* (1935), which repeats the memorable line "I am I because my little dog knows me."

17. See H.D.'s *End to Torment,* in which Pound plays Satyr to her Dryad, when her father finds the two in an armchair, an event she links to canto 74. She is also the Maenid of canto 79.

18. All quotations of H.D.'s poetry are from her *Collected Poems.* Line numbers are cited parenthetically in the text.

19. Moran has chosen the image of two pears for the cover of her book on Woolf and Mansfield, *Word of Mouth.*

20. See Gaard, "Toward a Queer Ecofeminism," for her discussion of "erotophobia," starting with the ascetic roots of early Christianity (29–32). The "matrifocal, matrilinear, peaceful agrarian era" preceding classical Greece and various migrations into Europe (Eisler 29) is suggested in H.D.'s ideas of Eleusis. See also Charlene Spretnak, *Lost Goddesses of Ancient Greece: A Collection of Pre-Hellenic Myths* (Boston: Beacon, 1981). Eisler and Spretnak are spiritual ecofeminists of the 1980s.

21. See my *Refiguring Modernism* for additional contextualizing of Harrison's work (1:50–51; 2:41–42). Chapter 6 returns to Harrison for rituals situated in nature.

22. "A Ship Comes into the Harbour," in *The Critical Writings of Katherine Mansfield* (Basingstoke: Macmillan, 1987), 56–57.

23. For more on Barnes's menagerie, see my "Barnes's Beasts Turning Human," chap. 2 of *Refiguring Modernism,* vol. 2, and "Revising the Human," chap. 5 of Rohman's *Stalking the Subject.*

24. I have long enjoyed constructing modernist intersections, the prime example being the "Tangled Mesh of Modernists" that illustrates the introduction of *The Gender of Modernism* (10).

2. Diversions of Darwin and Natural History

1. See Benjamin, *Science and Sensibility;* Harding (especially part 3, "Who Gets to Do Science?"); Breton (especially the chapter concerning the pioneer ecologist Ellen Swallow); and Gates, *Kindred Nature* (especially chap. 3, "Cataloging the Natural World").

2. An early example is Mrs. Fleming, who uses the phrase to describe her upbringing as one of thirteen children in *The Voyage Out.*

3. The description also qualifies as homophobic. It parodies exclusive male coteries at Cambridge, known for homosocial bonding. Jane Marcus has indicted the Cambridge Apostles for practices analogous to "fascist notions of fraternity" ("Liberty" 79–80). Piggford places Woolf in the company of Lytton Strachey and a Bloomsbury tradition of "camp biography," involving parodic strategies (101), which we might see in operation here.

4. Henry cites this incident and its capacity to stir Woolf's imagination in relation to astronomical perspective. Beer has written numerous studies related to science and the new physics, which also has entered into the recent work of Froula and Goldman. Like Henry, Alt's *Virginia Woolf and the Study of Nature* draws attention to scientific discourse, her work focusing on biology and incipient environmentalism, as they may have influenced Woolf.

5. Hankins, who has worked extensively on London's 1920s film culture, notes London Film Society showings of a "Bionomics Series" and "Nature Shorts." See also Laura Marcus 266.

6. See Gates and Shteir's *Natural Eloquence,* which demonstrates a nineteenth-century tradition for women writing science. Women popularized both natural history and disciplinary science, developing their own narrative techniques, emphases, and challenges.

7. Titles included White's *Natural History of Selborne* (1825) and his *Natural History and Antiquities of Selborne* (1901), W. S. Coleman's *British Butterflies* (1860), Robert Bentley's *Manual of Botany* (1882), George Bentham's *Handbook of British Flora* (1887), William Yarrell's *History of British Birds* (1856), and L. Howard Irby's *British Birds* (1892). As a girl, Woolf's mother had been awarded *Oeuvres Choisies de Buffon* (1858)—a work some see as a precursor of Darwin's theory of evolution.

8. An academic career at Cambridge required that he hold orders as a minister of the Church of England, which became an untenable position.

9. Leslie helped the family decide what to do in a dispute with Samuel Butler concerning rival interpretations of grandfather, Erasmus, whom Butler placed above Charles in importance (Desmond and Moore 648). Darwin's sons George and Francis visited regularly, and Francis married a Fisher cousin. Darwin's granddaughter Gwen frequented the younger generation's Bloomsbury gatherings. Her woodcuts depict streams, forests, bathing nymphs, and princesses. Woolf reports to Gwen and her husband, Jacques Riverat, that Jane Harrison had mentioned them during a recent visit. When Harrison expressed her woe over the religious revival among their mutual acquaintances, Woolf tried to cheer her with "There are thousands of Darwins," to which Harrison responded, "clasping her mittened hands and raising her eyes to Heaven . . . [,] 'The Darwins are the blackest of them all! With that name! . . . that inheritance! That magnificent record of the past!'" (*L* 3:58–59).

10. Gates and Shteir list "botany, the fern craze; geology, the rock-collecting craze;

entomology, the bug-hunting craze—all of these became female more than male pursuits" (10).

11. See the *Hyde Park Gate News* for items concerning the Stephen children's hiking and sailing. Adrian did not accompany Virginia, Thoby, and the Hunts on one sail, experiencing a disappointment akin to that of James in *To the Lighthouse*. Soon after, Leslie took both Adrian and Virginia sailing, and they spotted a porpoise (118). Another expedition led by "Mr. Stephen" goes to the "peninsular usually called the Island" to see the waves that accompany stormy days (120).

12. Nicholson interview, July 19, 2000.

13. None of the Stephens signed the Insect Room guest book in 1897, but it seems to have been kept irregularly, favoring visitors from afar. Today insects are found in a room called "Creepy Crawlies." Linnaean nomenclature is explained but rarely provided. While insect displays still illustrate their capacity for damage and spread of disease, there is greater interest in their ecological niche and adaptations. Concern over human degradation of birds' habitat is also expressed.

14. Mrs. Ramsay thinks of a storm-battered bird in *To the Lighthouse*.

15. Lee is among those who argue for the importance of shared literary interests (115).

16. See for example his dissection of the water ousel (*Natural History of Selborne* 68). He also describes research on the now rarely seen honey-buzzard. First a "bold boy" climbed a tree to extract the only egg in a nest. Subsequently the "hen-bird" was shot, then examined minutely to see if she resembled the species description and to find the content of her craw (109).

17. Walter Rothschild Zoological Museum, Tring, Mss Stephen Acc. 3149071001. In 1999, following her husband Quentin Bell's death, Ann Olivier Bell gave the manuscript to the Natural History Museum, deeming it an appropriate home for a work that "seemed to bear little relation to the largely literary and artistic nature of the rest" of Bell's family papers.

18. Jane Marcus's application of Darwin to the scene involves a conflation of the individual with evolution: "*The Years* asks the question, Is there a pattern? And *Between the Acts* gives a socio-biological answer. The origin of aggression, war, and oppression is in the origin of the species, in the drama of the battle of the sexes" ("Liberty" 77).

19. For example, Linnaeus based classes on the male stamen and lesser orders within them on the female pistils of flowers (Schiebinger 125).

20. Wallace was professor of agriculture at Edinburgh University. He encouraged Ormerod to write her autobiography. When she could not complete the task, he supplemented the latter narrative with extracts from her letters, arranged to show her work in controlling various insect infestations, and her campaign against the house sparrow, a.k.a. "the avian rat" (160).

21. Miss Ormerod identifies this incident as her "first insect investigation." Woolf adds details, such as a thumping of the table, to indicate the child's excitement. By the mid-1920s, Woolf would have been able to experience similar phenomena of nature at the cinema. The London Film Society aired a film on Dytiscus, "the common

carnivorous water beetle" in its fourth program, which describes "its exceptional voracity, both in the adult and the larval stages" as it exhibits its behavior "towards tadpoles and a full grown newt."

22. Ormerod's first important publication was "Notes for Observations of Injurious Insects," published in 1877, four years after her father's death. Gates argues that Ormerod was anything but obscure by the turn of the twentieth century and credits her with discovering how to "authorize herself in an area just outside 'high' science," agricultural economics (*Kindred Nature* 89).

23. Rachel Carson sounded the alarm on insecticides in the mid-twentieth century—an understanding of and approach to nature that complicates Ormerod's legacy, despite their common struggles against established practices.

24. Ormerod was, however, passed over for a lectureship in agricultural entomology at Edinburgh, as "Lady Professors are not admitted in Scotland." She reflected, "I think I could do all that is wanted, but then, oh! Shades of John Knox" (201).

25. Woolf identifies North as a "traveller" rather than a botanist or an artist in this essay.

26. In his "Pulp Fiction," Coyle cites incidents involving the "conjuring trick" of the paper flowers as moments of post-Romantic transcendence and accessibility in otherwise difficult texts. He focuses upon incidents in Proust's *A la recherche du temps perdu* and Joyce's *Ulysses,* but uses this quotation from Woolf centrally as evidence of her having "arch fun" over discovering worlds in small desiccated objects.

27. It seems oddly appropriate that in offering this formula, Halberstam and Livingston cite a performance of the rock group U2 that involves a disconcerting use of mirrors. "Bono's various couplings on stage with mirrors, cameras and video equipment fundamentally undermined otherwise stable relationships between the fan and star, disconcerting the technology of rock stardom by insisting that the star is a trick of the dazzling lights, a feedback effect rather than an emotional center that anchors the rock performance in time and space for each individual fan" (3).

Chapter 5 continues the discussion of posthuman bodies, with a focus on Haraway.

3. Limits of the Garden as Cultured Space

1. Sparks, "Woolf's Literary and Quotidian Flowers." Sparks notes that Greenaway was a friend of Violet Dickinson, whose garden figures in this account.

2. The exhibit "Virginia Woolf: A Botanical Perspective," at the 2003 Virginia Woolf Conference at Smith College, toured St. Ives, Kew Gardens, Monk's House, and Sissinghurst. It included botanical prints by Vanessa Bell and photographs from the Mortimer Rare Book Room.

3. Kathleen Karlson, "Cyclamen Flower Meanings," at *Living Arts Originals,* http://www.livingartsoriginals.com/flower-cyclamen.htm (last updated September 14, 2010).

4. In a previous entry, written after a walk with Stella, she describes these flowers

at an earlier stage and quotes with caution "a reverend gentleman" who had written to the *Times* to record a prodigiously early hawthorn flower (*PA* 52).

5. Sparks offers frequencies for flower types in Woolf's works. Roses are by far the most numerous (123 references), with carnations (33), violets (33) and lilies (29) following ("Woolf's Literary and Quotidian Flowers").

6. According to Geoffrey Young, Queen Caroline (wife of George III) posted servants at the entrances to assure that the "meanly clad" did not enter (49). Kensington Gardens dates back to William III's move to Kensington Palace.

7. Built in 1704 for Queen Anne, it may have been designed by Christopher Wren.

8. Her parents contributed to the positive outcome, with Julia sewing new sails and Leslie rigging them. Woolf's description of Sir Leslie "fixing the sails to the yard-arm after dinner" is touching. He said "with his little snort, half laughing, something like 'Absurd—what fun it is doing this'" (*MB* 77).

9. The younger Hooker's botanical expertise was valuable as Darwin assessed the plant species collected on the voyage of the Beagle. Hooker helped convince the scientific community that the theory of evolution originated with Darwin. See Emma Townshend, "Kew's Connection with Charles Darwin: An Evolutionary Relationship," *Kew Magazine,* September 29, 2009, http://www.kew.org/news/kew-connec tion-with-darwin.htm.

10. See Torgovnick, *Visual Arts* 131, and Hussey, *Singing* 70.

11. Stavely provides a detailed and insightful reading of the four conversations. She is particularly perceptive about the gender politics of what this couple is negotiating (49–50).

12. Woolf's short story "Happiness" presents a bachelor, Stuart Elton, to whom an afternoon alone at Kew represents his fragile sense of happiness, and his ability to keep the world (represented as a pack of wolves) at bay.

13. Sparks lists Dickinson among the master gardeners of Woolf's acquaintance, citing Dickinson's friendship with the gardening designers and authorities of her day, such as Gertrude Jekyll and William Robinson ("Woolf's Literary and Quotidian Flowers"). Like Caroline Stephen, Dickinson was an early mentor for Woolf.

14. Adding artistic features to the garden was a tradition that her son Quentin and grandson Julian later joined, with Quentin contributing both pottery and sculpture well into the 1970s.

15. The Charleston Trust (http://www.charleston.org.uk/) makes the gardens accessible to the public.

16. See also Grant's *The Doorway* (1925) and *Window, South of France* (1928), and Fry's *Spring in Provence* (1931).

17. Vanessa and Virginia have been cast both as sister artists and as rivals. In context, the remark is part of a discussion of color compatibility, where one of Vanessa's floral paintings needs a more harmonious choice of upholstery in the room, with Woolf distrusting her own aesthetics.

18. Woolf also mentions the thrush, though she hears the wood pigeon: "From the

deepest wells of silence the wood pigeon drew its bubble of sound, 'Safe, safe safe,' the pulse of the house beat softly" (*CSF* 122). As is characteristic of both sisters' art, the garden and the house merge, with apples and roses reflected in the window panes.

19. See especially chap. 8, "And No Birds Sing."

20. Case, Woolf's tutor in Greek, published articles on country life in the *Manchester Guardian*, later collected in *Country Diaries* (1939), which resided in the Woolfs' bookshelves.

21. Titles included *Bulb Gardening* (1925), *Flowering Trees and Shrubs* (1924), *The Real A B C of Gardening* (1924), *Gladioli* (1925), and *Soils and Fertilizers* (1926) by A. J. Macself; *Garden Construction* (1923), *Garden Development* (1924), and *Garden Renovation* (1926) by T. Geoffrey W. Henslow; *A Handbook of Garden Irises* (1924) by W. R. Dykes, *British Flora* (1925) by Gaston Bonnier, *A Handbook of Crocus and Colchicum for Gardeners* (1924) by E. A. Bowles, and *Garden Ponds and Pools* (1933) by A. E. Hodge.

22. See especially her essay entitled "Leonard's Vegetable Empire."

23. Nicholson interview, July 19, 2000; Nicholson, *Woolf: A Penguin Life* 73.

24. His meticulous records are preserved at the University of Sussex Library.

25. See Cramer ("Notes from Underground" 184) and Jane Marcus's discussion of Rose in *The Years* (*Languages of Patriarchy* 53). Greenaway lists "love" as the basic meaning for the rose, but has more varied definitions for various strains and colors. White and red roses stand for York and Lancaster, respectively, combatants in the Wars of the Roses, but white and red roses together signify "unity" to her.

26. For a fine comparative analysis modernist representations of pear trees (Lily's in *TTL* with Janie's in Zora Neal Hurston's *Their Eyes Were Watching God*), see Oxindine.

27. DiBattista suggests that "one is the genius of the shore, the other of the garden, offering their protection against 'the reign of chaos'" (74).

28. Mrs. Ramsay has gone through several stages of critical evaluation, as Lilienfeld has ably summarized in "Where the Spear Plants Grew." To one group, she is the "motherly, all-giving Angel in the House" and subject to her "harassment by her desiccated husband." Others view her as a "feather-brained self-satisfied manipulator" responsible for her husband's unhappiness (148–49). Lilienfeld finds that Woolf resists representing the Ramsay marriage as the union between naturally given masculine and feminine principles, interpreting this as a feminist position.

29. Written by Charles Elton, a relative of Lytton Strachey, this poem was apparently not published until 1945, in a collection edited by Vita Sackville-West and Harold Nicholson (Hussey, "Notes to TTL" 227). Lives "full of trees and changing leaves" correspond well to Woolf's own flora; by quoting a stanza on "kings" going by with "palm leaves," she implicates the planting of empire.

30. DiBattista notes that this poem supports "the novel's veiled myth of marriage as a paradisiacal Edenic state in which the relationship between the subject and object, self and world is spiritualized into the union of lover and beloved" (86).

31. In "Britannia Rules *The Waves*," Marcus sees Elvedon, its staff of sweepers, and

its woman writer as "the patriarchal representation of Woman as Culture" (139). It oppresses the working class and is complicit with imperial projects (140–41).

32. One photograph in Leslie Stephen's album reveals a very extensive greenhouse to the side of Talland House.

33. The lines also owe much to Edward Thomas's despairing poem "Old Man," which uses the same scented herb as a central metaphor and concludes with the memory of "an avenue dark, nameless, without end" (11).

34. This description has considerable resonance with West's *The Judge*, in which a leading female character, Marion, leaves on a similarly fatal walk, passing through her prized garden into a watery landscape. The focus on the heterosexual couple also has traction in West's *Black Lamb and Grey Falcon*. West's conception that Leonard made the garden for Virginia, though romantic, is undoubtedly an oversimplification.

4. The Art of Landscape, the Politics of Place

1. Buell notes "a porousness of ego boundaries bordering on panpsychism" in characters' shared urban environment. Woolf's flânerie is sensitive to the "interchangeability between nature and *techne*" (107). Much of Buell's brief analysis compares Woolf's vision of human "uncontrol" to the "more assertively politicized" vision of Henri Lefebvre (108)—a comparison that, like much early criticism of Woolf, depoliticizes her.

2. Leslie Stephen also affected the "cockney," though sometimes in a derogatory manner: "'The genuine British cockney in all his terrors,' was unmoved by 'the soft beauty of an Alpine valley'" (Schama 504).

3. As Goldman notes, she also recorded this statement in her reading notebook (*Cambridge Introduction* 39).

4. Cantrell offers a useful set of criteria for an idea of place that is distinct from thinking about landscape and that "necessarily includes the human presence" (34).

5. Woolf did not admire this strain of Brooke's poetry. She confesses in "The Intellectual Imagination," that "it has never happened to us, walking the woods, to hum over a line or two, and waking to find them his" (*E* 3:134). He lacked the "visionary imagination" she found in Keats and Shelley.

6. See Bazargan for a postcolonial analysis of Sackville-West's pastoral writing, from "The Land" through her Persian writings. Bazargan identifies "The Land" with a universalizing, masculine tradition of the pastoral that lays claim to the land, even as it naturalizes the poverty of rural laborers.

7. Julia Stephen posed for both Burne-Jones and Julia Cameron.

8. Watts embellished the walls of Little Holland House with mythical subjects in the image of the beautiful Pattle daughters—perhaps a remote source for Woolf's goddesses in *Mrs. Dalloway*, *Orlando*, and *The Waves*. Spalding opens her biography of Vanessa with a moving account of her 1903 visit to the studio of the aged Watts (1–2). Like Watts, Vanessa adorned interiors with her art, as Charleston still testifies.

9. I am grateful to Tony Inglis for his helpful explanation of this terrain. The

professional help and personal hospitality of his wife, Elizabeth Inglis, the former head of Special Collections at the University of Sussex, is legendary.

10. Sussex was a favorite haunt of the Stephen family long before her birth. Leslie took refuge in Brighton after Minny's death and later lodged in Seaford. He walked through Lewes castle with Julia and her son George while courting her.

11. Her narrative gives a feeling of spirited camaraderie with her siblings, including her half brother George, who in later accounts appears at best a bore, and at worst a sexual abuser.

12. With the exception of student years at Oxford, and occasional visits nearby, White spent his entire life in and around his native Hampshire village, Selborne, serving as a curate. Selborne boasted "one single straggling street, three-quarters of a mile in length," but the geography, flora, and fauna of this "sheltered vale" satisfied his investigations for life (*Natural History of Selborne* 4).

13. For a sobering explanation, raising the specter of sexual abuse, see DeSalvo. Though not dismissing the possibility of a sexually encoded message, I find this more likely in other texts, such as Rachel's nightmare tunnel beneath the Thames in *The Voyage Out*.

14. Millais's *Autumn Leaves* depicts four solemn-faced girls, collecting and burning leaves. A view to the flatlands of Perthshire leads along a line of sparse trees to a bright sunset, with a few dark clouds. Hunting and fishing in Perthshire gave Millais familiarity with this landscape.

15. In "The Island and the Aeroplane," Gillian Beer meditates upon the passing of an island conception of England, with the advent of the airplane as used in World War II. The older island concept, she suggests, is highly dependent upon the sea.

16. Among her sojourns on the downs were Playden (1907), Firle (where Woolf christened her 1911 abode "Little Talland House"), Asham House (leased 1911–19), and finally Monk's House (1919–41). Morris's *Travels with Virginia Woolf* offers detailed descriptions of English places she visited.

17. Something that annoyed Woolf about Wells was the frequent ringing of cathedral bells.

18. Woolf may have joined other modernists in an "anthropological turn" in the 1930s, again affecting attitudes toward Englishness (Southworth 197).

19. Qtd. by Malcolm Warner (73), who provides an excellent description of the painting and its reception in *The Victorians: British Painting, 1837–1901* (Washington, DC: National Gallery of Art, 1997).

20. In "An Essay in Aesthetics" (1909), he had said, "Alas! Nature is heartlessly indifferent to the needs of the imaginative life" (24). See 24–25 for a further discussion of art's uses of nature. In "Modern French Art at the Mansard Gallery" (1919), Fry discusses various streams of the modern movement, including its own version of naturalism. In recent cubists he found "ideas, symbolized by forms, could be juxtaposed, contrasted and combined almost as they can be by words on a page" (341). This did "almost precisely the same thing in paint that Virginia Woolf is doing in prose" (342), though he preferred her effect.

21. Charles Steele appears in the opening seascape of *Jacob's Room*. He needs Betty Flanders's form to contribute a "violet-black dab" to a landscape otherwise "too pale" (8).

22. Lily's paintings continue to inspire interpretation, as seen in the friendly competition between the artists Suzanne Bellamy and Isota Tucker Epes, each displaying her own versions at the 1999 Virginia Woolf Conference. See Bellamy and Epes in Ardis and Scott (244–56). Neither of their final paintings has a bold center line, but both offer the slim trunk of a tree. Bellamy also presents an energetic proliferation of triangles in her final painting and offers a central painting that eclipses landscape; she sees Lily as a would-be surrealist.

23. For a discussion of modernist women travelers and nationalism, see Rabinowitz (on lady painters) and Schulze (on poet/editor Harriet Monroe).

24. See the essays "Great Men's Houses" and "Character in Fiction" (*E* 3:420–438)—later with slight revisions titled "Mr. Bennett and Mrs. Brown"—for Woolf's description of the sexist domestic arrangements that oppressed the talented Jane Carlyle.

25. For the full climbing resumé, see Hollis.

26. Though less well known than his writing on art and architecture, his subjects included botany and geology, in the natural history tradition.

27. See Schama 503 for the image and Hollis for a sense of the impact of this accident.

28. Both Briggs (364, 395) and Hollis ("Virginia Woolf as Mountaineer") discuss the story in the light of Woolf's struggle with death during the last winter of her life.

29. In his poetry and his *Autobiography of a Super-Tramp* (1908), W. H. Davies showed that "nature worship which was, for many people the essence of Englishness" (Giles and Middleton 22).

30. Soon after Leslie Stephen's death in 1904, Woolf, Vanessa, and her brothers Thoby and Adrian visited Italy. The year 1905 brought a cruise to Spain and Portugal via France with Adrian. In 1906 Virginia, Vanessa, and Violet Dickinson traveled to Greece, where they met Adrian and Thoby; the women then traveled on alone to Constantinople. Woolf went to Italy in 1908 and 1909, and to Bayreuth and Dresden in 1909. By the 1920s, she went regularly to France, where Vanessa frequented Cassis. She returned to Spain and Germany with Leonard and visited Ireland in the mid-1930s.

31. See Jamie McDaniel's discussion of inheritance issues.

32. See Woolf's "Thunder at Wembley" (*E* 3:410–14), an essay testifying to her own experience of such exhibitions.

33. In *The Years,* Martin Pargiter also ventures to India, and he proves equally unheroic. He gets lost in the jungle, is down to his last match, and, to reestablish his track, climbs not a mountain but a small tree. His account is presented so as to make it seem unimportant, as Eleanor reads the numerous sheets of a letter in his small hand, in fits and starts, while riding through the streets of London.

34. Mitchell Leaska suggests that the impeded view of Pointz Hall may have been

inspired by Asham. Woolf complained builders had destroyed its view (notes to *Pointz Hall* 194).

5. Crossing the Species Barrier

1. In *Virginia Woolf*, Quentin Bell sees "Goat" emerging from Virginia's childhood "misadventures," such as losing her knickers in Kensington Gardens (24).

2. From a letter in a private collection, exhibited in "Virginia Woolf: This Perpetual Flight."

3. Woolf had identified herself with a whole group of monkeys, the "Singes," in family correspondence. The mandrill (signifying "man-ape") has an amusing place in English popular culture. "Happy Jerry," found at the Exeter Exchange in the 1820s, reportedly "drank grog, smoked a short clay pipe, and on one occasion dined . . . with George IV at Windsor Castle" (Blunt, *Ark in the Park* 95).

4. For an extensive list of nicknames, see *L* 1:509–10. Included are Apes, Sparroy (a sparrow monkey blend), Kangaroo and Wallaby for Virginia (the latter three with Violet Dickinson), Toad for Emma Vaughan, Barbary Ape for Madge Vaughan, Bruin (bear) for Ka Cox, Chipmunk for Clive Bell, Dolphin for Vanessa, and Wombat for the dog Hans. Later volumes of letters did not require extensive lists, suggesting fewer nicknames over time.

5. See also DeKoven's "Flush and Basket," on a panel she organized.

6. Art Spiegelman's graphic novel of holocaust survival, *Maus*, appropriates comparable animal representations of nationalities/ethnicities: Jews as mice; Germans, cats; Americans, dogs; British, fish; French, frogs. He both uses and challenges offensive cultural figurations.

7. Beth Rigel Daugherty's "Taking her Fences" offers a fine collection of Woolf's use of the trope.

8. See "In the House of the Paterfamilias," chap. 5 of DeSalvo's *Virginia Woolf* (134–61).

9. According to Mr. Pepper, Vinrace is a ship magnate, with ten ships that regularly ply their trade between Buenos Aires and London (*VO* 22). Rachel thinks of the welfare of the goats, rather than that of the native flora and fauna. The introduction of grazing stock to South America by Europeans has led to the destruction of indigenous animals and the dangerous reduction of native rain forests, as we realize today.

10. In *Virginia Woolf*, Quentin Bell observes that his aunt "nearly always had a dog, she took a dog with her when she went for a walk and, up to a point, controlled the creature" (175). Leonard played the alpha dog or "Sergeant-Major" with the dogs they shared. Woolf's earliest letters to Leonard after their marriage report on the adventures of Shot and Mike, cohabiting Asham House with her.

11. Haraway finds problems in cross-species encounters of Derrida and Deleuze and Guattari. Writing of his cat encountering him naked ("The Animal That Therefore I Am"), Derrida came "right to the edge of respect," but he was not "curious about what the cat might actually be doing, feeling, thinking, or perhaps making available to

him" (*When Species Meet* 20). In treating the wolf pack in *A Thousand Plateaus* (part of their study of "becoming animal"), Deleuze and Guattari show little respect for actual animals and attach undue sublimity to the wild wolf, versus the domestic dog, according to Haraway (29).

12. She wrote to Violet Dickinson of her "obituary notice of poor old Shag.... I hope Miss L will print it and make poor Sophies heart glad (*L* 1:164).

13. Woolf discusses adding a kitten to her life with Violet Dickinson in a May 1905 letter (*L* 1:191).

14. See Gilbert for a thorough account of the legislation and its overreaching enforcement as well as the opposition spearheaded by the National Canine Defense League.

15. Hans was a mixed-breed female acquired by Virginia and Adrian Stephen at a shelter.

16. For a dog-by-dog account of Woolf's life, see Maureen Adams.

17. For a collection of interpretations of the tailless cat in *A Room of One's Own*, see Hussey, *Virginia Woolf A-Z* (154). What it represents could be "silenced, mutilated women," according to Patricia Joplin, or "missing tales" of women in male colleges, as suggested by Jane Marcus. *Hyde Park Gate News* bore notice of the appearance of a "beautiful black but tailless cat" at the Stephen residence, reporting that the "juniors think it is a Manx, while the seniors think it not" (29).

18. Here Woolf inserts the name of a mixed-breed dog and a favorite with both Leonard and Virginia.

19. The study of Wilson survives mainly in a spirited six-page note, perhaps derived from an unpublished essay, "The Cook," based on Sophie's life (Light 71). In "Woolf's Dogs and Servants," Pamela Caughie compares Woolf's writing on servants and dogs, suggesting she had similar struggles in crossing class and species barriers.

20. See Vanita and Trombley. Vanessa contributed four drawings, decorating the inside covers of the first edition.

21. Aspects of this passage resonate with the primordial history Lucy Swithin reads in *Between the Acts*. This novel also offers a dog of ancient ancestry, Bart's Afghan hound Sohrab.

22. Jean Dubino has suggested that Woolf backed her whimsicality with historical research in breed books and on dynastic families, for her etymological explanations.

23. In discussing her impressions of country life, Woolf cites Mitford as the sort of country writer she did not wish to emulate. "I should not mind if the homes and haunts of Mary Russell Mitford were closed to the public for a century at least" (*AROO* 45). Mitford's "Walks in the Country" describes her dog puzzling over a tightly balled hedgehog.

24. One of the works Ritvo cites to represent the cult of the pet dog is one published in 1911 by Duckworth—Judith Neville Lytton's *Toy Dogs and Their Ancestry*.

25. He wrote numerous books related to sport fishing, including *A History of Fly Fishing for Trout* (1921), *The Golden River: Sport and Travel in Paraguay* (1922), *A*

Summer on the Test (1924), and *My Sporting Life* (1936), which Woolf reviewed, quoting generously (*E* 6:592–97).

26. See chaps. 6 and 8 of Goldman, *Feminist Aesthetics,* for interpretation of the aesthetics of the essay.

27. Two additional men in the family owe their deaths to hunting. Goldman's interpretation addresses the image of a mermaid in the crumbling plasterwork above the fireplace (*Feminist Aesthetics* 97–98). This fish/woman fits into women's associations with captured fish in the previous section of this chapter.

28. Letter from Thoby Stephen to Clive Bell, August 1902, University of Sussex. As evidence that Thoby did some shooting, he owned a cartridge belt, which he managed to leave behind on one vacation.

29. Diary, June 19, 1910, Leonard Woolf Collection, University of Sussex.

30. Though Virginia frequently referred to the couple's dogs, Mitzi comes in for surprisingly little attention in her diaries and letters. She did assign Leonard's pet a part in the play *Freshwater.*

31. Pippett called her early biography *The Moth and the Star,* recognizing the frequent presence of the moth in her work. Richter links the moth to Woolf's creative imaginary, while the "painted lady" butterfly expresses Vanessa Bell's creativity (17).

32. See Froula, "Out of the Chrysalis," concerning Rachel in *The Voyage Out.*

33. A sinister companion piece for this work is Katherine Mansfield's "The Fly," which follows a man's sadistic play with a fly he first liberates from sure death in his ink bottle, and then tests, with repeated doses of ink, unto death.

34. Thoby's devotion to birds emerges poignantly in a letter Woolf wrote to the desperately ill Violet Dickinson. Woolf tries to reassure Dickinson that Thoby is improving, when he had already died: "He asks [his nurse] why he cannot go for a ride with Bell, and look for wild geese. Then nurse says, 'won't tame ones do' at which we laugh" (*L* 1:250).

35. Septimus has various forms of communication with animals. He gets messages from sparrows and grasshoppers, and he is troubled by the hallucination of a terrier changing into a man.

36. I thank Jane Goldman for making this connection.

37. At the boys' boarding school in *The Waves,* another metallic bird, a brass eagle (symbol of military might), holds the Bible in the chapel (23–24).

38. Birds have a more limited presence in the remaining interludes. They build nests in interlude 5, have remote flight patterns in interlude 7, are represented by hawk and plover in interlude 8, and grow silent, no longer threatening the worm, as it darkens in interlude 9.

39. Woolf's description of the swallows' behavior, including haunting barns, may derive from White's *Natural History of Selborne* (see 30, 144) as well as Thoby's observations.

40. In one example, there are parallel representations of a "rich bitch" in fox furs and a "poor bitch" of a fox, shown dead and bleeding (202–7).

41. Woolf gets another dig at bird protectionists when she makes the little-admired Hugh Whitbred, of *Mrs. Dalloway*, a protector of owls of Norfolk.

42. Feathered hats resurface in *Mrs. Dalloway*, where Rezia Smith uses feathers in decorating hats and Lady Bradshaw wears ostrich plumes in a trophy-like painting hung in her husband's office.

43. This response would be used to clearer effect in *Three Guineas*, where Woolf obliges a male pacifist to listen to her arguments and priorities before she will support his cause. Even then, he gets only one of her three guineas.

44. For excellent backgrounds on the Plumage Bill, see Abbott. He reinforces Andrew McNeille's assessment of the importance of this essay for its "polemical panache" and sees it as a "direct prototype" for *A Room of One's Own* and *Three Guineas* (265–66).

6. Virginia Woolf and Ideas of Environmental Holism

1. See Beer, "Physics, Sound and Substance," in *Virginia Woolf: The Common Ground* (113–14).

2. Birkeland's list of environmental approaches includes eco-Marxists, eco-socialists, deep ecologists, "greens," social ecologists, and ecofeminists. For a comparative chart, see "Eco-feminism," figure 1 (31).

3. See for example Carol Christ, Charlene Spretnak, and Starhawk in Diamond and Orenstein's *Reweaving the World*.

4. Alaimo 168. Zimmerman connects lesbian love scenes in natural settings to the simultaneous women's and ecological movements of the 1960s and 1970s (137). See Rachel Stein's *New Perspectives on Environmental Justice* for work by Gaard, Sandilands, Unger, and Beth Berila. Sandilands and Erickson's *Queer Ecologies* adds to this list.

5. Woolf's library contained a copy of this 1918 work, inscribed by Harrison in 1923.

6. See, for example, the anthology *Decentering the Center: Philosophy for a Multicultural, Postcolonial, and Feminist World*, edited by Uma Narayan and Sandra Harding (Bloomington: Indiana University Press, 2000).

7. See DiBattista 35, on "Virginia Woolf's Momento Mori." DiBattista alludes to Woolf's late essay "Anon" for dismissing authorial ego in favor of anonymous sources.

8. See Cramer, "Notes from Underground" 178–79.

9. There are also allusions to *Antigone* in *To the Lighthouse*, *A Room of One's Own*, and *Three Guineas*.

10. Skeptical of political and kin-centered readings of Hegel, Lacan, and Irigaray, Butler finds that her performance of the speech act "is the occasion for a new field of the human . . . [,] the one that happens when the less than human speaks as human" (82). She also finds a measure of queer sexuality.

11. Woolf owned 1888 and 1904 editions of Richard Claverhouse Judd's translation

of *Antigone,* which I therefore quote. She did her own Greek translations, and when she refers to Judd in the notes of *Three Guineas,* she cites the disadvantages of working from a translation (170).

12. See Cramer, "Notes from Underground" (178, 181) and "Pearls and the Porpoise" (230, 232). Kitty, however, is her main focus for this analysis in *The Years.*

13. Isabella, if taken as an allusion to Boccaccio's tale from the *Decameron,* also resonates with Antigone. She saves the head of her slain beloved, Lorenzo, in a pot of basil. See also Keats's 1820 poem and William Holman Hunt's 1868 Pre-Raphaelite painting.

14. Froula cites Woolf's recent knowledge of quantum physics as a source for her abstract forms. In favoring a Kantian "nature as subject," Froula tends toward a postfeminist concept of artistic community that sets aside both gender and nature. The ecofeminist Josephine Donovan's reservation about Kant's androcentric uses of nature applies well to this.

15. This is post-Freudian thinking, falling closest to Freud's *Totem and Taboo.* Freud's idea of the fetish offers a similar form of alliance of the human with natural objects, sometimes associated with religious ritual.

16. Froula tags Clarissa's idea of a life spreading as "transcendental" (175).

17. Banfield and Froula offer new assessments of Woolf's philosophical heritage, both critics implicating nature. Banfield argues that Bertrand Russell has greater influence on Bloomsbury epistemology than G. E. Moore. Froula considers Immanuel Kant the "towering intellectual ancestor of modernity" (12), and the goal of Bloomsbury thinkers, a new civilization. "By creating 'another nature . . . out of the material that actual nature gives it,'" as would Kant, "the artist achieves 'completeness' nowhere found in nature" and "throws a bridge from nature's realm to the realm of freedom" (13).

18. See, for example, Shiv K. Kumar, *Bergson and the Stream of Consciousness Novel* (New York: New York University Press, 1963). Goldman finds that Bergsonian approaches to Woolf tend to be ahistorical and "neglect the feminist import" of Woolf's work (*Feminist Aesthetics* 4). They predate most feminist work.

19. Hussey's *The Singing of the Real World* is grounded in the phenomenology of Merleau Ponty, who also influences Cantrell's ideas of reciprocity. See also Henke's "Virginia Woolf's *The Waves:* A Phenomenological Reading." Poole, Henke, and DeSalvo were early contributors to the reading of trauma in Woolf's subjects. See Henke and Eberly.

20. See also J. M. Coetzee's *The Lives of Animals.*

21. Cantrell finds a relatively objective, dualistic landscape in *The Voyage Out,* which she contrasts with dialogic richness of place detected in *Between the Acts.*

22. Woolf's unifiers tend to be the very young or old and female. Children seek coherent patterns. Older women are readiest to disperse into a world that is woven through with connections for them.

Bibliography

Archives

Harvard Theatre Collection, Houghton Library, Harvard University, MA, USA
Modern Archives Centre, King's College, Cambridge, UK
Mortimer Rare Book Room, Smith College, MA, USA
Natural History Museum Archive, UK
Natural History Museum, Tring, at the Walter Rothschild Zoological Museum, UK
New York Public Library, Berg Collection
Tate Gallery Archive, Photographic Collection

Published Sources

Abbott, Reginalde. "'Birds Don't Sing in Greek': Virginia Woolf and 'The Plumage Bill.'" In Adams and Donovan, *Animals and Women*, 263–86.
Abel, Elizabeth. *Virginia Woolf and the Fictions of Psychoanalysis*. Chicago: University of Chicago Press, 1989.
Abel, Elizabeth, Marianne Hirsch, and Elizabeth Langland, eds. *The Voyage In: Fictions of Female Development*. Hanover, NY: University Press of New England, 1983.
Ackroyd, Peter. *T. S. Eliot: A Life*. New York: Simon and Schuster, 1984.
Adams, Carol J. *The Sexual Politics of Meat: A Feminist-Vegetarian Critical Theory*. New York: Continuum, 1990.
Adams, Carol J., and Josephine Donovan, eds. *Animals and Women: Feminist Theoretical Explorations*. Durham, NC: Duke University Press, 1995.
Adams, Maureen. *Shaggy Muses: Dogs Who Inspired Virginia Woolf, Emily Dickinson, Elizabeth Barrett Browning, Edith Wharton, and Emily Brontë*. New York: Ballantine Books, 2007.
Adams, Steven, and Anna Gruetzner Robbins, eds. *Gendering Landscape Art*. New Brunswick, NJ: Rutgers University Press, 2001.

Agamben, Giorgio. *The Open: Man and Animal*. Translated by Kevin Attell. Stanford, CA: Stanford University Press, 2004.

Alaimo, Stacy. *Undomesticated Ground: Recasting Nature as Feminist Space*. Ithaca, NY: Cornell University Press, 2000.

Alcorn, John. *The Nature Novel from Hardy to Lawrence*. New York: Columbia University Press, 1977.

Alt, Christina. "Virginia Woolf and the 'Naturalist Novelist.'" In Southworth and Sparks, *Woolf and the Art of Exploration*, 65–70.

———. *Virginia Woolf and the Study of Nature*. Cambridge: Cambridge University Press, 2010.

Anderson, Lorraine, ed. *Sisters of the Earth: Women's Prose and Poetry about Nature*. 2nd ed. New York: Vintage Books, 2003.

Annan, Noel. *Leslie Stephen: The Godless Victorian*. London: Weidenfeld and Nicolson, 1984.

Anscomb, Isabelle. *Omega and After: Bloomsbury and the Decorative Arts*. London: Thames and Hudson, 1981.

Anzaldúa, Gloria. *Borderlands/La Frontera: The New Mestiza*. San Francisco: Aunt Lute Books, 2007.

Ardis, Ann, and Bonnie Kime Scott, eds. *Virginia Woolf: Turning the Centuries*. New York: Pace University Press, 2000.

Armstrong, Tim. *Modernism, Technology, and the Body: A Cultural Study*. New York: Cambridge University Press, 1998.

Banfield, Ann. *The Phantom Table: Woolf, Fry, Russell and the Epistemology of Modernism*. Cambridge: Cambridge University Press, 2000.

Barnette, Martha. *A Garden of Words*. New York: ASJA Press, 2005.

Barrett, Eileen. "Matriarchal Myth on a Patriarchal Stage: Virginia Woolf's *Between the Acts*." *Twentieth Century Literature* 33.1 (Spring 1987): 18–37.

Bartkevicivius, Jocelyn. "Thinking Back through Our (Naturalist) Mothers: Woolf, Dillard and the Nature Essay." *ISLE: Interdisciplinary Studies in Literature and the Environment* 6 (Winter 1999): 41–50.

Bateson, Gregory. *Mind and Nature: A Necessary Unity*. New York: Dutton, 1979.

Bazargan, Susan. "The Uses of the Land: Vita Sackville-West's Pastoral Writings and Virginia Woolf's *Orlando*." *Woolf Studies Annual* 5 (1999): 25–55.

Beer, Gillian. *Darwin's Plots: Evolutionary Narrative in Darwin, George Eliot and Nineteenth-Century Fiction*. London: Routledge and Kegan Paul, 1983.

———. Introduction to *Between the Acts*. In *Virginia Woolf: Introductions to the Major Works*, edited by Julia Briggs, 395–424. London: Virago, 1994.

———. "The Island and the Aeroplane: The Case of Virginia Woolf." In Beer, *Virginia Woolf: The Common Ground*, 149–78.

———. *Open Fields: Science in Cultural Encounter*. New York: Oxford University Press, 1996.

———. "Virginia Woolf and Prehistory." In Beer, *Virginia Woolf: The Common Ground*, 6–28.

———. *Virginia Woolf: The Common Ground.* Ann Arbor: University of Michigan Press, 1996.

———. *Wave, Atom, Dinosaur: Woolf's Science.* London: Virginia Woolf Society of Great Britain, 2000.

Behn, Aphra. *Oroonoko.* London: Penguin, 2003.

Bell, Quentin. *Charleston Past and Present.* London: Hogarth, 1987.

———. *Virginia Woolf: A Biography.* Vol. 1, *Virginia Stephen, 1882–1912.* Vol. 2, *Mrs. Woolf, 1912–1941.* London: Hogarth, 1973.

Bell, Quentin, and Angelica Garnett, comp. *Vanessa Bell's Family Album.* London: Jill Norman and Hobhouse, 1981.

Bell, Vanessa. *Notes on Virginia's Childhood: A Memoir.* New York: Frank Hallman, 1974.

Bellamy, Suzanne. "'Painting the Words': A Version of Lily Briscoe's Paintings from *To the Lighthouse.*" In Ardis and Scott, *Virginia Woolf Turning the Centuries,* 244–50.

Benjamin, Marina, ed. *A Question of Identity: Women, Science, and Literature.* New Brunswick, NJ: Rutgers University Press, 1993.

———. *Science and Sensibility: Gender and Scientific Inquiry, 1780–1945.* Oxford: Basil Blackwell, 1991.

Bennett, Joan. *Virginia Woolf: Her Art as a Novelist.* Cambridge: Cambridge University Press, 1964.

Bhabha, Homi. "DissemiNation: Time, Narrative, and the Margins of the Modern Nation." In *Nation and Narration,* edited by Homi Bhabha, 291–322. New York: Routledge, 1990.

Bicknell, John W. "The Young Mr. Ramsay." In *Selected Letters of Leslie Stephen,* vol. 1, *1864–1882,* 11–19. Columbus: Ohio State University Press, 1996.

Birke, Lynda. *Feminism and the Biological Body.* New York: Rutgers University Press, 2000.

———. *Feminism, Animals, and Science: The Naming of the Shrew.* Philadelphia: Open University Press, 1994.

Birkeland, Janis. "Ecofeminism: Linking Theory and Practice." In Gaard, *Ecofeminism,* 13–59.

Bishop, Edward L. "Pursuing 'It' through 'Kew Gardens.'" *Studies in Short Fiction* 19.3 (Summer 1982): 269–75.

Blodgett, Harriet. "The Nature of *Between the Acts.*" *MLS* 13.3 (Summer 1983): 27–37.

Bloom, Harold, ed. *Women Writers of English and Their Works.* Philadelphia: Chelsea House, 1997.

Blunden, Edmund. *Nature in English Literature.* London: Hogarth, 1929.

Blunt, Alison, and Gillian Rose, eds. *Writing Women and Space: Colonial and Postcolonial Geographies.* New York: Guilford Press, 1994.

Blunt, Wilfrid. *The Ark in the Park: The Zoo in the Nineteenth Century.* London: H. Hamilton / Tryon Gallery, 1976.

———. *In for a Penny: A Prospect of Kew Gardens: Their Flora, Fauna, and Falballas.* London: H. Hamilton, 1978.

Blyth, Ian. "Woolf, Rooks, and Rural England." In Burrells et al., *Woolfian Boundaries,* 80–85.

Boone, Joseph Allen. "The Meaning of Elvedon in *The Waves.*" *Modern Fiction Studies* 27.4 (Winter 1981–82): 629–37.

Bordo, Susan. *Unbearable Weight: Feminism, Western Culture, and the Body.* Berkeley: University of California Press, 1993.

Bowlby, Rachel. *Virginia Woolf: Feminist Destinations.* New York: Basil Blackwell, 1988.

Braidotti, Rosi. *Metamorphoses: Towards a Materialist Theory of Becoming.* Cambridge: Blackwell, 2002.

————. *Nomadic Subjects: Embodiment and Sexual Difference in Contemporary Feminist Theory.* New York: Columbia University Press, 1994.

Breton, Mary Joy. *Women Pioneers for the Environment.* Boston: Northeastern University Press, 1998.

Briggs, Julia. *Virginia Woolf: An Inner Life.* Orlando: Harcourt, 2005.

Brontë, Charlotte. *Jane Eyre.* New York: Harper, 1876.

Brown, Jane. *Spirits of Place: Five Famous Lives in Their English Landscape.* London: Viking, 2001.

Buell, Lawrence. *Writing for an Endangered World: Literature, Culture, and Environment in the U.S. and Beyond.* Cambridge, MA: Belknap Press of Harvard University Press, 2001.

Burrells, Anna, Steve Ellis, Deborah Parsons, and Kathryn Simpson, eds. *Woolfian Boundaries: Selected Papers from the Sixteenth Annual International Conference on Virginia Woolf.* Clemson, SC: Clemson Digital Press, 2007.

Burrows, Victoria, and Hilary Fraser. "Virginia Stephen in George Duckworth's Family Album." *Australian Victorian Studies Journal* 5 (1999): 13–34.

Butler, Judith. *Gender Trouble: Feminism and the Subversion of Identity.* New York: Routledge, 1990.

Cantrell, Carol H. "'The Locus of Compossibility': Virginia Woolf, Modernism, and Place." In *The ISLE Reader: Ecocriticism, 1993–2003,* edited by Michael P. Branch and Scott Slovic, 33–46. Athens: University of Georgia Press, 2003.

Caramagno, Thomas. *"The Flight of the Mind": Virginia Woolf's Art and Manic-Depressive Illness.* Berkeley: University of California Press, 1992.

Carrington, [Dora]. *Letters and Extracts from Her Diaries.* Edited by David Garnett. Oxford: Oxford University Press, 1979.

Carson, Rachel. *Silent Spring.* Boston: Houghton Mifflin, 1962.

Caughie, Pamela. *Virginia Woolf and Postmodernism: Literature in Quest and Question of Itself.* Urbana: University of Illinois Press, 1991.

————, ed. *Virginia Woolf in the Age of Mechanical Reproduction.* New York: Garland, 2000.

————. "Woolf's Dogs and Servants." Paper presented at the 2009 Modernist Studies Conference, Montreal, Quebec, Canada.

Chambers, Douglas. *The Planters of the English Landscape Garden: Botany, Trees, and the Georgics.* New Haven, CT: Yale University Press, 1993.

Chapman, Wayne K., and Janet M. Manson. *Leonard and Virginia Woolf Working Together and the Hitherto Unpublished Manuscript of "In^L Re^{NS}."* London: Cecil Woolf, 1997.

Chaudhuri, Napur, and Margaret Strobel, eds. *Western Women and Imperialism: Complicity and Resistance.* Bloomington: Indiana University Press, 1992.

Cixous, Hélène, and Catherine Clement. *La Jeune Née.* Paris: Union générale d'éditions, 1975.

Clarke, Stuart Nelson. *A Bibliography of Virginia Woolf and the Bloomsbury Group.* London: S. N. Clarke, 1993.

Clement, Grace. "The Ethic of Care and the Problem of Wild Animals." In Donovan and Adams, *Feminist Care Tradition,* 301–15.

Corbett, David Peters. "Landscape, Masculinity and Interior Space." In Adams and Robbins, *Gendering Landscape Art,* 102–15.

Coyle, John. "Pulp Fiction: or, Proust and Joyce's Rhetorical Flourishes." *Glasgow Review.* http://www.arts.gla.ac.uk/ STELLA/COMET/glasgrev/issue3/coyle.htm.

Cramer, Patricia. "Notes from the Underground: Lesbian Ritual and the Writings of Virginia Woolf." In Hussey and Neverow-Turk, *Virginia Woolf Miscellanies,* 177–88.

———. "'Pearls and the Porpoise': Virginia Woolf and *The Years*—A Lesbian Memoir." In Barrett and Cramer, *Virginia Woolf: Lesbian Readings,* 222–40.

Crawford, Robert. *The Savage and the City in the Works of T. S. Eliot.* Oxford: Clarendon Press, 1987.

Cronon, William. "The Trouble with Wilderness, or Getting Back to the Wrong Nature." In *Uncommon Ground: Toward Reinventing Nature,* 69–90. New York: Norton, 1995.

Cuddy, Lois A. *T. S. Eliot and the Poetics of Evolution: Subversions of Classicism, Culture, and Progress.* Lewisburg, PA: Bucknell University Press, 2000.

Czarnecki, Kristin, and Carrie Rohman, eds. *Virginia Woolf and the Natural World: Selected Papers from the Twentieth Annual International Conference on Virginia Woolf.* Clemson, SC: Clemson University Digital Press, 2011.

Darwin, Charles. *The Effects of Cross- and Self-Fertilization in the Vegetable Kingdom.* New York: Appleton, 1877.

———. *The Origin of Species.* New York: New American Library, 1958.

Daugherty, Beth Rigel. "Taking Her Fences: The Equestrian Virginia Woolf." In Czarnecky and Rohman, *Virginia Woolf and the Natural World,* 61–70.

Davies, W. H. *Autobiography of a Super-Tramp.* New York: Alfred A. Knopf, 1917.

Davis, Karen. "Thinking Like a Chicken: Farm Animals and the Feminine Connection." In Adams and Donovan, *Animals and Women,* 193–212.

Davis, Laura, and Jeanette McVicar, eds. *Virginia Woolf and Her Influences: Selected Papers from the Seventh Annual Conference on Virginia Woolf.* New York: Pace University Press, 1998.

DeKoven, Marianne. "Flush and Basket: Woolf and Stein Writing as Dogs." Paper presented in the session "Woolf, Stein, and the Languages of the (Non)human Other: Dogs, Neighbors, Servants" at the 2009 Modernist Studies Conference, Montreal, Quebec, Canada.

———. *Rich and Strange: Gender, History, Modernism.* Princeton, NJ: Princeton University Press, 1991.

———. "Why Animals Now." Guest column. *PMLA* 124.2 (2009): 361–69.

Deleuze, Gilles, and Féliz Guattari. *Rhizome: Introduction.* Paris: Éditions de Minuit, 1976.

———. *A Thousand Plateaus.* Translated by Brian Massumi. Minneapolis: University of Minnesota Press, 1987.

Derrida, Jacques. "The Animal That Therefore I Am (More to Follow)." *Critical Inquiry* 28.2 (2002): 369–418.

———. *The Animal That Therefore I Am.* Edited by Marie-Louise Mallet. Translated by David Wills. New York: Fordham University Press, 2008.

———. *Dissemination.* Chicago: University of Chicago Press, 1981.

DeSalvo, Louise A. "As 'Miss Jan' Says: Virginia Woolf's Early Journals." In Jane Marcus, *Virginia Woolf and Bloomsbury,* 96–124.

———. "1897: Virginia Woolf at Fifteen." In Jane Marcus, *Virginia Woolf: A Feminist Slant,* 78–108.

———. *Virginia Woolf: The Impact of Childhood Sexual Abuse on Her Life and Work.* New York: Ballantine Books, 1990.

Desmond, Adrian, and James Moore. *Darwin: The Life of a Tormented Evolutionist.* New York: Warner Books, 1992.

Desmond, Ray. *The History of the Royal Botanical Gardens Kew.* London: Harvill, 1995.

Dettmar, Kevin J. H., and Stephen Watt, eds. *Marketing Modernisms: Self-Promotion, Canonization, Rereading.* Ann Arbor: University of Michigan, 1996.

Diamond, Irene, and Gloria Feman Orenstein, eds. *Reweaving the World: The Emergence of Ecofeminism.* San Francisco: Sierra Club Books, 1990.

DiBattista, Maria. *Virginia Woolf's Major Novels: The Fables of Anon.* New Haven, CT: Yale University Press, 1980.

Donovan, Josephine. "Animal Rights and Feminist Theory." In Gaard, *Ecofeminism,* 167–94.

———. "Attention to Suffering: Sympathy as a Basis for Ethical Treatment of Animals." In Donovan and Adams, *Feminist Care Tradition,* 174–97.

Donovan, Josephine, and Carol J. Adams, eds. *The Feminist Care Tradition in Animal Ethics.* New York: Columbia University Press, 2007.

Dubino, Jean. "Woolf, Darwin and *Flush;* or, The Origin of Spaniels." Paper presented at the 2010 International Conference on Virginia Woolf, Georgetown, KY.

Doyle, Laura. "Sublime Barbarians in the Narrative of Empire: or, Longinus at Sea in *The Waves.*" *Modern Fiction Studies* 42.2 (Summer 1996): 323–47.

Duncan, Carol. *The Aesthetics of Power: Essays in Critical Art History.* Cambridge: Cambridge University Press, 1993.

Dunn, Jane. *A Very Close Conspiracy: Vanessa Bell and Virginia Woolf.* London: Cape, 1990.

DuPlessis, Rachel Blau. *Genders, Races, and Religious Cultures in Modern American Poetry, 1908–1934.* Cambridge: Cambridge University Press, 2001.

———. "WOOLFENSTEIN." In *Breaking the Sequence: Women's Experimental Fiction,* edited by Ellen G. Friedman and Miriam Fuchs, 99–114. Princeton, NJ: Princeton University Press, 1989.

———. *Writing beyond the Ending: Narrative Strategies of Twentieth-Century Women Writers.* Bloomington: Indiana University Press, 1985.

Ebbatson, Roger. *Lawrence and the Nature Tradition: A Theme in English Fiction, 1859–1914.* Sussex: Harvester, 1980.

Eder, Doris L. "Louis Unmasked: T. S. Eliot in *The Waves.*" *Virginia Woolf Quarterly* 2.1–2 (Winter-Spring 1975): 13–27.

Edwards, Lee R. "War and Roses: The Politics of *Mrs. Dalloway.*" In *The Authority of Experience: Essays in Feminist Criticism,* edited by Arlyn Diamond and Lee R. Edwards, 161–77. Amherst: University of Massachusetts Press, 1977.

Eisler, Riane. "Gaia Tradition and the Partnership Future: An Ecofeminist Manifesto." In Diamond and Orenstein, *Reweaving the World,* 23–34.

Eliot, T. S. *The Complete Poems and Plays, 1909–1950.* New York: Harcourt, Brace and World, 1952.

———. "The Influence of Landscape upon the Poet." *Dedalus* 89 (Spring 1966): 421–22.

———. "Tradition and Individual Talent." In Faulkner, *A Modernist Reader,* 88–91.

———. *The Waste Land: A Facsimile and Transcript of the Original Drafts including the Annotations of Ezra Pound.* Edited by Valerie Eliot. New York: Harcourt Brace Jovanovich, 1971.

Esty, Joshua. *A Shrinking Island: Modernism and National Culture in England.* Princeton, NJ: Princeton University Press, 2004.

Faulkner, Peter, ed. *A Modernist Reader: Modernism in England, 1910–1930.* London: B. T. Batsford, 1986.

Felski, Rita. *The Gender of Modernity.* Cambridge, MA: Harvard University Press, 1995.

———. Introduction to *Rethinking Tragedy.* Baltimore: Johns Hopkins University Press, 2008. 1–25.

Forster, E. M. *Selected Letters of E. M. Forster.* Edited by Mary Lago and P. N. Furbank. Cambridge, MA: Harvard University Press, 1983–85.

Foucault, Michel. *Discipline and Punish: The Birth of the Prison.* Translated by Alan Sheridan. New York: Vintage Books, 1979.

———. *The Order of Things: An Archaeology of the Human Sciences.* New York: Vintage Books, 1973.

Frazer, James. *The Golden Bough.* 3rd ed. London: Macmillan, 1913.

Freedman, Melvin, ed. *Virginia Woolf: Revaluation and Continuity.* Berkeley: University of California Press, 1980.

Freud, Sigmund. *Civilization and Its Discontents.* Translated by Joan Riviere. London: Hogarth, 1930.

———. "Female Sexuality." Translated by Joan Riviere. *International Journal of Psychoanalysis* 13 (1932): 281–97.

Friedman, Susan. *Mappings: Feminism and the Cultural Geographies of Encounter.* Princeton, NJ: Princeton University Press, 1998.

———. *Psyche Reborn: The Reemergence of H.D.* Bloomington: Indiana University Press, 1981.

Froula, Christine. "'Out of the Chrysalis': Female Initiation and Female Authority in Virginia Woolf's *The Voyage Out.*" In Homans, *Virginia Woolf,* 136–61.

———. "Rewriting *Genesis:* Gender and Culture in Twentieth-Century Texts." *Tulsa Studies in Women's Literature* 7.2 (1988): 197–220.

———. *Virginia Woolf and the Bloomsbury Avant Garde: War, Civilization, Modernity.* New York: Columbia University Press, 2005.

Fry, Roger. *Vision and Design.* 1920. New York: Peter Smith, 1947.

Fuss, Diana. *Essentially Speaking: Feminism, Nature and Difference.* New York: Routledge, 1989.

———. *Human, All Too Human.* New York: Routledge, 1996.

Gaard, Greta, ed. *Ecofeminism: Women, Animals, Nature.* Philadelphia: Temple University Press, 1993.

———. "Living Interconnections with Animals and Nature." In Gaard, *Ecofeminism,* 1–12.

———. "Toward a Queer Ecofeminism." In Rachel Stein, *New Perspectives on Environmental Justice,* 21–44.

Garnett, Angelica. *Deceived with Kindness: A Bloomsbury Childhood.* Oxford: Oxford University Press, 1985.

Garvey, Michelle Jenneman. "Belonging to Nature: An Interdisciplinary, Feminist Analysis of Constructions of Nature." Master's thesis, San Diego State University, 2008.

Gates, Barbara. *Kindred Nature: Victorian and Edwardian Women Embrace the Living World.* Chicago: University of Chicago Press, 1998.

Gates, Barbara, and Ann B. Shteir, eds. *Natural Eloquence: Women Reinscribe Science.* Madison: University of Wisconsin Press, 1997.

A General Guide to the British Museum (Natural History). London: William Clowes and Sons, 1887.

A General Guide to the British Museum (Natural History). London: William Clowes and Sons, 1897.

Gerrard, Deborah. "Brown-ness, Trees, Rose Petals, and Chrysalises: The Influence of Edward Carpenter's Mystical Evolutionary Socialism on the Writing of Virginia Woolf, with Particular Reference to *The Years.*" In Burrells et al., *Woolfian Boundaries,* 15–21.

Gervais, David. *Literary Englands: Versions of "Englishness" in Modern Writing.* Cambridge: Cambridge University Press, 1993.

Gilbert, Geoff. *Before Modernism Was: Modern History and the Constituency of Writing.* London: Palgrave Macmillan, 2004.

Giles, Judy, and Tim Middleton, eds. *Writing Englishness, 1900–1950: An Introductory Sourcebook on National Identity.* London: Routledge, 1995.

Gillespie, Diane F., ed. *The Multiple Muses of Virginia Woolf.* Columbia: University of Missouri Press, 1993.

———. *The Sisters' Arts: The Writing and Painting of Virginia Woolf and Vanessa Bell.* Syracuse, NY: Syracuse University Press, 1988.

Gillespie, Diane F., and Leslie K. Hankins, eds. *Virginia Woolf and the Arts: Selected Papers from the Sixth Annual Conference on Virginia Woolf.* New York: Pace University Press, 1997.

Gilligan, Carol. *In a Different Voice: Psychological Theory and Women's Development.* Cambridge, MA: Harvard University Press, 1982.

Ginsberg, Elaine K., and Laura Moss Gottleib, eds. *Virginia Woolf: Centennial Essays.* Troy, NY: Whitston, 1983.

Glendinning, Victoria. *Vita: A Biography of Vita Sackville-West.* New York: Alfred A. Knopf, 1983.

Goldman, Jane. *The Cambridge Introduction to Virginia Woolf.* Cambridge: Cambridge University Press, 2006.

———. "'Ce chien est à moi': Virginia Woolf and the Signifying Dog." In Burrells et al., *Woolfian Boundaries,* 100–107.

———. *The Feminist Aesthetics of Virginia Woolf: Modernism, Post-Impressionism and the Politics of the Visual.* Cambridge: Cambridge University Press, 1998.

Goody, Jack. "The Secret Language of Flowers." *Yale Journal of Criticism* 3 (1990): 133–52.

Gordon, Lyndall. *T. S. Eliot: An Imperfect Life.* New York: W. W. Norton, 1998.

Greenaway, Kate. *The Language of Flowers.* London: George Routledge, 1884. http://www.illuminated-books.com/viewer-en.php?book=flowers.

Gregory, Eileen. "Rose Cut in Rock: Sappho and H.D.'s *Sea Garden.*" In *Signets: Reading H.D.,* edited by Susan Stanford Friedman and Rachel Blau DuPlessis, 129–54. Madison: University of Wisconsin Press, 1990.

Griffin, Susan. *Woman and Nature: The Roaring inside Her.* New York: Harper and Row, 1980.

Grosz, Elizabeth A. *The Nick of Time: Politics, Evolution, and the Untimely.* Durham, NC: Duke University Press, 2004.

Guiguet, Jean. *Virginia Woolf and Her Works.* New York: Harcourt Brace Jovanovich, 1965.

Halberstam, Judith, and Ira Livingston. Introduction to *Posthuman Bodies,* edited by Judith Halberstam and Ira Livingston, 1–19. Indianapolis: Indiana University Press, 1995.

Haller, Evelyn. "Isis Unveiled: Virginia Woolf's Use of Egyptian Myth." In Jane Marcus, *Virginia Woolf: A Feminist Slant,* 109–31.

Hankins, Leslie. "Cinéastes and Modernists: Writing on Film in 1920s London." In Bonnie Kime Scott, *Gender in Modernism*, 809–24.

Haraway, Donna. *The Companion Species Manifesto: Dogs, People, and Significant Otherness*. Chicago: Prickly Paradigm, 2003.

———. *Modest_Witness@Second_Millennium.FemaleMan©Meets_OncoMouse™: Feminism and Technoscience*. New York: Routledge, 1997.

———. *Simians, Cyborgs, and Women: The Reinvention of Nature*. New York: Routledge, 1992.

———. *When Species Meet*. Minneapolis: University of Minnesota Press, 2008.

Harding, Sandra, ed. *The "Racial" Economy of Science: Toward a Democratic Future*. Bloomington: Indiana University Press, 1993.

Harrison, Jane Ellen. *Ancient Art and Ritual*. 1913. New York: Greenwood, 1969.

———. *Prolegomena to a Study of Greek Religion*. 1908. Cambridge: Cambridge University Press, 1922.

Haule, James M., and Philip H. Smith Jr. *A Concordance to the Novels of Virginia Woolf*. New York: Garland, 1991.

Hawkes, Ellen. "Woolf's Magical Garden of Women." In Jane Marcus, *New Feminist Essays*, 1–60.

Hayles, N. Katherine. *How We Became Posthuman: Virtual Bodies in Cybernetics, Literature, and Informatics*. Chicago: University of Chicago Press, 1999.

H.D. (Hilda Doolittle). *Bid Me to Live*. London: Virago, 1984.

———. *Collected Poems, 1912–1944*. New York: New Directions, 1983.

———. "Notes on Thought and Vision." In Bonnie Kime Scott, *Gender of Modernism*, 93–109.

Hecht, Roger. "'I Am Nature's Bride': Orlando and the Female Pastoral." In *Re: Reading, Re: Writing, Re: Teaching Virginia Woolf*, edited by Eileen Barrett and Patricia Cramer, 22–28. New York: Pace University Press, 1995.

Helsinger, Elizabeth. *Rural Scenes and National Representation: Britain, 1815–1850*. Princeton, NJ: Princeton University Press, 1997.

Henke, Suzette. "Virginia Woolf's *The Waves*: A Phenomenological Reading." *Neophilologus* 73 (1989): 461–44.

Henke, Suzette, and David Eberly, eds. *Virginia Woolf and Trauma: Embodied Texts*. New York: Pace University Press, 2007.

Henry, Holly. *Virginia Woolf and the Discourse of Science: The Aesthetics of Astronomy*. Cambridge: Cambridge University Press, 2003.

Hill, Marylu. *Mothering Modernity: Feminism, Modernism, and the Maternal Muse*. New York: Garland, 1999.

Hill-Miller, Katherine C. *From the Lighthouse to Monk's House: A Guide to Virginia Woolf's Literary Landscapes*. London: Duckworth Publishers, 2001.

Holleyman and Treacher. *Catalogue of Books from the Library of Leonard and Virginia Woolf: Taken from Monks House, Rodmell, Sussex and 24 Victoria Square, London and Now in the Possession of Washington State University, Pullman, U.S.A.* Brighton: Holleyman and Treacher, 1975.

Hollis, Catherine W. *Leslie Stephen as Mountaineer: "Where does Mont Blanc end, and where do I begin?"* London: Cecil Woolf, 2010.

———. "Virginia Woolf as Mountaineer." In Czarnecki and Rohman, *Virginia Woolf and the Natural World*, 184–90.

Holtby, Winifred. *Virginia Woolf.* London: Wishart, 1932.

Homans, Margaret. *Bearing the Word: Language and Female Experience in Nineteenth-Century Women's Writing.* Chicago: University of Chicago Press, 1986.

———, ed. *Virginia Woolf: A Collection of Critical Essays.* Englewood Cliffs: Prentice-Hall, 1993.

Hulme, T. E. "From 'Romanticism and Classicism' 1911." In *Modernism: An Anthology of Sources and Documents,* edited by Vassiliki Kolocotroni, Jane Goldman, and Olga Taxidou, 178–85. Chicago: University of Chicago Press, 1998.

Hussey, Mark. "Notes to *To the Lighthouse.*" In Woolf, *To the Lighthouse,* 213–37.

———. *The Singing of the Real World: The Philosophy of Virginia Woolf's Fiction.* Columbus: Ohio State University Press, 1986.

———. *Virginia Woolf A-Z: A Comprehensive Reference for Students, Teachers and Common Readers of Her Life, Work and Critical Reception.* New York: Oxford University Press, 1995.

———, ed. *Virginia Woolf and War: Fiction, Reality and Myth.* Syracuse, NY: Syracuse University Press, 1991.

Hussey, Mark, and Vara Neverow-Turk, eds. *Virginia Woolf Miscellanies: Proceedings of the First Annual Conference on Virginia Woolf.* New York: Pace University Press, 1992.

Huxley, Thomas Henry. *Lay Sermons: Addresses and Reviews.* New York: Appleton, 1883.

Irigaray, Luce, "Ce sexe que n'en est pas un." Translated by Claudia Reeder. In *New French Feminisms: An Anthology,* edited by Elaine Marks and Isabelle de Courtivron, 99–106. New York: Schocken Books, 1981.

Jacobus, Mary, Evelyn Fox Keller, and Sally Shuttleworth, eds. *Body Politics: Women and the Discourses of Science.* New York: Routledge, 1990.

Jamison, Kay Redfield. *Touched with Fire: Manic-Depressive Illness and the Artistic Temperment.* New York: Free Press Paperbacks, 1993.

Jeffery, Ian. *The British Landscape, 1920–1950.* London: Thames and Hudson, 1984.

Jones, Ann Rosalind. "Inscribing Femininity: French Theories of the Feminine." In *Making a Difference: Feminist Literary Criticism,* edited by Gayle Greene and Coppélia Kahn, 80–112. London: Nethues, 1985.

Joyce, James. *Finnegans Wake.* New York: Viking, 1939.

———. *A Portrait of the Artist as a Young Man.* 1916. New York: Viking, 1964.

———. *Selected Letters of James Joyce.* Edited by Richard Ellmann. New York: Viking, 1975.

———. *Ulysses: A Critical and Synoptic Edition.* Edited by Hans Walter Gabler. New York: Garland, 1984.

Keller, Evelyn Fox, and Helen E. Longino. *Feminism and Science.* Oxford: Oxford University Press, 1996.

———. "Secrets of God, Nature, and Life." In Lederman and Bartsch, *Gender and Science Reader*, 98–110.

Kheel, Marti. "From Heroic to Holistic Ethics." In Gaard, *Ecofeminism*, 243–71.

———. "The Liberation of Nature: A Circular Affair." In Donovan and Adams, *Feminist Care Tradition*, 39–57.

———. "License to Kill: An Ecofeminist Critique of Hunters' Discourse." In Adams and Donovan, *Animals and Women*, 85–125.

Kirkpatrick, B. J. *A Bibliography of Virginia Woolf.* Oxford: Clarendon Press, 1997.

Kolodny, Annette. *The Lay of the Land: Metaphor as Experience and History in American Life and Letters.* Chapel Hill: University of North Carolina Press, 1975.

Kostkowska, Justyna. "'Scissors and Silks,' 'Flowers and Trees,' and 'Geraniums Ruined by the War': Virginia Woolf's Ecological Critique of Science in *Mrs. Dalloway.*" *Women's Studies: An International Journal* 32.2 (March–April 2004): 183–98.

Kreutziger, Joseph. "Darwin's Temporal Aesthetics: A Brief Sketch in Time from Pater to Woolf." In *Woolf in the Real World: Selected Papers from the Thirteenth Annual International Conference on Virginia Woolf,* edited by Karen V. Kukil, 64–69. Clemson, SC: Clemson Digital Press, 2005.

Laity, Cassandra. "H.D.'s Romantic Landscapes: The Sexual Politics of the Garden." In *Signets: Reading H.D.,* edited by Susan Stanford Friedman and Rachel Blau DuPlessis, 110–28. Madison: University of Wisconsin Press, 1990.

Lambert, Elizabeth. "Evolution and Imagination in *Pointz Hall* and *Between the Acts.*" In Neverow-Turk and Hussey, *Virginia Woolf: Themes and Variation,* 83–89. New York: Pace University Press, 1993.

———. "Proportion Is in the Mind of the Beholder: Mrs. Dalloway's Critique of Science." In *Selected Papers from the Third Annual Conference on Virginia Woolf,* edited by Mark Hussey, Vara Neverow, and Jane Lilienfeld. New York: Pace University Press, 1994.

Lawrence, D. H. *Women in Love.* London: Penguin, 1995.

Leaska, Mitchell. Notes to *Pointz Hall: The Earlier and Later Typescripts of "Between the Acts,"* by Virginia Woolf. New York: University Publications, 1983.

Lederman, Muriel, and Ingrid Bartsch, eds. *The Gender and Science Reader.* New York: Routledge, 2001.

Lee, Hermione. *Virginia Woolf.* New York: Knopf, 1997.

Leopold, Aldo. *A Sand Country Almanac and Sketches Here and There.* New York: Oxford University Press, 1989.

Lewis, Wyndham. *Men without Art.* Santa Rosa: Black Sparrow Press, 1987.

Light, Alison. *Mrs. Woolf and the Servants.* New York: Bloomsbury Press, 2008.

Lilienfeld, Jane. "'Where the Spear Plants Grew': The Ramsays' Marriage in *To the Lighthouse.*" In Jane Marcus, *New Feminist Essays,* 148–69.

Linett, Marin Tova. *Modernism, Feminism, and Jewishness.* Cambridge: Cambridge University Press, 2007.

Longley, Edna. "'The Business of the Earth': Edward Thomas and Ecocentrism." In

High and Low Moderns, edited by Maria DiBattista and Lucy McDiarmid, 107–31. New York: Oxford University Press, 1996.

Loring, Marti T., Robert Geffner, and Janessa March, eds. *Animal Abuse and Family Violence: Linkages, Research, and Implications for Professional Practice.* Binghamton, NY: Haworth Maltreatment and Trauma Press, 2007.

Lorsch, Susan. *Where Nature Ends: Literary Responses to the Designification of Landscape.* Rutherford, NJ: Fairleigh Dickinson University Press, 1983.

Maika, Patricia. *Virginia Woolf's "Between the Acts" and Jane Harrison's "Con/spiracy."* Ann Arbor, MI: UMI Research Press, 1987.

Maitland, Frederic William. *The Life and Letters of Leslie Stephen.* Detroit: Gale Research, 1968.

Marcus, Jane. "Britannia Rules *The Waves.*" In *Hearts of Darkness: White Women Write Race,* 59–85. New Jersey: Rutgers University Press, 2004.

———. "Liberty, Sorority, Misogyny." In *Virginia Woolf and the Languages of Patriarchy,* 75–95. Bloomington: Indiana University Press, 1987.

———, ed. *New Feminist Essays on Virginia Woolf.* Lincoln: University of Nebraska Press, 1981.

———. "'Taking the Bull by the Udders': Sexual Difference in Virginia Woolf—a Conspiracy Theory." In Jane Marcus, *Virginia Woolf and Bloomsbury,* 146–69.

———, ed. *Virginia Woolf: A Feminist Slant.* Lincoln: University of Nebraska Press, 1983.

———, ed. *Virginia Woolf and Bloomsbury: A Centenary Celebration.* Blasingstoke, UK: Macmillan, 1987.

Marcus, Laura. *The Tenth Muse: Writing about Cinema in the Modernist Period.* Oxford: Oxford University Press, 2007.

Marder, Herbert. *The Measure of Life: Virginia Woolf's Last Years.* Ithaca, NY: Cornell University Press, 2000.

Marx, Leo. "The Puzzle of Anti-Urbanism in Classic American Literature." In *Literature and the Urban Experience: Essays on the City and Literature,* edited by Michael Jaye and Ann Chalmers Watts, 63–81. New Brunswick, NJ: Rutgers University Press, 1981.

McAllester Jones, Mary. *Gaston Bachelard, Subversive Humanist: Texts and Readings.* Madison: University of Wisconsin Press, 1991.

McDaniel, Jamie. "'I'm Dead Sir!': The Writing of C. P. Sanger and the Influence of Intestacy Law in *Orlando.*" Paper presented in session 499, "Orlando's 'House that Was No Longer Hers Entirley': Property in Virginia Woolf," at the 2008 MLA Convention, San Francisco, CA.

McGee, Patrick. "Woolf's Other: The University in Her Eye." *Novel* 23 (1990): 229–46.

Mellor, Mary. *Feminism and Ecology.* Cambridge: Polity Press, 1997.

Merchant, Carolyn. *The Death of Nature: Women, Ecology, and the Scientific Revolution: A Feminist Reappraisal of the Scientific Revolution.* San Francisco: Harper and Row, 1979.

———. "Dominion over Nature." In Lederman and Bartsch, *Gender and Science Reader,* 68–81.

———. *Earthcare: Women and the Environment.* New York: Routledge, 1995.

Miletic-Vejzovic, Laila. *A Library of One's Own: The Library of Leonard and Virginia Woolf.* London: Cecil Woolf, 1997.

Mills, Sara. *Discourses of Difference: An Analysis of Women's Travel Writing and Colonialism.* London: Routledge, 1991.

Mirrlees, Hope. "Paris." Edited and annotated by Julia Briggs. In Bonnie Kime Scott, *Gender in Modernism,* 261–303.

Mitford, Mary Russell. "Walks in the Country: The Wood." In *In Nature's Name,* edited by Barbara T. Gates, 185–88. Chicago: University of Chicago Press, 2002.

Moi, Toril. *Sexual/Textual Politics: Feminist Literary Theory.* New York: Methuen, 1985.

Monroe, Harriet. *The Difference and Other Poems.* New York: Macmillan, 1925.

Moore, Madeline. "Nature and Community: A Study of Reality in *The Waves.*" In *Virginia Woolf: Revaluation and Continuity,* edited by Ralph Freedman, 219–40. Berkeley: University of California Press, 1980.

———. "On Female Versions of Pastoral: *The Voyage Out* and Matriarchal Mythologies." In Jane Marcus, *New Feminist Essays,* 82–104.

Moore, Marianne. "Hymen." In Bonnie Kime Scott, *Gender of Modernism,* 350–52.

Moran, Patricia. *Word of Mouth: Body Language in Katherine Mansfield and Virginia Woolf.* Charlottesville: University of Virginia Press, 1996.

Morgan, Susan. *Place Matters: Gendered Geography in Victorian Women's Travel Books about Southeast Asia.* New Brunswick, NJ: Rutgers University Press, 1996.

Morrell, Ottoline. *Lady Ottoline's Album.* Edited by Carolyn Heilbrun. New York: Knopf, 1976.

Morris, Jan. *Travels with Virginia Woolf.* London: Hogarth, 1993.

Myers, Elyse. "Virginia Woolf and the 'Voyage Out' from Victorian Science." In Ardis and Scott, *Virginia Woolf Turning the Centuries,* 298–304.

Nalbantian, Suzanne. *Aesthetic Autobiography: From Life to Art in Marcel Proust, James Joyce, Virginia Woolf and Anaïs Nin.* New York: St. Martin's, 1997.

Naremore, James. "Nature and History in *The Years.*" In Freedman, *Virginia Woolf: Revaluation and Continuity,* 241–62.

Neverow-Turk, Vara, and Mark Hussey, eds. *Virginia Woolf: Themes and Variations: Selected Papers from the Second Annual Conference on Virginia Woolf.* New York: Pace University Press, 1993.

Nicolson, Nigel. Interview by Bonnie Kime Scott. July 19, 2000, Sissinghurst, UK.

———. *Virginia Woolf: A Penguin Life.* New York: Penguin, 2000.

———. "Vita and Virginia and Vanessa." In *A Cézanne in the Hedge,* edited by Hugh Lee, 86–92. Chicago: University of Chicago Press, 1992.

Ormerod, Eleanor. *Eleanor Ormerod, LL.D., Economic Entomologist: Autobiography and Correspondence.* Edited by Robert Wallace. New York: E. P. Dutton, 1904.

Ortner, Sherry. "Is Female to Male as Nature Is to Culture?" In *Woman, Culture and*

Society, edited by Michelle Zimbalist Rosaldo and Louise Lamphere, 67–87. Stanford, CA: Stanford University Press, 1974.

Oxindine, Annette. "Pear Trees beyond Eden: Women's Knowing Reconfigured in Woolf's *To the Lighthouse* and Hurston's *Their Eyes Were Watching God.*" In *Approaches to Teaching Woolf's "To the Lighthouse,"* edited by Beth Rigel Daugherty and Mary Beth Pringle, 163–68. New York: Modern Language Association, 2001.

Paul, Janis M. *The Victorian Heritage of Virginia Woolf: The External World in Her Novels.* Norman, OK: Pilgrim Books, 1987.

Phillips, Kathy J. *Virginia Woolf against Empire.* Knoxville: University of Tennessee Press, 1994.

Piggford, George. "Camp Sites: Forster and the Biographics of Queer Bloomsbury." In *Queer Forster,* edited by George Piggford, 89–112. Chicago: University of Chicago Press, 1997.

Pippett, Aileen. *The Moth and the Star: A Biography of Virginia Woolf.* Boston: Little, Brown, 1955.

Plumwood, Val. *Environmental Culture: The Ecological Crisis of Reason.* London: Routledge, 2002.

———. *Feminism and the Mastery of Nature.* London: Routledge, 1993.

Poole, Roger. *The Unknown Virginia Woolf.* 3rd ed. Atlantic Highlands, NJ: Humanities Press International, 1990.

Pound, Ezra. "A Retrospect." 1918. In Faulkner, *Modernist Reader,* 59–71.

———. Translator's postscript to *The Natural Philosophy of Love* by Remy Du Gourmont. 1922. New York: Collier, 1961.

Pratt, Mary Louise. *Imperial Eyes: Travel Writing and Transculturation.* London: Routledge, 1992.

Preston, Carrie J. *Modernism's Mythic Pose: Gender, Genre, Solo Performance.* New York: Oxford University Press, 2011.

Rabinowitz, Paula. "Great Lady Painters, Inc.: Icons of Feminism, Modernism, and the Nation." In *Modernism, Inc.: Body, Memory, Capital,* edited by Jani Scandura and Michael Thurston, 193–218. New York: New York University Press, 2001.

Rado, Lisa, ed. *Modernism, Gender, and Culture: A Cultural Studies Approach.* New York: Garland, 1997.

Raitt, Suzanne. *Vita and Virginia: The Work and Friendship of Vita Sackville-West and Virginia Woolf.* Oxford: Oxford University Press, 1993.

Reed, Christopher. "Through Formalism: Feminism and Virginia Woolf's Relation to Bloomsbury Aesthetics." In Gillespie, *Multiple Muses of Virginia Woolf,* 11–35.

Reid, Panthea. *Art and Affection: A Life of Virginia Woolf.* New York: Oxford University Press, 1996.

Richardson, Dorothy. *Backwater.* In *Pilgrimage I.* London: Virago, 1979.

———. *The Tunnel.* In *Pilgrimage II.* London: Virago, 1979.

Richter, Harvena. "Hunting the Moth: Virginia Woolf and the Creative Imagination." In Freedman, *Virginia Woolf: Revaluation and Continuity,* 13–28.

———. *Virginia Woolf: The Inward Voyage.* Princeton, NJ: Princeton University Press, 1970.

Ritvo, Harriet. *The Animal Estate: The English and Other Creatures in the Victorian Age.* Cambridge, MA: Harvard University Press, 1987.

Rohman, Carrie. *Stalking the Subject: Modernism and the Animal.* New York: Columbia University Press, 2009.

Roof, Judith. "Hocus Crocus." In Ardis and Scott, *Virginia Woolf Turning the Centuries,* 93–102.

Rosendale, Steven. *The Greening of Literary Scholarship: Literature, Theory, and the Environment.* Iowa City: University of Iowa Press, 2002.

Roskill, Mark. *The Languages of Landscape.* University Park: Pennsylvania State University Press, 1997.

Ruskin, John. *Sesame and Lilies.* New Haven, CT: Yale University Press, 2002.

Sacks, Peter. Introduction to *The Poems of Edward Thomas,* xi–xxvi. New York: Handsel Books, 2003.

Sackville-West, Vita. *The Letters of Vita Sackville-West to Virginia Woolf.* Edited by Louise DeSalvo and Mitchell A. Leaska. London: Macmillan, 1984.

———. *A Passenger to Teheran.* New York: Moyer Bell, 1990.

———. *Twelve Days: An Account of a Journey across the Bakhtiari Mountains in Southwestern Persia.* London: Hogarth Press, 1928.

Sandilands, Catriona. *The Good-Natured Feminist: Ecofeminism and the Quest for Democracy.* Minneapolis: University of Minnesota Press, 1999.

Sandliands, Catriona, and Bruce Erickson, eds. *Queer Ecologies: Sex, Nature, Politics, Desire.* Bloomington: Indiana University Press, 2010.

Sartiliot, Claudette. *Herbarium Verbarium: The Discourse of Flowers.* Lincoln: University of Nebraska Press, 1993.

Schama, Simon. *Landscape and Memory.* London: Harper Collins, 1995.

Schiebinger, Londa. "The Private Life of Plants: Sexual Politics in Carl Linnaeus and Erasmus Darwin." In Benjamin, *Question of Identity,* 121–43.

Schuchard, Ronald. *Eliot's Dark Angel: Intersections of Life and Art.* New York: Oxford University Press, 1999.

Schug, Charles. *The Romantic Genesis of the Modern Novel.* Pittsburgh: University of Pittsburgh Press, 1979.

Schulze, Robin G. "Harriet Monroe's Pioneer Modernist Nature, National Identity, and Poetry." *Legacy* 21.1 (2004): 50–67.

Schwartz, Sanford. *The Matrix of Modernism: Pound, Eliot and Early Twentieth-Century Thought.* Princeton, NJ: Princeton University Press, 1985.

Scott, Bonnie Kime, ed. *Gender in Modernism: New Geographies, Complex Intersections.* Urbana: University of Illinois Press, 2007.

———, ed. *The Gender of Modernism.* Bloomington: Indiana University Press, 1990.

———. *Refiguring Modernism.* Vol. 1, *The Women of 1928.* Bloomington: Indiana University Press, 1995.

———. "Virginia Woolf, Ecofeminism, and Breaking Boundaries in Nature." In Burrells et al., *Woolfian Boundaries*, 108–15.

Scott, Heidi C. M. "Apocalypse Narrative, Chaotic System: Gilbert White's *Natural History of Selborne* and Modern Ecology." *Romanticism and Victorianism on the Net (RaVoN)* 56 (November 2009). http://id.erudit.org/iderudit/1001095ar.

Scott-James, Ann. *Sissinghurst: The Making of a Garden.* London: Michael Joseph, 1975.

Sellei, Nora. *Katherine Mansfield and Virginia Woolf: A Personal and Professional Bond.* Frankfurt: P. Lang, 1996.

Shiva, Vandana. *Stolen Harvest: The Hijacking of the Global Food Supply.* Cambridge, MA: North End Press, 2000.

Shone, Richard. *The Art of Bloomsbury: Roger Fry, Vanessa Bell and Duncan Grant.* London: Tate Gallery, 1999.

Showalter, Elaine. *The Female Malady: Women, Madness, and English Culture, 1830–1980.* New York: Pantheon, 1985.

Shteir, Anne B. *Cultivating Women, Cultivating Science: Flora's Daughters and Botany in England, 1760–1860.* Baltimore: Johns Hopkins University Press, 1996.

Silver, Brenda. *Virginia Woolf's Reading Notebooks.* Princeton, NJ: Princeton University Press, 1983.

Sinclair, May. "The Poems of 'H.D.'" In Bonnie Kime Scott, *Gender of Modernism*, 453–67.

Smith, Paul. "Cézanne's Maternal landscape and Its Gender." In Adams and Robins, *Gendering Landscape Art*, 116–32.

Sophocles. *Antigone.* Translated by Richard Claverhouse Jebb. In *Greek Dramas by Aeschylus, Sophocles, Euripides, and Aristophanes*, 105–39. New York: D. Appleton, 1904.

Southworth, Helen. "Virginia Woolf's 'Wild England': George Borrow, Autoethnography, and *Between the Acts.*" *Studies in the Novel* 39.2 (Summer 2007): 196–215.

Southworth, Helen, and Elisa Kay Sparks, eds. *Woolf and the Art of Exploration: Selected Papers from the Fifteenth International Conference on Virginia Woolf.* Clemson, SC: Clemson Digital Press, 2006.

Spalding, Frances. *Vanessa Bell.* London: Weidenfeld and Nicolson, 1983.

Sparks, Elisa Kay. "Accounting for the Garden: What Leonard's Record Books Show Us about the Garden at Monk's House." *Virginia Woolf Miscellany* 72 (Fall/Winter 2007): 61–64.

———. "Leonard's Vegetable Empire: A History of the Garden at Monk's House." *Virginia Woolf Bulletin* (January 2003): 10–19.

———. "Virginia Woolf's Literary and Quotidian Flowers: A Bar-Graphical Approach." Paper presented at the Twentieth Annual Conference on Virginia Woolf, Georgetown College, KY, 2010.

Squier, Susan Merrill. *Virginia Woolf and London: The Sexual Politics of the City.* Chapel Hill: University of North Carolina Press, 1985.

————, ed. *Women Writers and the City: Essays in Feminist Literary Criticism.* Knoxville: University of Tennessee Press, 1984.

Staveley, Alice. "Conversations at Kew." In *Trespassing Boundaries: Virginia Woolf's Short Fiction,* edited by Kathryn N. Benzel and Ruth Hoberman, 39–62. New York: Palgrave, 2004.

————. "'Kew will do': Cultivating Fictions of Kew Gardens." In Gillespie and Hankins, *Virginia Woolf and the Arts,* 57–66.

Steele, Elizabeth. *Virginia Woolf's Literary Sources and Allusions: A Guide to the Essays.* New York: Garland, 1983.

Stein, Gertrude. *Selected Writings of Gertrude Stein.* New York: Vintage, 1990.

————. "Transatlantic Interview 1946." In Bonnie Kime Scott, *Gender of Modernism,* 502–16.

Stein, Rachel. *New Perspectives on Environmental Justice: Gender, Sexuality and Activism.* New Brunswick, NJ: Rutgers University Press, 2004.

————. *Shifting the Ground: American Women Writers' Revisions of Nature, Gender, and Race.* Charlottesville: University of Virginia Press, 1997.

Stephen, Julia Duckworth. *Julia Duckworth Stephen: Stories for Children, Essays for Adults.* Edited by Diane F. Gillespie and Elizabeth Steele. Syracuse, NY: Syracuse University Press, 1987.

Stephen, Leslie. *Men, Books and Mountains: Essays by Leslie Stephen.* Edited by S. O. A. Ullmann. Minneapolis: University of Minnesota Press, 1956.

————. *The Playground of Europe.* Oxford: Blackwell, 1936.

————. *Selected Letters of Leslie Stephen.* Vol. 2, *1882–1904.* Edited by John W. Bicknell. Columbus: Ohio State University Press, 1996.

————. *Sir Leslie Stephen's Mausoleum Book.* Edited by Alan Bell. Oxford: Clarendon Press, 1977.

Stephen, Thoby. *Notes on Birds and Mammals Observed in England, Wales and Parts of Europe, 1902–1906.* Ms. in the Ornithological Library, Natural History Museum, Tring, UK.

Sturgeon, Noel. *Ecofeminist Natures: Race, Gender, Feminist Theory.* New York: Routledge, 1997.

Sultzbach, Kelly. "The Fertile Potential of Virginia Woolf's Environmental Ethic." In Southworth and Sparks, *Woolf and the Art of Exploration,* 71–77.

Sutcliffe, Anthony, ed. *Metropolis, 1890–1940.* London: Mansell, 1984.

Symons, Julian. *Makers of the New: The Revolution in Literature, 1912–1939.* London: Andre Deutsch, 1987.

Thackray, John C. *A Guide to the Official Archives of the Natural History Museum.* London: Society for the History of Natural History, 1998.

Thomas, Edward. *The Poems of Edward Thomas.* New York: Handsel Press, 2003.

Torgovnick, Marianna. "'The Bloomsbury Fraction' versus War and Empire." In *Seeing Double: Revisioning Edwardian and Modernist Literature,* edited by Carola M. Kaplan and Anne B. Simpson, 131–48. New York: St. Martins, 1996.

———. *Gone Primitive: Savage Intellects, Modern Lives.* Chicago: University of Chicago Press, 1990.

———. *Primitive Passions: Men, Women, and the Quest for Ecstasy.* New York: Knopf, 1997.

———. *The Visual Arts, Pictorialism, and the Novel: James, Lawrence, and Woolf.* Princeton, NJ: Princeton University Press, 1985.

Trautmann, Joanne. *The Jessamy Brides: The Friendship of Virginia Woolf and V. Sackville-West.* University Park: Pennsylvania State University Press, 1973.

Tremper, Ellen. *Who Lived at Alfoxton? Virginia Woolf and English Romanticism.* Lewisburg, PA: Bucknell University Press, 1998.

Trombley, Stephen. *All That Summer She Was Mad: Virginia Woolf, Female Victim of Male Medicine.* New York: Continuum, 1982.

Ullmann, S. A. O. Introduction to *Men, Books, and Mountains* by Leslie Stephen, 7–15.

Unger, Nancy C. "Women, Sexuality and Environmental Justice in American History." In Rachel Stein, *Shifting the Ground,* 45–60.

Vanita, Ruth. "'Love Unspeakable': The Uses of Allusion in *Flush.*" In Neverow-Turk and Hussey, *Virginia Woolf: Themes and Variations,* 248–57.

Velicu, Adrian. *Unifying Strategies in Virginia Woolf's Experimental Fiction.* Uppsala, Sweden: Uppsala University, 1985.

"Virginia Woolf: A Botanical Perspective." Church Exhibition Gallery, Botanic Garden of Smith College, Northampton, MA, May 9–September 30, 2003.

"Virginia Woolf: This Perpetual Flight: Love and Loss in Virginia Woolf's Intimate Circle." Curated by William Beekman and Sara Funke. Exhibit at the Grolier Club of New York, September 17–November 22, 2008.

Vlasopolos, Anca. "Shelley's Triumph of Death in Virginia Woolf's *Voyage Out.*" *Modern Language Quarterly* 47.2 (June 1986): 130–53.

Wagner-Martin, Linda. *"Favored Strangers": Gertrude Stein and her Family.* New Brunswick, NJ: Rutgers University Press, 1995.

Walker, Charlotte Zoe. "The Book 'Laid on the Landscape': Virginia Woolf and Nature." In *Beyond Nature Writing: Expanding the Boundaries of Ecocriticism,* edited by Karla Armbruster and Kathleen R. Wallace, 143–61. Charlottesville: University of Virginia Press, 2001.

Walkowitz, Rebecca. *Cosmopolitan Style: Modernism beyond the Nation.* New York: Columbia, 2006.

Waller, L. Elizabeth. "Writing the Real: Virginia Woolf and an Ecology of Language." In *New Essays in Ecological Feminist Criticism,* edited by Glynis Carr. *Bucknell Review* 44.1 (2000): 137–56.

Warren, Karen J. *Ecofeminist Philosophy: A Western Perspective on What It Is and Why It Matters.* Lanham, MD: Rowman and Littlefield, 2000.

Waterhouse, Charles O. *Notes on the Various Collections of Insects in the Insect Room of the British Museum.* London: William Clowes and Sons, 1900.

Webb, Caroline. "'All was dark; all was doubt; all was confusion': Nature, Culture, and Orlando's Ruskinian Storm Cloud." In *Virginia Woolf Out of Bounds,* edited by Jessica Berman and Jane Goldman, 243–49. New York: Pace University Press, 2001.

———. "The Room as Laboratory: The Gender of Science and Literature in Modernist Poetics." In Rado, *Modernism, Gender and Culture,* 337–52.

Westling, Louise. "Virginia Woolf and the Flesh of the World." *New Literary History* 30 (1999): 855–75.

Whatmore, Sarah. *Hybrid Geographies: Natures, Cultures, Spaces.* London: Sage, 2002.

White, Gilbert. *The Journals of Gilbert White.* Edited by Francesca Greenoak. 2 vols. London: Century, 1986.

———. *The Natural History of Selborne.* 1789. Edited by R. M. Lockley. London: J. M. Dent, 1949.

Wilde, Alan. "Touching Earth: Virginia Woolf and the Prose of the World." In *Philosophical Approaches to Literature: New Essays on Nineteenth- and Twentieth-Century Texts,* edited by William E. Cain, 140–64. Lewisburg, PA: Bucknell University Press, 1984.

Williams, Raymond. *The Country and the City.* New York: Oxford University Press, 1973.

Wilson, Jean Moorcroft. *Virginia Woolf: Life and London: A Biography of Place.* London: Cecil Woolf, 1987.

Woolf, Leonard. *Beginning Again: An Autobiography of the Years 1911 to 1918.* San Diego: Harcourt Brace Jovanovich, 1964.

———. *Growing: An Autobiography of the Years 1904–1911.* San Diego: Harcourt Brace Jovanovich, 1961.

Woolf, Virginia. "Across the Border." In *Essays of Virginia Woolf,* 2:217–20.

———. "Anon." In Bonnie Kime Scott, *Gender of Modernism,* 679–96.

———. *Between the Acts.* 1941. Annotated edition. Orlando: Harcourt, 2008.

———. *A Cockney's Farming Experience.* London: Cecil Woolf, 1994.

———. *The Collected Essays of Virginia Woolf.* Edited by Leonard Woolf. 4 vols. London: Hogarth, 1966–67.

———. *The Complete Shorter Fiction of Virginia Woolf.* Edited by Susan Dick. 2nd ed. San Diego: Harcourt Brace Jovanovich, 1989.

———. *The Diary of Virginia Woolf.* Edited by Anne Olivier Bell and Andrew McNeillie. 5 vols. San Diego: Harcourt, Brace Jovanovich, 1977–84.

———. *The Essays of Virginia Woolf.* Edited by Andrew McNeillie. 4 vols. San Diego: Harcourt Brace Jovanovich, 1986–94.

———. *The Essays of Virginia Woolf.* Edited by Stuart N. Clarke. Vol. 5, *1929–1932.* Boston: Houghton Mifflin, 2010. Vol. 6, *1933–1941.* London: Hogarth, 2011.

———. "A Faithful Friend." In *Essays of Virginia Woolf,* 1:12–15.

———. *Flush: A Biography.* 1933. New York: Harcourt Brace Jovanovich, 1961.

———. "Friendships Gallery." *Twentieth-Century Literature* 25.3–4 (1979): 270–302.

———. "Great Men's Houses." In *Essays of Virginia Woolf,* 5:294–301.

———. "Heard on the Downs: The Genesis of Myth." In *Essays of Virginia Woolf*, 2:40–42.

———. "How Should One Read a Book." In *Essays of Virginia Woolf*, 5:572–584.

———. *Jacob's Room.* 1922. San Diego: Harcourt Brace Jovanovich, 1978.

———. *The Letters of Virginia Woolf.* Edited by Nigel Nicolson and Joanne Trautmann. 6 vols. New York: Harcourt Brace Jovanonvich, 1975–80.

———. "The Man Who Loved His Kind." In *Complete Shorter Fiction*, 195–200.

———. "Mr. Bennett and Mrs. Brown." In *Essays of Virginia Woolf*, 3:420–38, as "Character in Fiction."

———. *Mrs. Dalloway.* 1925. Annotated edition. Orlando: Harcourt, 2005.

———. "The Novels of Thomas Hardy." In *Essays of Virginia Woolf*, 5:561–72.

———. *Orlando.* 1928. San Diego: Harcourt Brace Jovanovich, 1956.

———. *A Passionate Apprentice.* Edited by Mitchell A. Leaska. San Diego: Harcourt Brace Jovanovich, 1990.

———. "The Plumage Bill." In *Essays of Virginia Woolf*, 3:241–45.

———. *Roger Fry.* Middlesex: Penguin, 1979.

———. *A Room of One's Own.* 1929. Annotated edition. Orlando: Harcourt, 2005.

———. *The Second Common Reader.* 1932. New York: Harcourt, Brace and World, 1960.

———. "A Sketch of the Past." In *Moments of Being: Unpublished Autobiographical Writings*, edited by Jeanne Schulkind, 61–137. New York: Harcourt Brace Jovanovich, 1976.

———. "Street Haunting: A London Adventure." In *Essays of Virginia Woolf*, 4:480–91.

———. "A Summing Up." In *Complete Shorter Fiction*, 208–11.

———. *Three Guineas.* 1938. Annotated edition. Orlando: Harcourt, 2006.

———. *To the Lighthouse.* 1927. Annotated edition. Orlando: Harcourt, 2005.

———. *Travels with Virginia Woolf.* Edited by Jan Morris. London: Hogarth, 1993.

———. *The Virginia Woolf Manuscripts from the Monk's House Papers at the University of Sussex.* Brighton, UK; Woodbridge, CT: Research Publications, Harvester Microform, 1985.

———. *The Virginia Woolf Manuscripts: From the Henry W. and Albert A. Berg Collection at the New York Public Library.* Woodbridge, CT: Research Publications International, 1993. Microform.

———. *The Voyage Out.* 1915. New York: Harcourt Brace and World, 1948.

———. "Walter Sickert: A Conversation." In *Essays of Virginia Woolf*, 6:36–51.

———. *The Waves.* 1931. Annotated edition. Orlando: Harcourt, 2006.

———. *The Waves: The Two Holograph Drafts.* Edited by John W. Graham. Toronto: University of Toronto Press, 1976.

———. "White's Selbourne." In *Essays of Virginia Woolf*, 6:189–94.

———. *The Years.* Annotated edition. Orlando: Harcourt, 2008.

Woolf, Virginia, and Vanessa Bell, with Thoby Stephen. *Hyde Park Gate News.* Edited by Gill Lowe. London: Hesperus Press, 2005.

Worthen, John. *D. H. Lawrence: The Early Years, 1885–1912.* Cambridge: Cambridge University Press, 1991.

Young, Geoffrey. *Walking London's Parks and Gardens.* London: New Holland Publishers, 1998.

Young, Suzanne. "The Unnatural Object of Modernist Aesthetics: Artifice in Woolf's *Orlando*." In *Unmanning Modernism: Gendered Re-readings,* edited by Elizabeth Jane Harrison and Shirley Peterson, 168–87. Knoxville: University of Tennessee Press, 1997.

Zimmerman, Bonnie, ed. *Safe Sea of Women: Lesbian Fiction, 1969–1989.* Boston: Beacon, 1990.

Zwerdling, Alex. *Virginia Woolf and the Real World.* Berkeley: University of California Press, 1986.

Index

Page numbers in italics refer to figures.

Woolf, Virginia (*continued*)
50, 53, 70, 90, 108, 113, 136, 139, 149, 162, 164, 170, 183, 194, 205, 222n15, 232n21; "Kew Gardens," 60, 77, 88–90, 96, 184, 205, 227n2, 228n11; letters, 155, 233n2, 233n4, 233n10, 234n13, 235n28, 235n34; "A Man Who Loved His Kind," 80; "The Mark on the Wall," 60, 154; "Mr. Bennett and Mrs. Brown," 16–17, 126, 232n24; *Mrs. Dalloway,* 1, 4–5, 6, 41, 44, 66, 67, 75, 77, 90, 97, 100–102, 108, 113, 132, 137, 144, 156, 164, 170, 175, 185, 193, 199, 203–4, 206, 208, 213, 216–17, 219, 230n8, 235n35, 236nn41–42; *Night and Day,* 38, 44, 108, 208; "Novels of Thomas Hardy," 122, 208; "On a Faithful Friend," 167; *Orlando,* 6, 9, 40, 60, 65, 82, 84, 98, 114, 142–44, 146, 150, 168, 170, 173, 181, 188, 194, 210, 214–15, 230n8; pets, 158, *159,* 166, 167–69, 171, 172, 180, 181, *182;* "Reading," 13, 111; *A Room of One's Own,* 3, 9, 34, 44, 82, 99, 149, 157, 160–61, 165, 169, 173, 178, 185, 191, 198, 200, 206, 214, 215, 234n17, 236n44, 236n9 (chap. 6); "A Scribbling Dame," 42; "The Shooting Party," 179; "A Sketch of the Past," 5, 6–8, 23, 37, 53, 60, 71, 73, 76, 77, 103, 113, 116, 128, 193, 213; "Slater's Pins Have No Points," 79; "Street Haunting," 80, 161; "The Sun and the Fish," 177; "The Symbol," 134; "Terrible Tragedy in a Duck Pond," 121; *Three Guineas,* 3, 44, 66, 114, 163, 190, 236nn43–44, 236n9 (chap. 6); "Thunder at Wembley," 206, 232n32; *To the Lighthouse,* 6, 21, 30, 37, 41, 53, 62, 66, 79, 86, 88, 92, 102–3, 105, 113, 123, 128, 134, 136, 146, 164, 176, 182, 185, 190, 198, 200, 202–3, 205–6, 209, 215, 217, 219, 226n11, 226n14, 229n28, 236n9; travel, 111, 113, 116, 118–23, 131, 137–39, 169, 232n30; *The Voyage Out,* 6, 21, 37, 60, 127–28, 139, 141, 145, 148, 158, 164–65, 182, 184, 200, 205, 208, 215, 218, 225n2, 231n13, 235n32, 237n21; *The Waves,* 1, 4, 5, 19, 25, 28, 37, 57, 60, 71, 75, 76, 79, 90, 105–6, 109, 113, 116, 119, 121, 123, 137, 144, 148, 156, 162, 176, 181, 183, 184, 186–87, 195, 198, 200, 202, 204–5, 209–10, 214, 216, 218–19, 222n10, 229n31, 230n8, 235nn37–38, 237n19; "White's Selbourne," 120; *The Years,* 6, 48, 76, 123, 149, 167, 184, 187, 198, 200, 202, 209, 219, 226n18, 229n25, 232n33, 237n12

zoos, 4, 39, 52–53, 77, 178, 222n15